PLACES TO GO WITH CHILDREN IN MIAMI AND SOUTH FLORIDA

CHERYL LANI JUÁREZ AND DEBORAH ANN JOHNSON

Completely Revised and Expanded

D1542539

CHRONICLE BOOKS

SAN FRANCISCO

Copyright © 1994 by Cheryl Lani Juárez and Deborah Ann Johnson.
All rights reserved. No part of this book may be reproduced in any form without written permission from the publisher.

Printed in the United States of America.
SECOND EDITION

Library of Congress Cataloging-in-Publication Data
Juárez, Cheryl Lani.
    Places to go with children in Miami and south Florida / Cheryl Lani
Juárez & Deborah Ann Johnson.
      p.   cm.
    ISBN 0-8118-0479-8 (pb.)
    1. Miami (Fla.)—Guidebooks.   2. Florida—Guidebooks.
3. Family recreation—Florida—Miami—Guidebooks.   4. Family
recreation—Florida—Guidebooks.   I. Johnson, Deborah Ann,
1958–   . II. Title.
F319.M6J83   1994
917.59'3—dc20   93-37798
                                                              CIP

Design and illustration: Karen Smidth
Composition: Words & Deeds

Distributed in Canada by Raincoast Books, 112 East Third Ave.,
Vancouver, B.C. V5T 1C8

10 9 8 7 6 5 4 3 2 1

Chronicle Books
275 Fifth Street
San Francisco, CA 94103

CONTENTS

INTRODUCTION

Tell me and I forget.
Teach me and I remember.
Involve me and I learn.
—BENJAMIN FRANKLIN

Let's play a guessing game. You guess the place. Here are some clues. Key lime pie. Pink flamingos. Arroz con pollo. Key West sunsets. Alligators. Palm Beach polo matches. Waving coconut palm trees. Hurricane Andrew.

Did you guess South Florida? Good job! Let's play again. Here goes. Seminole Indian villages. Butterfly gardens. Nesting Loggerhead sea turtles. Churros con chocolate. Water taxis. Japanese gardens. Baseball. An ancient Spanish monastery. Okay, what was your guess? No, not some far-off land. It's spectacular South Florida, where children of all ages can explore unique sights, sounds, and flavors.

We've discovered that the area known as South Florida, from Tequesta in Palm Beach County, to the Dry Tortugas (68 miles west of the southernmost point in the continental United States), and west to the Everglades, provides hundreds of wonderful places to go with children of all ages. This book, our second edition, aims to help families get out and explore the land known as South Florida.

In the years since *Places to Go with Children in Miami and South Florida* first hit the bookstands in 1990, we've discovered many more places that appeal to children and their adult companions. You'll find fascinating new museums, sparkling new performing arts centers, sensational additions to the South Florida sports scene, captivating ecotourism destinations, family-friendly restaurants, and an amazing variety of indoor playgrounds. In South Florida we're not just rebuilding after Hurricane Andrew in August 1992, we're making it an even better place for children.

We believe this guidebook will be particularly helpful to many of you "at-home" moms and dads, working parents, "weekend" parents, grandparents, and other relatives. Teachers, homeschoolers, and babysitters will find lots of suggestions for trips, too. (We even know of a group of realtors who purchased a box of books to give as gifts to new-comers to South Florida!) Whether you have just arrived for a short visit, have relocated to South Florida, or have lived here for years, this book will help you find some very special places to make memories with the children in your life.

And now for a word about the places listed in this book. Most are appropriate for children up to 12 years of age and cover a broad range of interests. Most are free or cost no more than the price of a movie. Each chapter provides alphabetical, county-by-county listings for Dade, Broward, Palm Beach, and Monroe counties. We've included mailing addresses if you want to write ahead for brochures, maps, schedules, or reservations. Note that the weeks from mid-December to after Easter are South Florida's coolest, driest, and busiest. This means that reservations are a must. You'll also find that during summer months some schedules change to accommodate children's vacations and to get the most out of those wonderfully long summer evenings. Other places, however, close until after Labor Day.

If you are familiar with the first edition of this book, you'll note that we decided to make a few changes in this edition. The most important addition is a new chapter called "Across Alligator Alley," which we hope will entice you to explore the southwest coast of Florida.

We also made a change regarding our party-planning chapter—it's no longer included. After much research, we found that the business of providing birthday party environments is a booming and ever-changing one here in South Florida. As you read through this new edition, keep in mind that most places listed here are happy to work with you to host a special party. Many offer various party packages. If you're still stumped for ideas, *South Florida Parenting* magazine publishes an annual birthday party issue every February. The magazine, available at over 1,500 distribution points, will keep you up to date on the latest ideas for your child's party. If you can't find a copy, call (305) 448-6003, or write to *South Florida Parenting*, 4200 Aurora Street, Suite R, Coral Gables, FL 33146.

Many of our listings offer discounts to special groups (AAA members even get discounts at turnpike rest areas shops!). State and county resident passes are available at museums, parks, and attractions. Golden Eagle passports ($25 per year covers everyone in car) for free admission to federally administered recreation areas are worth investigating. Most zoos and museums have reciprocal agreements with sister organizations throughout the country, so if you're from another state, or another area of Florida, bring your membership cards with you, and *always* ask about discounts before you pay the full ticket price.

Here's a checklist that may be helpful:

- Buckle up...it's the law!
- Bring along quarters for phone calls and toll booths, and plan on spending several dollars if you travel on the Florida Turnpike.
- Pack light, but always carry essentials: sunscreen, sunglasses, a lightweight jacket, drinks, a few toys.
- Stop by tourist information centers for goodies like brochures, discount tickets, and orange juice.
- Most listings are appropriate for field trips for school and other groups. When you call, be prepared to provide information about group size, age, and times you can visit.
- We've used the following credit card abbreviations: AE = American Express; C = Choice; CB = Carte Blanche; DC = Diner's Club; DIS = Discover; IC = International Card; IGT = In Good Taste; MC = MasterCard; and V = Visa.
- When getting directions for locations in the Florida Keys, addresses usually include "Mile Markers," which refer to the number of miles traveled north from the beginning of U.S. 1 in Key West, and tell whether sites are on the oceanside or bayside of the highway. For example, John Pennekamp Coral Reef State Park in Key Largo is at Mile Marker 102.5, oceanside.

In a fast-growing area like South Florida, it's very important to **call before you go.** We have confirmed and reconfirmed the information in this book, but you should call ahead anyway to check the address, hours, cost, and other relevant information, such as wheelchair and stroller access. Most people are happy to give you directions, which is important because maps often do not reflect the area's rapid development.

We have not received any compensation from the organizations or companies listed in this book, nor have we maliciously omitted anyone. As you explore on your own, if you find a favorite spot that we have not mentioned in this guide, please share it with us through Chronicle Books, 275 Fifth Street, San Francisco, California 94103.

We've enjoyed working on this project and hope it is helpful to all of you who realize that children need to be involved in our world if they are to make it theirs.

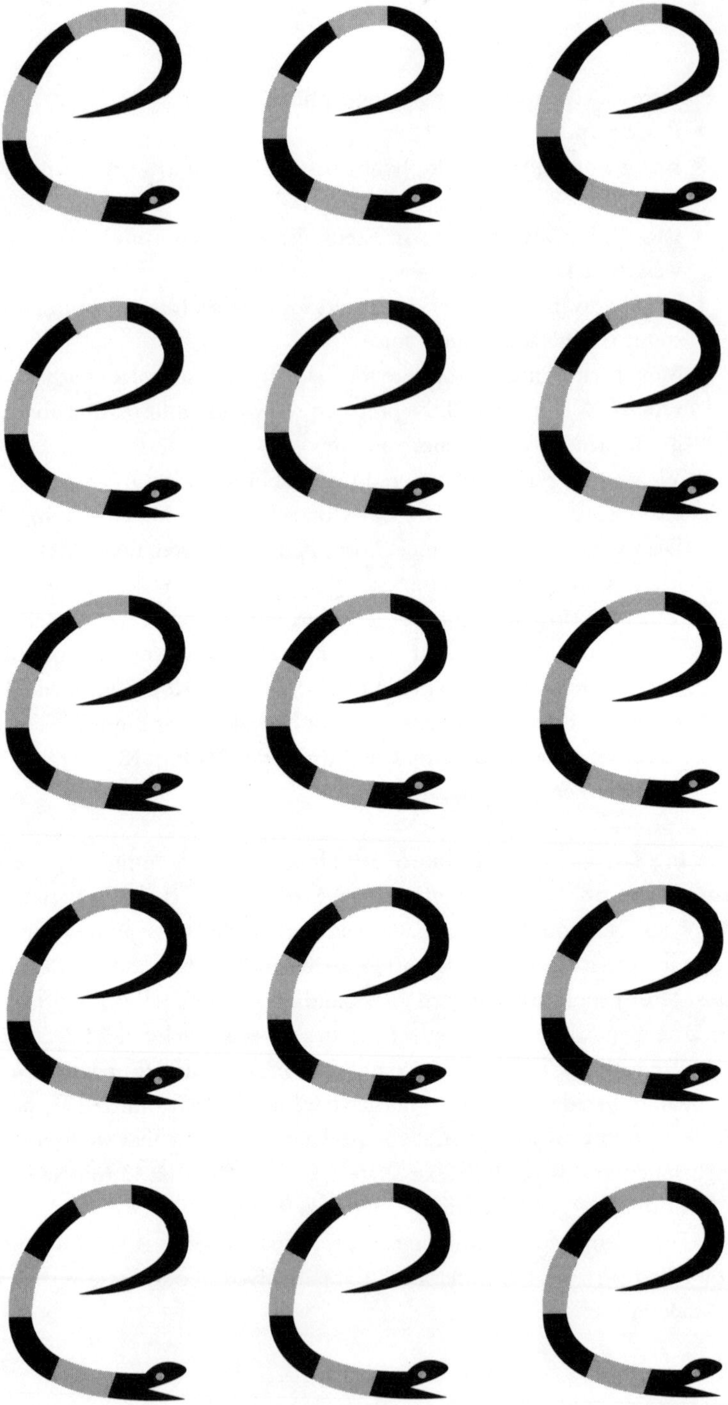

ON SAFARI IN SOUTH FLORIDA

Grab the kids, the camera, a compass, and a backpack full of snacks and get ready to be entertained the South Florida way! This is a land full of adventures waiting to happen. As you "safari" through South Florida, try riding an elephant (that's so safari-ish) or on an airboat through a "river of grass"; explore a shipwreck full of golden treasures or a chickee hut on an Indian reservation; inspect butterflies in a park of their own or a baby sea turtle about to head to sea; come face-to-face with a kissable sea lion or a talking parrot; touch the walls of the oldest building in the Western Hemisphere or a spiny sea urchin living in a touch tank. No matter which destinations are on your itinerary, just make sure you take the time to create a special memory with the children in your life.

DADE COUNTY

◆ American Police Hall of Fame and Museum

3801 Biscayne Boulevard, Miami 33137. Located half block north of I-195 junction. (305) 573-0070. Daily, 10 A.M.–5:30 P.M. Closed Christmas Day. Adults, $6; seniors, $4; children 6 to 12, $3; police officers, $1.

You know you're at the right place when you see the life-size squad car on the outside wall of the museum building. As the nation's only memorial and museum dedicated solely to police, this one-acre facility has a three-fold purpose: to remember, to serve, and to educate. The names of about 4,000 police officers who have lost their lives in the line of duty have been etched on marble walls that make up the memorial hall. Next to the memorial is an interdenominational chapel open to the public.

The museum, housed in the former Miami FBI headquarters, features law enforcement artifacts, such as uniforms, photographs, vehicles, and firearms, that make up a collection of over 10,000 items. New memorabilia are constantly added. Groups of 25 or more can request a guided tour (multilingual), and educational programs for children of all ages are offered. **Tip:** Allow one hour to tour.

♦ The Ancient Spanish Monastery

16711 West Dixie Highway, North Miami Beach 33160. (305) 945-1462. Monday through Saturday, 10 A.M.–4 P.M.; Sunday, noon–4 P.M. Closed major holidays. Adults, $4; seniors, $2.50; children under 12, $1. AE accepted.

Built in 1141, The Ancient Spanish Monastery is the oldest building in the Western Hemisphere and is listed on the National Register of Historic Places. It was built in Spain and moved to Miami by William Randolph Hearst after he saw it when visiting Spain in 1925. He had it dismantled and shipped to the United States, where the boxes were quarantined (due to an outbreak of hoof-and-mouth disease!). The carefully numbered and boxed stones were jumbled together and kept in a warehouse for 26 years. In 1952, they were bought and shipped to Miami; 19 months and $1.5 million later, they were reassembled. **Tips:** Plan on spending about 40 minutes to tour the monastery, now an Episcopal church. Group tours can be arranged. Picnic facilities are available.

♦ Bayside Marketplace

401 Biscayne Boulevard, Miami 33132. From I-95 north, take Biscayne Boulevard exit; from I-95 south, take I-395 Miami Beach east and exit at Biscayne Boulevard. (305) 577-3344. Monday through Thursday, 10 A.M.–10 P.M.; Friday and Saturday, 10 A.M.–11 P.M.; Sunday, 11 A.M.–8 P.M. Charged parking is available in the Bayside Garage.

To experience the real international flavor of Miami, visit this popular South Florida attraction—a dash of shopping, a sprinkle of entertainment, and a pinch of great food! Located on a busy waterway, the open-air market displays crafts and wares from other countries. Upstairs in the eatery section, there are lots of different ethnic foods for children to try, and you can take your tray out to the patio and enjoy watching boats and birds in the bay while you eat. On that rare cool day or evening, try the hot chocolate served at the Cuban coffee counter—it's thick, rich, and delicious (not made from a packet!). There's usually some type of special entertainment going on in the evenings.

♦ Coral Castle

28655 South Dixie Highway, Homestead 33030. (305) 248-6344. Daily, 9 A.M.–5 P.M. Adults, $7.75; children 6 to 12, $4.50; children under 6, free.

Mystery surrounds this stone castle, built by Latvian immigrant Edward Leedskalnin over a 20-year period, from 1920 to 1939. To impress the woman who left him the night before their wedding, he single-handedly dug the 1,000 tons of coral used for the huge sculptures. In 1984 the Coral Castle was placed on the National Register of Historic

Places. **Tip:** A covered shelter and restrooms are located behind the gift shop building.

◆ Everglades Alligator Farm

40351 SW 192nd Avenue, Homestead 33090. Located at the main entrance of the Everglades National Park. From Florida Turnpike, take Florida City exit and go west on Palm Drive two miles. Turn left on 192nd Avenue and head south for four miles to entrance. (305) 247-2628. Daily, 9 A.M.–6 P.M. Airboat rides and farm: adults, $11; children 4 to 12, $6. Farm and shows only: adults, $5; children 4 to 12, $3. AE, DISC, MC, and V accepted.

Here's your chance to see alligators up close and personal. Before entering the gift shop, filled with about a zillion alligator toys, souvenirs, and shirts, pose for a picture with a life-size, wacky wooden gator near the walkway. Stroll around the farm and take in one of the snake and alligator shows that run continuously throughout the day. Schedules are posted at the entrance, in the gift shop, and announced over the PA system, so you shouldn't miss out! You'll see the life stages of alligators—from hatchlings to adults. Breeding ponds are located behind the gift shop and offer a natural setting for the alligators to, well, breed. Baby alligators live in the "grow out" pen. A crocodile pond and wildlife exhibit are also located at the farm. To feed alligators, purchase a bag of food for $1.25 in the gift shop and ask about feeding details.

The narrated airboat ride is about 30 minutes in length. Your guide will point out interesting species that inhabit the canals around the property, including osprey, blue herons, turtles, and fish. Then, be prepared for a fast ride into the 'glades! **Tips:** Group rates for 15 or more are available with advance reservations. A snack bar offers hot dogs, ice cream, and, of course, those ever-popular gator nuggets. For more information about the tours, see listing in "By Land, Sea, and Air."

◆ Florida Gold Coast Railroad Museum

12450 SW 152nd Street, Miami 33177. Follow signs to Metrozoo; the museum is on the right as you approach the Metrozoo's west parking lot. (305) 253-0063. Call for hours. Adults, $3; children 3 to 11, $2.

The museum was once the homesite of a U.S. Navy air blimp station. The large "hangars" at one time held six blimps that were sent out on surveillance missions over the Atlantic Ocean during World War II. Today, the same "hangars" hold old railroad cars, including the "Ferdinand Magellan" (U.S. Presidential Car #1). The best part of your visit may be the ride on a real train through the forest. The museum has hopes of adding a narrow-gauge "toy" train, which would run on air or steam on a two-track path.

This is a common destination for field trips and birthday parties. Children particularly enjoy the room full of miniature trains. **Tip:** Strollers do not fit on the trains, so bring an alternative or be prepared to leave it outside while you're inside.

◆   Holocaust Memorial

1933 to 1945 Meridian Avenue, Miami Beach 33139. (305) 538-1663. Daily, 9 A.M.–9 P.M. Free admission.

Guided tours are available through this memorial building that pays tribute to the six million Jewish victims of Nazi terror during World War II. Through art, sculpture, photographs, and etchings, visitors will be touched and inspired. **Tip:** Use discretion when bringing young children.

◆   The Little Farm

13401 SW 224th Street, Goulds. Mailing address is P.O. Box 397, Goulds 33170. (305) 258-3186. Open exclusively for school field trips on weekdays, September through June, 9 A.M.–noon; minimum field trip cost $100. Open to families one Saturday morning per month, November through May, 10 A.M.– noon, $3 per person. Reservations are necessary.

Take advantage of an opportunity to feed a baby pig, touch a rooster, or milk a goat. It's not often that city kids get the chance to see life on a working farm, but at the Little Farm (formerly Spotted Acres), they can get the idea! Teachers can take their classes here on a field trip, or families can come on one of the Saturdays designated each month (call first for dates and required reservations).

In the spring children may see a baby animal come into the world— not something they see every day! They may also touch and caress the various animals and get a good idea of the way a farm is run. If time permits, kids will get to ride a horse. Make sure there are plenty of adults to help supervise children, especially for large groups.

The Little Farm can also travel to your school, church, or home. Classroom materials can be sent to teachers ahead of time if requested. Inquire about cost. **Tips:** Recommended for children 3 and up. Plan to spend about 90 minutes to tour, and bring drinks with you. You must have a reservation—be sure to schedule far in advance. No restroom facilities on grounds.

◆   Metrozoo

12400 SW 152nd Street (Coral Reef Drive), Miami 33177. Located one- quarter mile west of the Florida Turnpike Homestead/Key West Extension;

three miles west of U.S. 1 (South Dixie Highway). Zoo information, (305) 251-0400; educational programming, (305) 255-5551. Daily, 9:30 A.M.– 5:30 P.M.; ticket booth closes at 4:30 P.M. Adults, $5 plus tax; children 3 to 12, $2.50 plus tax; children under 3, free. Inquire at information booth about family memberships. AE, MC, V accepted.

Although devastated by Hurricane Andrew in August 1992, Metrozoo friends and employees worked gallantly to clean and rebuild its many exhibits. Within months the zoo had reopened nearly 80 percent of the park. At time of printing, restoration efforts were being made to open the monorail, aviary, Asian elephant exhibit, and the koala exhibit. Despite this hurricane damage, one of the best entertainment and educational investments local families can make is to become a member of this 285-acre cageless zoo.

Pick up a map at the entrance booth and begin your journey to each section of the zoo. Along the way you'll see the stars of the zoo: chimps and chinchillas, flamingos and felines, gorillas and giraffes! Bring a camera along to get some great shots for your children's scrapbook.

PAWS, the children's zoo completed in early 1989, lets you and your children view animals up close. A petting yard, an amphitheater show, and elephant rides and performances are among the highlights. A small play area, a snack shop, and a gift store are also found in the PAWS vicinity.

The entire family can take part in the zoo's educational and recreational programs, sponsored by the Zoological Society of Florida. There are camps for kids, family or group sleep-overs, early-morning breakfasts, after-school programs, and behind-the-scene tours. But don't let all of these events steal the show, because the animals themselves really make the zoo what it is—a fascinating and educational experience for everyone.

Tips: Best time to visit is in the morning or late afternoon, when the weather is cool and the animals are ready to perform. Not a lot of shade; be prepared to do a lot of walking. Rental strollers for children are available. Diaper-changing table in the PAWS' restroom. On Sunday mornings, the Southern Cross Astronomical Society usually sets up telescopes at the entrance of Metrozoo for free public viewing; for information about the Southern Cross Astronomical Society, see listing in "Exploring Science and Nature."

◆ Miami Seaquarium

4400 Rickenbacker Causeway, Key Biscayne 33149. Take I-95 south to Key Biscayne exit, then take Rickenbacker Causeway to Seaquarium. (305) 361-5703. Daily, 9:30 A.M.–6:00 P.M.; tickets sold until 5 P.M. Shows begin at

*10 A.M.; last show begins at 4 P.M. Adults, $17.95 plus tax; children 3 to
12, $12.95 plus tax; children under 3, free. Group rates for field trips.
Stroller rental, $3 per day. AE, MC, V accepted. Rainchecks available.*

A close-up view of a 10,000-pound killer whale doing tricks in the
water, dolphins performing acrobatics, and sea lions kissing little gig-
gling children all make for wonderful Kodak (or Fuji) moments. Be sure
to pack your camera for this outing!

A family favorite since 1955, Seaquarium added a few hot new shows
and exhibits in 1990. A new manatee exhibit is one of the more popular
additions. Here you can see manatee families—mothers and calves—
interacting and playing. Since Seaquarium has a very active rescue and
breeding program for marine life, new members are added to this area
periodically. As a matter of fact, just shortly after Hurricane Andrew in
1992, three manatee calves were born at the facility after the mothers were
rescued from the storm. A reef-feeding demonstration at a 50,000-gallon
aquarium features over 200 fish.

At least six different shows run continuously throughout the day, so
be prepared to move from one area to another to get all the shows in by
the end of the day. Perhaps your child's favorite part of the day will be
peering inside one of the 40 aquariums that line the walls of the main
building, where tropical fish will keep them entertained for a long time.
Children can be seated on a ledge that runs along the aquariums. The
shark feeding show seems to be a big hit, especially for boys! **Tips:** Cafeteria and snack shops on grounds. Picnic areas outside of gate; playground
directly inside gate. Film available in gift shop. Approximately four hours
to tour—best time to visit is prior to 4 P.M., to see all shows. Strollers
available to rent, but not all shows have stroller access—you must either
fold it and carry it with you, or park it outside the arenas. Summer
camp—all hands-on—is offered. Rickenbacker Causeway toll is $1. Birth-
day parties are offered here.

♦ Miami Youth Museum

*5701 Sunset Drive, South Miami 33143. Located in the Bakery Centre, third
level. (305) 661-3046. Monday and Friday, 10 A.M.–5 P.M.; Tuesday
through Thursday, 1–5 P.M.; Saturday and Sunday, 11 A.M.–5 P.M. Adults
and children over age 1, $3. Memberships available.*

This museum features rotating and permanent exhibits designed
especially for children, as well as related hands-on activities that allow
kids to explore many different artistic expressions. Toddlers may enjoy
these activities, but they'll feel more at home in Kidspace, an area made

just for them, where they can climb and crawl to touch different textures and shapes.

A gift shop is located at the museum, where children can buy small bags of recycled materials that can be used for arts and crafts projects. "Ed-U-Kits," offered for rent at the museum's resource center, will interest elementary school age children. Each kit includes hands-on materials that teach children about art, Florida's environment, patchwork quilting, Miami's history, and more. **Tips:** You'll need to spend about 90 minutes with your children to tour; please stay with them in the museum. Plans are underway to move the museum to a 40,000-square-foot location in West Kendall sometime in 1995. Inquire about birthday parties.

◆ Miccosukee Indian Village and Airboat Tours

Twenty-five miles west of the Florida Turnpike on Tamiami Trail (U.S. 41). Mailing address is P.O. Box 440021, Miami 33144. (305) 223-8380 (weekdays); 223-8399 (weekends). Daily, 9 A.M.–5 P.M. Adults, $5; children 5 to 12, $3.50; children 4 and under, free. Airboat rides start at $6 per person. Parking is free.

Located on the north side of Tamiami Trail (U.S. 41), the village is actually home to tribal members who live in traditional village fashion. Their homes, called "chickees," are thatch-roofed, open-sided structures. Watch men and women at work as they demonstrate craft specialties such as basketry, beading, doll-making, patchworking, and woodcarving. An alligator wrestling match is offered throughout the day. The museum, located at the rear of the village, features a film, artifacts, and artwork that represent the Miccosukee tribe. Annual events at the village include a music and crafts festival in July and an Indian arts festival in December. The airboat rides are located across the street. Try some of the tribal delights such as fry bread, pumpkin bread, or frog legs at the Miccosukee Restaurant; for more information, see listing in "Come and Get It!" **Tips:** Guided tours begin at 10 A.M. Special combination ticket packages are available for the village, airboat rides, and restaurant. For event information, see listings in "Mark Your Calendar"; for tour information, see listing in "By Land, Sea, and Air."

◆ Monkey Jungle

14805 SW 216th Street, Miami 33170. From the north, take the Florida Turnpike's Homestead Extension (Highway 821) south to SW 216th Street (exit 11). Get into the westbound lane and go west five miles. Or, take U.S. 1 south to SW 216th Street, go west 3.5 miles. (305) 235-1611. Daily,

9:30 A.M.–5 P.M. Adults, $10.50; seniors, $9.50; children 4 to 12, $5.35; children under 4, free. Resident passes available. AE, MC, V accepted. Rainchecks available in gift shop if weather dictates.

In 1935 Monkey Jungle opened with the purpose to study primate behavior in a natural environment. When research funds were depleted, tourists' money helped to pay for the monkey's food and care.

Today over 500 primates, most running free, live in this 25-acre reserve (plans are underway to expand the facility). Stroll the protected walkways while monkeys roam around you. Some species, including gibbons, black spider monkeys, and golden-lion tamarins, are in cages. Sumatran orangutans, lowland gorillas, and squirrel monkeys can be observed within the jungle. Children can feed many of the monkeys by placing raisins and peanuts (available at the concession area) in metal bowls that swing on a chain. The Java monkeys will anxiously watch and then pull up the chain to reach in for their snack. These monkeys are excellent skin divers in the wild; see a demonstration of their swimming skills during a show at the Monkey Swimming Pool.

When you enter the attraction you'll be given a show schedule that details the times and places to see the Wild Monkey Swimming Show, Ape Encounter, and the Chimpin' with Colin and Colleen show. Field trips and special educational presentations can be made by appointment. Call for topics. **Tips:** Check out show schedules and plan your stay around these. Remember to keep an eye on younger children and especially on little fingers—the monkeys may bite. Concession and picnic areas on grounds. Stroller maneuvering is difficult in some areas due to bark-chip paths.

◆ Parrot Jungle and Gardens

11000 SW 57th Avenue (South Red Road), Miami 33156. Located 2.5 miles east of U.S. 1. (305) 666-7834. Daily, 9:30 A.M.–6 P.M.; tickets sold until 5 P.M. Adults, $10.50 plus tax; seniors, $9.50 plus tax; children 3 to 12, $7 plus tax; children under 3, free. Memberships and group rates available. AE, MC, and V accepted.

Open since 1936, with over 12 million visitors passing through its entrance gate, Parrot Jungle is a well-known South Florida attraction. The jungle will delight you and your children, but before you go too far into the foliage, stop just beyond the entrance for a pose with a friendly parrot.

As you wind your way through the lush tropical forest, have some fun identifying strange trees and unusual plants (there are signs to help!). The shady trail will take you near an alligator pool, a parrot island, a cactus garden, and famous Flamingo Lake, where scenes from "Miami Vice,"

"The Miss Universe Pageant," and other television specials have been filmed. Over 1,000 exotic birds, giant tortoises, peacocks, iguanas, and flamingos call this place home. In the rear of the park you will find an area just for children, with a petting zoo and play area.

Trained-bird shows begin at 10:30 A.M., and the last show is presented at 5 P.M. The parrots here will amaze you and your youngsters with their acrobatic routines, bicycling tricks, high-wire acts, and roller-skating demonstrations.

Planned expansion includes a new aviary and an updated educational building. **Tips:** Plan to spend two hours to tour. Stroller rentals available for $1; wheelchairs available free of charge. Restrooms are located at the rear of the Parrot Bowl Theater and in the Parrot Cafe. The Parrot Cafe opens for breakfast daily at 8 A.M. Lunch and snacks are also served there. Snacks also available near Flamingo Lake and the original entrance building within the gardens. Picnic tables located near parking lot outside entrance.

♦ Vizcaya Museum and Gardens

3251 South Miami Avenue, Miami 33129. Take the Metrorail to the Vizcaya exit. (305) 579-2708. Daily, 9:30 A.M.–5:30 P.M.; tickets sold until 4:30 P.M. Museum building closes at 5 P.M.; gardens close at 5:30 P.M. Closed Christmas. Adults, $8; children 6 to 12, $4. Memberships are available. AE accepted.

Built by James Deering, co-founder of International Harvester, Vizcaya (from a Basque word meaning "elevated place") was completed in 1916 and is now operated by the Metro-Dade County Department of Parks and Recreation. Ten acres of formal gardens overlooking Biscayne Bay surround this 70-room Italian palace, which houses a collection of European art from the 15th through 19th centuries. Sound and light shows are held here, as well as the annual Shakespeare Festival, Italian Renaissance Festival, and a beautiful Christmas tree display. Learning packets are available for children who visit with school groups; coloring books are available in the gift shop.

Plan to spend at least two hours here in order to take the 45-minute tour of the first floor and then explore the second floor and gardens on your own. Only 34 of the 70 rooms are open to the public.

In 1984, the Ellis A. Gimbel Garden for the Blind, located at the south end of the formal gardens, was dedicated. Many of the plants here have unique textures, are especially aromatic, and need no identifying labels. They include blue sage, rosemary, lavender, mint, white butterfly ginger, lemon grass, and society garlic, as well as bay, allspice, eucalyptus, and camphor trees. On the west side of the formal gardens, you can get a good idea of different architectural features by feeling marble, terra-cotta, limestone, and wrought-iron textures on the building. A narrative tape is available by contacting Vizcaya personnel at (305) 579-2808. **Tips:** Strollers are not allowed inside the mansion and are somewhat difficult to maneuver on the grounds and in the gift shop. On the bayside of the grounds, there is no barrier, so hold onto young explorers. No food or refreshments may be brought on the premises. For special event information, see listings in "Mark Your Calendar."

♦ Weeks Air Museum

14710 SW 128th Street, Miami 33186. Located at Kendall-Tamiami Executive Airport. (305) 233-5197. Daily, 10 A.M.–5 P.M. Closed on Christmas and Thanksgiving. Adults, $5; seniors 65 and over, $4; children 3 to 12, $3; children under 3, free. AE, MC, and V accepted. Annual memberships and discounts for groups of 20 or more available.

The museum was opened to the public in 1987 by champion acrobatic pilot Kermit Weeks. It has an interesting collection of aircraft from the beginning of flight to the end of the World War II era.

Nearly 50 aircraft are on display, and some date back to 1916. Many of the aircraft have been rebuilt and restored and are in flying condition. A wide variety of engines, propellers, and model planes can be examined. Video booths offer information on the museum's history and memorabilia and on aircraft-related topics. Members can rent movies ranging from how to fly specific aircraft to *The Great Waldo Pepper*. **Tips:** There is a coffee shop at the airport and a new and improved post–Hurricane Andrew gift shop. Plan to spend 30 minutes to two hours to tour. Member's Days are held four times a year. Recommended for older children; guided tours can be arranged with prior notification.

≡ BROWARD COUNTY

♦ Butterfly World

3600 West Sample Road, Coconut Creek 33073. Located in Tradewinds Park, just west of the Florida Turnpike, or four miles west of I-95. (305) 977-4400. Monday through Saturday, 9 A.M.-5 P.M.; Sunday, 1-5 P.M.; admission closes at 4 P.M. Adults, $8.95; seniors, $7.95; children 3 to 12, $5; children under 3, free. AE, MC, and V accepted. Resident passes, group rates, and tours available. Additional fee charged at Tradewinds Park entrance on weekends.

The first of its kind; the largest in the world! Those are impressive credentials for this live butterfly park, home to thousands of delicate butterflies representing over 150 species from around the world. Three main aviaries house the creatures, so visitors are able to study the butterflies up close and personal.

Purchase an official program before venturing around the facilities. This full-color magazine gives insight into the life stages of butterflies, as well as the vegetation that has been planted to attract them. This can become an important learning tool after you and your child tour the park.

To take the self-guided tour, follow your map through the laboratory (where eggs and larva are kept), the aviaries, the emerging area, a tropical rain forest (stop to feed the fish!), and other points of interest. Along the way you'll learn about the life span of a butterfly and what food caterpillars prefer.

Make notes of the various plantings throughout the aviaries...maybe you'd like to create a butterfly garden of your own.

Field trips have been created for all age levels, and include pre-visit activities, reduced rates, and a knowledgeable guide to lead your troop. Call for a reservation. **Tips:** Snack bar and picnic facilities on grounds. Plan to spend one hour to tour. Gift shop has souvenirs and film. Field trips are available by reservation. The staff requests that adults accompany children while touring the facility. Best time to visit is on sunny days between 10 A.M. and 3 P.M. For information on Tradewinds Park, see listing in "Under the Sun." This is a popular place for birthdays.

◆ Flamingo Gardens

3750 Flamingo Road, Davie 33330. Take I-95 to 595 west (S.R. 84); go west to exit 2/Flamingo Road, head south for 2.5 miles to entrance. (305) 473-0010. Daily, 9 A.M.–5 P.M. Adults, $7; children 3 to 11, $3.50; 20% discount for seniors and AAA members. Memberships available. AE accepted. Rainchecks are available.

This 60-acre botanical garden (which blossomed from a working citrus grove) has a little bit to offer everyone. Visitors get to see crocodiles, alligators, monkeys, flamingos, river otters, and exotic birds. A new free-flight aviary was recently added, and you can actually feed the birds, which are bred for release into the wild. Walk among the hummingbird, fragrance, and xeriscape gardens, and visit the historic Wray Home. An Everglades nature center is very interesting. Book Corner, located in the center, contains a wealth of information on Florida plants, animals, and environments. There's a mile-long tram ride through a citrus grove; future dreams include creation of a citrus arboretum. Be sure to sample fresh citrus at the Fresh Fruit Patio from October through July.

Children's programs include "Green Machine," a puppet program designed for ages 5 to 9, "Wildlife Encounter," "Gardens and Galaxies," and "Adaptation Artistry," which teaches older children about birds and how they are able to fly. **Tips:** Gift shop, film, and snacks available on grounds. Plan to spend about three hours to tour. Picnic areas are located within the park.

◆ Fort Lauderdale Swap Shop

3291 West Sunrise Boulevard, Fort Lauderdale 33311. Located between I-95 and Florida Turnpike. (305) 791-7927 or 800-345-SWAP. Daily, 5 A.M.–6:30 P.M. Free.

There's more than you'd ever imagine inside the Swap Shop. Not only will you be able to shop for bargains from the 2,000 vendors located on the 80 acres, but you can attend free daily circus shows featuring the Hanneford Family Circus, Arabian horses, and dozens of animals. Amusement rides, a video arcade, and an 11-screen drive-in movie theater also help to attract 12 million visitors a year. **Tip:** There's an International Food Court on the grounds.

◆ Goodyear Blimp *Enterprise*

1500 NE Fifth Avenue, Pompano Beach 33060. (305) 946-4629. Daily, 9 A.M.–5 P.M. Free admission.

The *Enterprise* is one of only three touring Goodyear blimps in the world, traveling as far west as Dallas and as far north as Montreal. Take a look at the airship and operating hangar at Pompano Beach Air Park (November through May—the *Enterprise* tours during the other months). **Tips:** Your self-guided tour will take about 20 to 30 minutes. No rides offered. Be sure to call ahead of time because the blimp has an active tour schedule.

◆ International Swimming Hall of Fame

1 Hall of Fame Drive, Fort Lauderdale 33316. Located one block west of A1A between East Las Olas Boulevard and 17th Street Causeway. (305) 462-6536. Exhibition Hall: daily, 9 A.M.–7 P.M. Adults, $3; students and seniors, $1; children under 5, free. Hall of Fame: Monday through Friday, 9 A.M.–5 P.M.; Saturday and Sunday, 10 A.M.-4 P.M. Donations accepted. The Henning Library: Monday through Friday, 9 A.M.–4:30 P.M. or by appointment. Pool: 501 Seabreeze Boulevard (next to museum). (305) 468-1580. Monday through Friday, 8 A.M.–4 P.M. and 6–8 P.M.; Saturday and Sunday, 8 A.M.–4 P.M. Hours subject to change if there is a swim meet. Fort Lauderdale residents: adults, $2; students, seniors, and military personnel, $1.50; children under 6, $1. Nonresidents: adults, $3; students, seniors, and military personnel, $2; children under 6, $1.50.

In 1992 this museum reopened after undergoing a $12 million renovation and expansion project. For years this has been the world's premier resource for technical and historical aquatics information. Today the museum offers visitors a look at swimming history through state-of-the-art exhibits. The new 10,000-square-foot exhibition hall, shaped like a giant wave, showcases multimedia and hands-on exhibits. Two 50-meter pools, a teaching pool, and a diving pool are used to host nearly 50 events each year.

The Hall of Honor contains trophies, artifacts, and memorabilia from its 300 members from water's great sports, including swimming, diving, water polo, and synchronized swimming. Featured swimmers are Johnny Weissmuller, Mark Spitz, and Donna de Varona. A reference library houses historical films and videos, periodicals, and hundreds of books about the sport. An art gallery is also open. **Tips:** Plan to spend one hour to tour. Gift shop on grounds. This facility is open to the public for water aerobics and swimming lessons. For swimming information, see listing in "On Your Mark, Get Set, Go!"

♦ Museum of Discovery and Science and Blockbuster IMAX Theater

401 SW Second Street, Fort Lauderdale 33312-1707. Take I-95 to Broward Boulevard. Go east on Broward Boulevard to SW Fifth Avenue (Commodore Brook) and turn south. Go one block. Parking: west of the museum at the Arts & Sciences garage. Museum: (305) 467-6637; IMAX: (305) 463-4629. Monday through Friday, 10 A.M.–5 P.M.; Saturday, 10 A.M.–8:30 P.M.; Sunday, Noon–5 P.M. Museum admission is free for members; adults, $6; children 3 to 12 and seniors 65 and over, $5. Combination admission to the museum and IMAX theater: adults, $8; children and seniors, $7.

If you live anywhere near Fort Lauderdale, you'll want to invest in an annual membership in this museum, because one visit won't be enough for anyone in the family. Completed in late 1992, at a cost of over $30 million, the 85,000-square-foot museum provides a wonderful focus on science and a beautiful addition to Riverwalk along the New River.

Traveling exhibits complement the seven permanent exhibit areas, many of which center on South Florida's environment. Walk through a bi-level ecology mountain at "Florida EcoScapes"; journey to the stars on a moving space vehicle, or try to repair the space station hanging from a jet-propelled Manned Maneuvering Unit (there's always a line for these rides) in the "SpaceBase." "No Place Like Home" teaches home safety and water conservation. "Choose Health" lets children interact with restaurants to learn about food choices and measures their reaction times and respiration.

"KidScience" includes a musical staircase and stage for bold children to try to learn dance steps; the "Florida Sunshine Grove" provides hands-on learning about how oranges are harvested. And don't miss the exhibition about sound, to explore how it's made, recorded, and modified by technology.

South Florida's only IMAX theater presents outstanding "you are there" effects. (IMAX stands for "image maximum.") It will change the way you hear, see, and perceive motion pictures, possibly because its screen is five-stories high and 80-feet wide! The movies will change periodically, but you might catch one about a tropical rain forest or a journey into outer space. Call for titles and show times.

During your visit, be sure to inquire about the many fascinating and top-notch programs offered for children. They range from summer camp-ins to Saturday morning programs on wacky inventions. Teachers should ask for details about the MODSquad program, which allows the museum to come to you. The variety of programs appeals to young children and adults. Ask for an information packet.

◆ Native Village

3551 North S.R. 7 (between Stirling and Sheridan roads), Hollywood 33314. (305) 961-4519. Monday through Saturday, 10 A.M.–4 P.M. Alligator wrestling show and guided tour: adults, $8; children under 12, $6. Guided tour only: adults, $6; children under 12, $5. Self-guided tour: adults, $4; children under 12, $3.

A trip to the Native Village will educate your child about wild animals, venomous and nonvenomous snakes, alligators, and Seminole Indian culture. An alligator wrestling show is presented throughout the day. The one-acre village features Seminole and other Indian tribal crafts—you can watch an Indian woman creating beaded artwork. The craft shop is usually open one hour after the ticket booth closes. Children will enjoy examining the artifacts on the touch tables and seeing the thatch-roofed chickee huts. **Tip:** Plan on spending an hour for the guided tour; less for the self-guided tour.

◆ Ocean World

1701 SE 17th Street Causeway, Fort Lauderdale 33316. Take I-95 to exit 28/Davie Boulevard. Head east to U.S. 1; turn south on U.S. 1 to the next traffic light (SE 17th Street); go east on SE 17th Street to entrance. (305) 525-6611. Daily, 10 A.M.–6 P.M.; ticket gates close at 4:30 P.M. Adults, $10.95; children 4 to 12, $8.95; children under 3, free with a paying adult. MC and V accepted. Group rates and resident passes available.

Ocean World, Fort Lauderdale's famed aquatic park, has seven shows you won't want to miss. The stars include dolphins, sharks, alligators, sea lions, and turtles. The aviary, complete with parrots and toucans, adds a twist to this marine-life park. Ocean World's own cruise boat, *Miss Ocean World,* jaunts along the Intracoastal Waterway for a fun 45-minute sightseeing adventure. **Tips:** Plan on approximately two hours to tour and see all the shows. Eating facilities, gift shop, and film on grounds. For cruise information, see listing in "By Land, Sea, and Air."

PALM BEACH COUNTY

◆   Burt Reynolds Ranch and Film Studios

16133 Jupiter Farms Road, Jupiter 33478. Located two miles west of the Florida Turnpike (exit 706) and the Indiantown Road exit off I-95. Turn south on Jupiter Farms Road and travel two miles. Look for the ranch sign on the right. (407) 746-0393. Daily, 10 A.M.–5 P.M. Guided tours: adults, $10; children 6 to 12, $5. Free admission to the petting farm. MC, V accepted.

Tucked away from the bustle of the city, Burt's enormous complex includes a feed store, gift shop, film studio, and a small petting farm. There are two entrances to the complex. The first takes you to the feed store, which is packed with pet and livestock items. Go through the second entrance at the white iron gates, and look to the right for the winding, boardwalk path that leads inquisitive visitors to see llamas, ponies, turkeys, sheep, goats, and other animals. Bring some quarters to pop in the food machines and give a treat to a friendly goat. If you take time to read the signs, you will discover how Mr. Reynolds came to own the various animals.

To buy tickets for the film studio tour, you will need to stop in the western wear store. Don't be frightened by the large preserved bear named Ted, who greets you at the door! The tour will take you around the 160-acre ranch, and you'll see parts of the sets from Burt's television series, "B.L. Striker," and his movie *Smokey and the Bandit.* **Tips:** There is a pizza shop behind the western wear store. Soda and snack machines are near the petting zoo. There is a nice country store and restaurant down the street.

◆   Children's Museum of Boca Raton

498 Crawford Boulevard, Boca Raton 33432. Located two miles east of I-95 on Crawford Boulevard off Palmetto Park Road. (407) 368-6875. Monday through Sunday, noon–5 P.M. Closed holidays and month of September. Admission, $1; children under 2, free. Cash payment only.

One of Florida's oldest houses, Singing Pines, is home for this museum designed just for children. Play in a pioneer kitchen, make a discovery in the insect room, and pretend in a child-size supermarket. Traveling exhibits also set up shop at the museum. Wonderful programming and special events are held throughout the year, including "KidsFest" in April and a summer camp. Field trips are very popular, and each trip provides new exhibits and educational opportunities for children. Teachers may request a *Gallery Guide for Students* to help prepare for their visit.

Schools and groups located in neighboring counties can also take advantage of "The Traveling Museum." Request a brochure about the many science, arts, and humanities programs that can be brought to your school or group. **Tips:** Free parking is located behind the museum. Group tours must be reserved. Gift shop, picnic tables, and soda machines are available. For more information about special annual events, see listing in "Mark Your Calendar."

◆ Dreher Park Zoo

1301 Summit Boulevard, West Palm Beach 33405. Located just east of I-95; follow the signs. (407) 547-WILD. Daily, 9 A.M.–5 P.M.; tickets sold until 4:15 P.M. Extended hours in the summer. Adults, $5; seniors over 60, $4.50; children 3 to 12, $3.50; children under 3, free. Groups of 15 or more receive a 50% discount. MC and V accepted. Annual memberships available.

This 22-acre zoo is located within Palm Beach County's Dreher Park and is home to nearly 100 species of domestic and exotic animals. A map provided at the ticket gate will give you a good idea of what to expect as you walk along the paved trails. Start out on the trail to the far right (it passes alongside the education building) to avoid missing some of the endangered species. You'll see a Florida panther (the rarest large mammal in North America) and a pair of American bald eagles, among a host of others. Large trees provide plenty of shade along your journey. Across from the Diana monkeys you'll find water fowl splashing in a long, winding pond. Look for the bright scarlet ibis — you can't miss them! The giant Aldabra tortoises, Brazilian tapirs, and Bengal tiger are also in the neighborhood.

The reptile exhibit is quite impressive with both venomous and non-venomous snakes, including an albino king snake. Take this opportunity to reintroduce wildlife safety rules to your children. At the children's area, called ARK (Animals Reaching Kids), an attendant will greet you with a small critter to touch. Guinea pigs, baby turkeys, rabbits, and turtles are among the species your children can examine at eye level. Miniature horses, goats, and other farm animals stay in this area. A nature trail is located at the rear of the zoo, just beyond the ARK area.

Vending machines are located throughout the zoo, and just beyond the entrance is a small red barn where sandwiches, drinks, and ice cream treats are served. There are a few picnic tables scattered under the trees. Special events are held on a regular basis, and summer camps are very popular. The next time you need to come up with a gift for a birthday party, consider adopting one of the zoo's animals in the birthday child's name (and give him or her a stuffed replica to make believe with). Adoptions start at $10. **Tips:** Plan to spend two hours to tour. A small gift shop has film and souvenirs. No feeding of the animals is permitted. The South Florida Science Museum is also located within Dreher Park.

♦ Hallpatee Seminole Village at Knollwood Groves

8053 Lawrence Road, Boynton Beach 33032. Located off Lawrence Road, between Hypoluxo Road and Boynton Beach Boulevard. (407) 582-5947; (800) 624-2730. Adults, $5; seniors, $4.50; children 12 and above, $3. Group rates available. MC, V accepted.

A trip to this attraction will help children understand the Seminole Indian culture that is such an important part of South Florida's history. By observing cooking (sample a few treats like alligator tail!) and craft demonstrations at the Indian Village, located just beyond the parking lot, visitors will get a sense of the past. Pick up a map of the village and groves as you buy tickets, and plot out your journey. Take a tram ride through the citrus groves, walk the paths of the Natural Jungle Hammock, and inquire about airboat rides. Don't miss the alligator wrestling show offered throughout the day! **Tip:** Gift shop, snack area, and restrooms are available.

♦ Hoffman's Chocolate Shoppe and Gardens

5190 Lake Worth Road, Greenacres 33463. Located east of the Florida Turnpike (exit 93) and west of Military Trail on south side of Lake Worth Road. (407) 967-2213 or (800) 545-0094. Monday through Saturday, 9 A.M.–6 P.M.; Sunday 12–6 P.M. Free.

As you approach *this* chocolate factory, you might be reminded of Willy Wonka's! Hoffman's is a true delight, from the outside building and gardens to the gift shop and working factory. You might want to bring your children here to pick out a special gift for a teacher or grandparent. There are literally hundreds of shapes, sizes, and flavors of chocolate in the gift and chocolate shop. During the summer months, the cooking schedule is a bit relaxed, so you'll view a video of the chocolate-making procedure. However, most of the year visitors can enjoy watching the busy candy-makers in the kitchen through large viewing windows (benches are provided).

Take a walk outside to the back of the building, where you'll discover a delightful garden area. Look for the shrub-sculptured animals in the various garden plots, and be sure to walk around the path to find the electric train that weaves around a small village. Bring your camera for a special photo opportunity near the waterfall, then sit very still and watch for butterflies to come sip nectar from the various plants. **Tips:** Restrooms are located inside. There are other Hoffman's Chocolate Shoppes located throughout the area, but this location is the only one of its kind. Plan a trip around Christmas for a special surprise in the garden area!

◆ Lion Country Safari

Southern Boulevard (S.R. 80), West Palm Beach. Ninety minutes from downtown Miami; 15 miles west of Florida Turnpike exits 93 or 99. From I-95 take exit 50; from the coastal areas, go west on Southern Boulevard. Mailing address is P.O. Box 16066, West Palm Beach 33416-6066. (407) 793-1084; campground, (407) 793-9797. Daily, 9:30 A.M.–5:30 P.M.; tickets sold until 4:30 P.M., when wildlife preserve closes. Adults, $11.95; children 3 to 15, $9.95; children under 3, free. Group rates available. AE, MC, and V accepted.

Yield the right-of-way to rhinos, elephants, and zebras! As you drive through 500 acres of natural wildlife preserve, you'll be amazed how the 1,000 wild beasts, including lions, giraffes, elephants, zebras, chimpanzees, antelopes, ostriches, and rhinos, roam freely in a natural setting. Open since 1967, Lion Country Safari is North America's first cageless zoo. It's as interesting for adults as it is for kids. Visitors are permitted to drive through as often as they like (just remember to give the right-of-way to the animals).

And when the kids are ready for a change of pace—from jungle to civilization—take them to Safari World Amusement Park (included in your admission price), where you'll find boat rides, jeep tours, nature trails, a free-flight aviary, reptile displays, a dinosaur replica park, miniature golf, and an "old-tyme" carousel. The Great American Farm Yard has a variety of domestic and exotic animals, often including zebras, llamas, miniature horses, and baby ostriches. You can purchase bottles of milk at the barn to feed the animals. An unusual collection of chickens gather here as well, including some that have feathered feet, lay different-colored eggs, or whose wild plumage gives them a "punk" look!

Adventurers can cruise on the Safari Queen, which will take them past Gibbon apes, flamingos, and spider monkeys. Paddleboats can be rented. The complete KOA campground facilities, located to the right of the entrance, include a swimming pool, children's playground, and general store. **Tips:** Gift shop, snacks, and refreshments on grounds. A pet hotel is located to the left of the entrance. Watch in newspapers for special discount price coupons; souvenir program is a nice keepsake. Changing table available in women's restroom behind film/gift area. Picnic area with lots of trees just past entrance on right. Note that convertible cars are banned from entering the preserve. Rental vehicles are available.

MONROE COUNTY

Don't miss a stop at the Visitors' Center, located just south of U.S. 1 and SW 334th Street (Palm Drive), next to the Hurricane Andrew Motor Inn in Homestead, on your way down the Keys! The friendly people who work here are very interested in sharing maps, discount tickets, and menus with you, free of charge. They can also give you tidbits of information if you have questions about where to stay, weather concerns, directions, etc. The Key West Welcome Center is also worth a visit. Open daily from 9 A.M. to 5 P.M., it is located at 3840 North Roosevelt Boulevard, Key West 33440; (305) 296-4444 or (800) 352-8538.

Have fun exploring this unusual chain of islands. On your adventure driving down the Keys, be sure to make note of the Seven Mile Bridge leading from Marathon to the Lower Keys. The bridge is a doozy, but it's actually just under 7 miles—6.79 miles to be exact! Robbie's Dock at Mile Marker 77.5 in Matecumbe is noted as one of the world's best spots to catch gamefish. For $1.50 you can buy a bucket of fish chunks and feed tarpon and other fish. Look for the six-footers that weigh 100 pounds!

◆ African Queen

Mile Marker 100, Key Largo 33037. Docked at the ocean-access canal adjoining the Holiday Inn. (305) 451-4655. Free to look at; $15 per person to tour.

The legendary ship *The African Queen,* from the 1951 movie by the same name (starring Humphrey Bogart and Katherine Hepburn), is now docked outside the Key Largo Holiday Inn for all to see.

After appearing in the movie, the 30-foot boat was used in Africa as a government supply vessel. In 1968 she was brought to the U.S. and used as a fund-raiser for cancer research. In the early 1980s the boat was refurbished and has appeared in parades and races. She has sailed around the world twice.

Upon request and reservation, the *Queen* can take passengers on a short trip to the Atlantic Ocean and back. Inquire by calling the number listed above.

◆ Dolphin Research Center

Mile Marker 59 (bayside), Grassy Key. Mailing address is P.O. Box 2875, Marathon Shores 33052. (305) 289-1121 or 289-0002. Wednesday through Sunday, 9 A.M.–4 P.M.; closed Mondays and Tuesdays. Walking tours: adults, $7.50; children 4 to 12, $4.50. Dolphin Insight: $65. Dolphin Swimming Encounters: $80.

From its name, you can tell this is first a research facility. During the week, however, interested visitors can come to the center for an educational tour or for one of the other programs that will give them a sense of the world of dolphins. The Dolphin Insight program allows humans to touch and interact with the dolphins without swimming with them. On the other hand, "Dolphin Encounters" are available for visitors to actually get in the water and swim with the dolphins. You must be a strong swimmer to participate in the swim program. Make reservations well in advance.

◆ Dolphin's Plus

Mile Marker 100, Key Largo. Located oceanside on Ocean Bay Drive. At Mile Marker 100 traffic light, turn east, go one block and make the first right hand turn; go one more block, and make the first left hand turn; proceed about eight blocks and turn right just before small bridge. Mailing address is P.O. Box 2728, Key Largo 33037. (305) 451-1993. Animal Assisted Therapy: 453-0051. Daily programs: 9 A.M. and 2 P.M. (1:30 P.M. during winter months). Cost for swimming programs starts at $65 plus tax. Observers, $5 plus tax for visitors 6 and older.

Dolphin's Plus is a marine mammal research and education center, where the public can come to learn more about dolphins and/or swim with them in their natural habitat. Visitors who want to participate in the swimming or snorkeling program must participate in a pre-swim orientation and have prior swimming experience. Swim fins and a face mask are a must; they are provided by Dolphin's Plus, or visitors may bring their own. Therapeutic encounters with dolphins for special needs children and adults are provided. Please call for more information and to make reservations.

◆ Jules' Undersea Lodge

Mile Marker 103.2, Key Largo 33037. Located one-half mile north of the entrance to John Pennekamp Coral Reef State Park. (305) 451-2353. Call for hours and prices.

Located within Key Largo Undersea Park, Jules' Undersea Lodge is the world's only underwater hotel. It is five fathoms deep and can accommodate up to six divers. Reservations are required. Meals are served. At the park lagoon, adventurers can dive, snorkel, and swim. Snorkelers will be able to observe an underwater research laboratory and marine archaeologists searching for shipwrecks. Snorkeling instruction and rental equipment are offered. Call for details.

◆ Key West Hand Print Fabrics

201 Simonton Street, Key West 33040. Located at the corner of Greene Street. Turn right at Sloppy Joe's, and go two blocks. (305) 294-9535. Daily, 10 A.M.-6 P.M. Free.

This working factory and design shop is located in the historic Curry Warehouse, which was a tobacco holding warehouse in the late 1800s. If you stop in to look around, ask about a free tour of the factory. Watch the paints being mixed, observe the designers as they transfer designs to the screens that are used to print the fabrics, get involved in the printing process, and then visit the sewing room to see how the seamstresses create the clothing and other goods sold in the shop area.

◆ Little White House Museum

111 Front Street, Key West 33040. Located in the Truman Annex. (305) 294-9911. Daily, 9 A.M.–5 P.M.; last tour leaves at 4:30 P.M. Adults, $6; children 2 to 12, $3.

This is the restored vacation home of Harry S. Truman, the 33rd president of the United States. The home, used during Truman's administration, features the piano that he played during his trips (he was an accomplished pianist) and other furnishings dear to the former president. A short video about Truman is presented to visitors, and a 15-minute tour gives insight into his life. Tour guides are dressed in the typical "Key West" attire that Truman so enjoyed.

◆ Mallory Dock

Mallory Square, Key West. Head south on Overseas Highway until you reach the end of the road. Turn right and head toward old Key West. Turn right on Duval Street. Look for a place to park. (800) 648-6269.

The sunset is breathtaking (how many colors can you find?), the entertainment is unusual, and both are free (although a hat may be passed). The street theater performed here changes daily, but expect to see fire-eaters, trained cats, contortionists, tight-rope walkers, comedians, magicians, mimes, and jugglers. Locally produced art is also on display and for sale. Most hotels and shops in Key West post daily sunrise and sunset times, so there's no excuse to miss this free show.

While you're in the area, head down to South Beach to find baby crabs to watch or chase near the pier. Or watch the fishing boats unload their catch of the day around 6 P.M. at Land's End Village.

◆ Maritime Museum of the Florida Keys

Mile marker 102, Key Largo 33037. Located bayside across from John Pennekamp Coral Reef State Park. (305) 451-6444. Daily, 10 A.M.–5 P.M. Adults, $5; children 6 to 12, $3; under 5, free. Group rates available.

This mighty fortress contains over 500 years of historical displays, including treasures from the sea like jewels, coins, glassware, and pottery. The impressive display of pirate history is fun to look at. (Don't spread this around, but treasure maps are for sale here!) This museum is also known as Kimbell's Caribbean Shipwreck Museum.

◆ Mel Fisher's Maritime Heritage Society Museum

200 Greene Street, Key West 33040. (305) 294-2633. Daily, 9:30 A.M.– 5:00 P.M. Adults, $6; children 7 to 12, $2; children under 6, free. AE, MC, V accepted.

See gold, silver, jewelry, coins, and gems that Mel Fisher, the world-renowned treasure-seeker, found during his many quests under the sea. Many of the treasures were recovered from two Spanish ships that sank 40 miles off Key West in 1622. Perhaps most impressive are the artifacts from the *Atocha*, discovered by two of Fisher's divers in 1985. Valued at $250 million, they make up the richest find ever, and many items remain to be brought to the surface from the underwater site. There is a video presentation and a souvenir shop as well.

◆ Museum of Natural History of the Florida Keys and the Florida Keys' Children's Museum

Mile Marker 50, Marathon 33050. Located bayside in Crane Point Ham-mock. (305) 743-9100. Monday through Saturday, 9 A.M.–5 P.M.; Sunday, noon–5 P.M. Admission for both museums: adults, $5; seniors, $4; students, $2; children under 12, free. MC, V accepted. Memberships available.

Opened in 1991, the museum complex is located in 63.5 acres of natural Keys environment, and its displays help adults and children learn about the local geology, geography, history, and wildlife. The land was once the site of a Bahamian village, and the hammock (a fertile land area made up of densely grown hardwood trees) holds pre-Columbian and prehistoric Indian artifacts.

The children's museum, located behind the main museum, is housed in an authentic restored Conch House. Travel over a tropical lagoon (be on the lookout for fish!) by way of a boardwalk to the porch of the children's museum. Here you'll find a variety of touch tanks and sea-life tanks for observation. Hermit and horseshoe crabs, sea anemones, and other indigenous sea creatures occupy the tanks. A Flagler Railroad exhibit is being created outside the entrance. Visit a ticket house and try a telegraph machine; negotiations are in progress for a real caboose!

Inside the museum you'll find four main areas: the library, where children can snuggle up on a pillow and look at unusual books; the science activity center, where children can peer into a microscope to examine interesting samples (mosquito larvae is one!) or study a jar of scorpions (not alive!); the Do Not Touch area (the only one in the museum), which demonstrates safety tips regarding snakes and insects that live in the area; and the Spanish Galleon, a re-creation of a pirate vessel, complete with treasure chest and pirate dress-up clothes. If your child is interested in art, there are a few murals and paintings worth pointing out and discussing.

Before adventuring out on the nature trail, stop by the authentic Miccosukee Indian Huts, which were actually built for the museum by Indian friends. Be sure to say hello to Mr. Iggy and his bride-to-be, "Sweet Pea," the resident iguanas. **Tips:** Admission includes the two museums and a one-quarter mile nature trail. Groups on field trips can use the amphitheater as a meeting place. A water fountain and soda machines are available. Allow at least one hour to tour. The parking lot is small, so if there is no room for your vehicle, parking is also available at the Nation's Bank next door. Birthday parties are welcome, although no set package is available. Parents can set up food in the amphitheater area with prior permission.

◆ Ripley's Believe It or Not!

527 Duval Street, Key West 33040. Located in the old Strand Theater. (305) 293-9694; (800) 998-4418. Sunday through Thursday, 10 A.M.– 11 P.M.; Friday and Saturday, 10 A.M.–midnight. Adults, $9.75; children 4 to 11, $6.75; children under 4, free. AE, DISC, MC, and V accepted.

Robert Ripley, cartoonist and collector, has museums like this one all over the country. When this museum opened in 1992, it became the 20th of its kind—an odditorium that focuses on the unusual. The theme is felt the moment you enter. The museum features collections of dive gear and reef exhibits, and the 250 exhibits in the 10,000-square-foot museum include artifacts, videos, illusions, music, and interactive displays.

A 28-foot-high gallery showcases mammoth sea life with a giant periscope you can try. Children will be amazed at the nearly 30,000 match sticks that make up a replica of the *Santa Maria*. Try the noise box exhibit: push a block and get a different noise! One exhibit area may be a bit grotesque for youngsters (or maybe for mom). It displays shrunken heads and death masks, and you might want to bypass this stop. **Tips:** Group rates are available. The gift shop has unusual souvenirs. Allow one hour to tour.

◆ Southernmost Point
Corner of Whitehead and South streets, Key West.

The southernmost point in the continental United States can't help but be thrilling, even if only to say "I was there!" It's free and a good place to meet people from around the world.

◆ Theater of the Sea
Mile Marker 84.5, Islamorada. Mailing address is P.O. Box 407, Islamorada 33036. (305) 664-2431. Daily, 9:30 A.M.–5:45 P.M.; box office closes at 4 P.M. Adults, $11.75 plus tax; children 3 to 12, $6.25 plus tax; children 3 and under, free. Dolphin Adventure: $65. AE, MC, V accepted. Annual membership for local residents available. Rainchecks available if needed.

You can't miss the large sign and flags waving you down! Open since 1946, Theater of the Sea is the second-oldest marine-life park in the world. It is known for its famous dolphins, sea lions, and marine exhibits.

Shows run continuously throughout the day. Have the video camera ready as volunteers from the audience get kissed by sea lions, touch dolphins, sea turtles, and sharks, or feed stingrays. Kids can also experience marine life firsthand when they hold a sea urchin or examine crabs from the tidal pool. The glass-bottom boat rides also give insight into life below.

The Dolphin Adventure is offered to people who are very interested in these creatures. A seminar to educate visitors is held prior to the swim. Advance reservations are necessary. **Tips:** Snack bar on grounds. Gift shop sells film and souvenirs. Guided tours and group rates available. Plan on 90 minutes to tour. Birthday parties can be fun here; ask for information.

◆ Turtle Kraals
2 Land's End Village (where Margaret Street meets the Gulf), Key West 33040. (305) 294-2640. Monday through Saturday, 11 A.M.–11 P.M.; Sunday, noon–11 P.M. Free admission.

Turtle Kraals, located in the famous shrimp-dock area, is home of the Florida Marine Conservancy, where sick and injured marine life find refuge. The huge loggerhead turtles that weigh up to 400 pounds can be observed here. Kids will enjoy the touch tank filled with marine life. There's an aviary here as well, and if you're hungry, try the full-service waterfront restaurant. For more information about the restaurant, see listing in "Come and Get It!"

TRACING THE PAST

Indians, pirates, Spanish explorers, wreckers, slaves, pioneers, English soldiers, railroad workers, and immigrants from all over the world play important roles in South Florida's past, present, and future. Fortunately, South Florida has many ways for children to touch the past and wonder about the future—the best ways are listed here.

The first known human presence in South Florida can be traced to about 8000 B.C., when Paleo-Indians inhabited the area. Then came the Hobe, Tequesta, Creek, Miccosukee, and Seminole Indians. Spanish explorer Ponce de León, in search of the Fountain of Youth, saw Biscayne Bay in 1513. He and other European explorers brought smallpox and other diseases to the Tequesta Indians, who had inhabited the area since 2000 B.C., and by 1763 the few surviving families (less than 100) departed for Cuba.

England gained control of Florida in 1763; Florida became a United States territory in 1821, gained statehood in 1845, seceded from the Union in 1861, and reunited with the United States in 1868. A long and bloody war with the Seminole Indians broke out in 1835; the Third Seminole War ended in 1858. A peace treaty between the Seminoles and the U.S. has yet to be signed.

Fitzgerald, Flagler, Tuttle, Brickell, Merrick, and Matheson are a few of the names you'll encounter as you explore South Florida's more recent past. The actions of these pioneer men and women during the late 19th and early 20th centuries shaped the past and influence the present. A trip to Miami Beach on the Tuttle Causeway, a drive down Flagler Street, or a visit to the city of Tequesta will be more interesting when children know something about Julia Tuttle, Henry Flagler, and the Tequesta Indians.

Many South Floridians have ethnic roots in countries throughout the Caribbean and Latin America, Africa, Europe, and Asia. South Florida's immigrants have had many motives for developing communities here; Bahamians, African-Americans, Conchs, wreckers, Cubans, Haitians, Nicaraguans, Norwegians, Finns, Japanese, Mexicans, and others have influenced the area's history and geography.

DADE COUNTY

◆ Art Deco District

From 6th to 23rd streets on Miami Beach, between Lennox Avenue and Ocean Drive. Tours (minimum of 10 people per group) can be arranged by contacting the Dade Heritage Trust at (305) 638-6064.

Come see the world-renowned pastel buildings along the streets of this designated historic district, a one-square-mile area with more than 800 buildings representing the famous architectural styles of the 1920s, 1930s, and 1940s. **Tips:** Note that the 90-minute tour on Saturday morning, sponsored by the Miami Design Preservation League, is not appropriate for children. Call (305) 672-2014 for more information about alternatives. Some areas are not safe to visit in the evenings. For information about Art Deco Weekend Festival, see listing in "Mark Your Calendar."

◆ Barnacle State Historic Site

3485 Main Highway, Coconut Grove 33133. (305) 448-9445. Tours: Thursday through Monday, 10:30 A.M., 1, and 2:30 P.M. Admission, $1; children under 6, free.

In 1886 Commodore Ralph Middleton Munroe, early pioneer, naval architect, photographer, and community leader, moved to the area he named Cocoanut Grove and built his beautiful and ingenious frame home. He was the head, or commodore, of the Biscayne Yacht Club for 22 years, from whence came his nickname "Commodore" (Commodore Plaza, across the highway, was named after him). The shed and *Micco*, the boat built in 1891, were destroyed and will not be replaced; the home, boathouse, and grounds suffered some damage from Hurricane Andrew but are being restored. An hour here provides a great way to imagine life in Miami at the turn of the century. **Tips:** Tours start promptly, so get to the entrance several minutes early; the guide will unlock the door to take anyone waiting, and lock the door behind him. Tours last at least an hour, commencing with a tour of the grounds before entering the house. Toddlers and small children will be tempted to play with the antiques that are displayed in the house, so be prepared to carry your children or hold their hands. No stroller access in the house.

◆ The Biltmore Hotel

1212 Anastasia Avenue, Coral Gables 33134. (305) 445-1926. Free 30-minute historic tours depart from the hotel lobby at 1:30, 2:30, and 3:30 P.M. on Sundays.

This National Historic Landmark was a holiday haven for the wealthy of the 1920s and 1930s. The 26-story tower is a replica of the Giralda

Tower in Sevilla, Spain. After World War II, the hotel was used as a veterans' hospital. It was vacant from 1968 until its restoration was completed in 1986. It now houses two restaurants, a spa, and North America's largest hotel pool. **Tips:** The tour is interesting for older children accompanied by an adult. Customized tours are available if you have younger children or large groups; call for reservations. For information on Christmas at the Biltmore, see listing in "Mark Your Calendar."

♦ Black Archives History and Research Foundation of South Florida

Caleb Center, First Floor, Building B, Suite 101, 5400 NW 22nd Avenue, Miami 33142. (305) 636-2390. Monday through Friday, 9 A.M.–5 P.M.

This nonprofit organization was incorporated in 1977 to spearhead African-American heritage observances throughout Dade County. These include programs in the humanities and in the literary, visual, and performing arts. The research center is a treasure chest of original materials such as letters, photographs, historical records, clippings, manuscripts, and recorded oral histories that document the various black communities in Dade County from 1845 to the present.

The Black Archives sponsors the ongoing development of the Historic Overtown Folklife Village, which will encompass eight blocks from NW Eighth Street north to NW Tenth Street, with NW Second Avenue on the east and NW Third Avenue on the west. They also hold an annual Black Heritage Fair, an Adopt-a-Pioneer history program, and many other activities. **Tips:** Tours can be arranged for a minimum of 10 people. Call for individual appointments.

♦ Cape Florida Lighthouse

1200 South Crandon Boulevard, Key Biscayne 33149. Located in Bill Baggs/Cape Florida State Recreation Area, south of Miami off the Rickenbacker Causeway. (305) 361-5811. Park: daily, 8 A.M.–sunset. Admission: $3.25 per vehicle, plus $.50 per person; $1.50 for walk-ins or bikers. Rickenbacker Causeway toll: $1.

Built in 1825, the lighthouse is currently undergoing major renovations and is due to open in 1995. You can get into the park, walk around the lighthouse (and take some great Florida vacation pictures), and then visit the lightkeeper's home to find out how a lightkeeper might have lived in the early 1900s. While you're in the past, imagine the battle between the Seminole Indians and the settlers in 1836, when the Seminoles killed the lightkeeper's aide and tried to burn down the lighthouse. For more information, see Bill Baggs/Cape Florida State Recreation Area listing in "Under the Sun."

◆ Cauley Square

22400 Old Dixie Highway (one block west of South Dixie Highway, across the railroad tracks), Goulds 33170. (305) 258-3543. Monday through Saturday, 10 A.M.–4:30 P.M.

When William H. Cauley built most of this complex in 1919, it included a commissary, offices, luxury apartments, restaurants, and warehouses. Those buildings, together with the woodframe houses that make up the rest of the old-style southern village, house a unique shopping area. Now under restoration, the Tea Room restaurant, the main building, and landscaping suffered major damage during Hurricane Andrew. Many of the shops are strictly for older children and adults because of the variety of small and fragile items. For older kids it's like taking a tour of great-grandma's attic! There are plenty of unusual treasures here—this could almost be classified as a museum area! **Tips:** Much of the area outside is covered with pine bark chips, which can make stroller access difficult. For special event information, see listing in "Mark Your Calendar."

◆ Chapman House Ethnic Heritage Children's Folklife Education Center

1200 NW Sixth Avenue, Miami 33136. Call the Black Archives History and Research Foundation of South Florida for information: (305) 636-2390. Open during school year, Monday through Friday, 9 A.M.–3 P.M. Field trips can be arranged. Free admission.

Dr. W. A. Chapman, a black physician, was called to serve as the first "colored consultant" for the State Board of Health in Jacksonville in the 1930s. He was also a church and civic leader in the area known as Colored Town (renamed Overtown in the 1940s), and he built his 17-room, 2 1/2-story home near Booker T. Washington High School, where it stands today. The Chapman House was declared a historic site by the City of Miami Commission and is listed in the National Register of Historic Places.

The Ethnic Heritage Children's Folklife Education Center opened in Chapman House in April 1993. It focuses on the folk arts and the lives of children who have come to South Florida in migrant and immigrant groups from around the world. Dade County reports that over 120 languages are spoken by students in the district, and one exhibit features flags from most of the countries represented. Center staff visit the schools to record oral histories of students from around the world, and these tapes are stored at the center. Traveling exhibits change periodically.

The next phase of development in what is known as the Historic Overtown Folklife Village area is the Dorsey House, once owned by Dana Dorsey, Miami's first African-American millionaire and an important community benefactor. His home, at 250 NW Ninth Street, is under complete reconstruction and will serve as the Children's Folklife Museum. The Lyric Theatre is also set for restoration.

Field trips can be arranged to include the Chapman House, a tour of the Historic Overtown Folklife Village area (see listing under "Black Archives" earlier in this chapter), and a visit to the planetarium at Booker T. Washington Middle School at 1200 NW Sixth Avenue, (305) 324-8900. **Tip:** These trips are best for children in 4th to 12th grades.

◆ Charles Deering Estate

16701 SW 72nd Avenue, Miami 33157. (305) 235-1668.

The history of this 350-acre bay-front estate spans 10,000 years, beginning with the Paleo-Indians who hunted and gathered food in the area. Tequesta Indian archaeological sites located on the grounds date back to around 500 A.D. Remains of a late nineteenth-century town, Cutler, can be seen, as can the Richmond Cottage, built in 1896. In 1916, Charles Deering (brother of James Deering of Vizcaya) bought the entire property and built his Mediterranean Revival–style mansion. In 1985 the state of Florida and Metropolitan Dade County bought the property and opened it to the public. In 1992 Hurricane Andrew destroyed much of the construction, and rebuilding is underway. Call for information about tours. When operation is restored, this is an excellent place for school field trips.

◆ Dade Heritage Trust

Historic Preservation Center, 190 SE 12th Terrace, Miami 33131. (305) 358-9572.

Call the office or stop by to pick up their excellent materials designed to help children and adults get to know Dade County as it once was. The friendly staff is willing to help you provide age-appropriate outings that introduce children to the history around them. If you are interested in exploring old Dade County sites (rather than just driving past them), the staff can arrange tours for children ages one and older. They request that groups have at least 10 people. A coloring book for younger children, a preservation activity book for older children, and other materials describing Dade County's historic sights are available at the office.

◆ First Coconut Grove Schoolhouse

3429 Devon Road (on grounds of Plymouth Congregational Church), Coconut Grove 33133.

School-age children will enjoy visiting the first public school in what is now Dade County. Built across from the Peacock Inn in 1889 to serve as a Sunday school, the school was constructed of lumber that Coconut Grove pioneers salvaged from wrecked ships. It was sold in 1902 to serve as a home; the Ryder Corporation bought it in 1969, donated it to Plymouth Congregational Church, moved it to church property, and restored its original appearance. **Tip:** Tours can be arranged for groups of at least 10 people. Call the Dade Heritage Trust at (305) 638-6064.

◆ Florida Pioneer Museum

826 North Krome Avenue (east side, north of Silver Palm; just look for the yellow and white buildings), Florida City 33034. (305) 246-9531. Daily, except Christmas and New Year's, 1–5 P.M. Adults, $1.50; children, $.75.

Hurricane Andrew flattened much of this museum, but rebuilding is underway. The original plans and over 700 black-and-white photograph negatives dating back to 1903 survived the storm in a bank vault, so the station and front building were rebuilt exactly as they were. A railroad agent's 10-room home and a caboose are under restoration. New copies of the old photos have been printed as well. The buildings, painted "Flagler yellow," as prescribed by Henry Flagler for his Florida East Coast Railway Company buildings and hotels, were constructed around 1904 from Dade County pine.

◆ Hialeah Park

Corner of East Fourth Avenue and 79th Street, Hialeah 33010. Mailing address is P.O. Box 158, Hialeah 33011. (305) 885-8000; (800) 423-3504, in Florida. Daily, 9:30 A.M.–4:30 P.M. except during racing season (April and May). Free admission during off season. Cost varies according to seating location; children 17 and under admitted to races free with adult.

Whether you prefer watching the horses run for fun or for money, you and the little ones will enjoy a few hours at this National Historic Site during the racing season. The clubhouse opened in 1925—look for displays of thoroughbred racing silks. During the season gates open early on designated Saturday and Sunday mornings to let you eat breakfast (7:30–9:30 A.M.), watch the horses work out, and count the several hundred Cuban flamingos. **Tips:** If you take the Metrorail to Hialeah station, located in the park, the information booths and gift shops will give you a free return Metrorail pass. For more information, see listing in "On Your Mark, Get Set, Go!"

◆ Historic Coral Gables House

907 Coral Way, Coral Gables 33134. Sunday, 1–4 P.M.; Wednesday, 10 A.M.– 4 P.M. Group tours may be arranged on other days. Adults, $1; children, $.50.

Call the Chamber of Commerce at (305) 446-1657 for information.

Get an idea of life in Coral Gables during the 1920s by touring the boyhood home of the city's founder, George Merrick. The city acquired the home in 1976, restored it, and opened it to the public. Keep an eye on toddlers and small children, as there are many things that they will want to touch but shouldn't. The annual Christmas party is great for children; call for information.

◆ Historical Museum of Southern Florida

101 West Flagler Street, Miami 33130. (305) 375-1492. Monday through Wednesday, Friday and Saturday, 10 A.M.–5 P.M.; Thursday, 10 A.M.– 9 P.M.; Sunday, noon–5 P.M. Adults, $4; children 6 to 12, $2; contributions only on Monday. Ask about special discounts on joint admission tickets to the Center for the Fine Arts next door. Annual memberships available.

A great place for children and adults to see, hear, and feel the drama of 10,000 years of South Florida and Caribbean history. You'll enjoy life-size displays of Indian families, Florida animals and marine life, a Spanish galleon (complete with treasure chest), and more. Several hands-on exhibits teach children about various aspects of Florida life.

The museum sponsors about 25 different outings between September and June that include historical boat trips and tours of old Miami neighborhoods. The museum has extensive educational programs for children's groups (schools, camps, etc.) that feature ancestral stories, Miami neighborhoods, and the many cultural traditions of the peoples of Southern Florida. For information about The Harvest, a festival featuring 350 crafts booths, food, re-enactments, and continuous folklife performances, see listing in "Mark Your Calendar."

◆ Ichimura Miami-Japan Garden

Located on Watson Island, opposite downtown Miami on the north side of MacArthur Causeway, east of the bridge. (305) 665-2459. Tuesday, 9 A.M.– 1 P.M.; Thursday and Sunday, 1–5 P.M.; Saturday, 11 A.M.–3 P.M. (Call to confirm hours.) Call the City of Miami Parks, Recreation, and Public Facilities Operations Division, (305) 575-5256, to arrange for tours, field trips, and rentals. Free admission.

This one-acre garden was built and donated to the city of Miami by Kyoshi Ichimura, a Japanese industrialist and founder of the Ricoh Corporation's copy machine company. The garden was completely restored in 1988, and a new *hakkaku-do* (the octagonal pavilion) as well as the original pagoda, lanterns, and stone *Hotei* figures can be seen as you wander down winding paths.

♦ Little Havana/Calle Ocho

Area from State Road 836 (Dolphin Expressway) and Miami River south to Dixie Highway, I-95 on the east and SW 27th Avenue on the west. The main street is Calle Ocho (SW Eighth Street/Tamiami Trail). From 27th Avenue east, Calle Ocho is one-way, so you need to take SW Seventh Street to travel west. Call Little Havana Development Authority, (305) 324-8127, for tour information. The office is open Monday through Friday, 9 A.M.–5 P.M.

Whether you live in Miami or are just here for a visit, plan to spend a couple of hours getting to know this part of town. And don't worry if you don't speak Spanish—shop and restaurant owners, and even people on the street, will be happy to find someone who can help you find what you need. There are several historic sites in this area, and the Little Havana Development Authority can provide you with a written, self-guided tour on request, or they can tell you where to visit. Be sure to see:

- **Cuban Memorial Plaza,** Memorial Boulevard and Eighth Street, dedicated to the "Martyrs of the Assault, April 17, 1961."
- **Máximo Gómez Park,** popularly known as "Domino Park." The game is taken very seriously, and dominoes is the only thing people play here.
- Open **fruit and vegetable market** on Calle Ocho.
- **Casa de los Trucos** and **La Casa de las Piñatas.**
- **El Crédito Cigars,** 1106 SW Eighth Street, (305) 858-4162. This cigar manufacturer has been operating since 1907, and you can watch them make cigars by hand.

≡ BROWARD COUNTY

♦ Ah-Tha-Thi-Ki Museum

Mini-museum: Seminole Tribe of Florida, 5845 South S.R. 7 (on the Seminole Reservation at S.R. 7 and Stirling Road), Fort Lauderdale 33314. (305) 792-0745. Wednesday through Sunday, 9 A.M.–4 P.M. Donations accepted. Major museum: Big Cypress Reservation. Take Alligator Alley to Snake Road (Shell gasoline station on corner), go north 17 miles to West Boundary Road. Call (305) 967-8997 for information about hours, admission cost, and exhibits.

The Seminole name of these museums means "a place to learn, a place to remember," and it perfectly describes this beautiful place. The tribe maintains the mini-museum in Hollywood to make exhibits about Seminole culture and art easily accessible to the public. The $10 million museum on the Big Cypress Seminole Indian Reservation began construction in 1993 and will include seven buildings set on 60 acres, nature walks, ceremonial grounds, and more. Both museums strive to preserve and teach Seminole culture and traditions. Call for information concerning special events and programs. For more information about Billie Swamp Safari, located about two miles west on West Boundary Road, see listing in "On Safari in South Florida."

◆ Bonnet House

900 North Birch Road, Fort Lauderdale 33301. (305) 563-5393. Tours available Tuesday through Friday, 10 and 11 A.M., 1 and 2 P.M.; Sunday, 1 and 2 P.M. Reservations required for groups of four or more. Adults, $7; students to 18 and seniors 60 and older, $5; children ages 5 and under, free.

Built in the 1920s by Frederic and Evelyn Bartlett, the Bonnet House (also known as the Bartlett Home) is part of a $36 million, 35-acre estate on Fort Lauderdale Beach. It has been restored to its original elegance and is available for tours of the home and grounds, including a lagoon with swans. The tours last about 75 minutes. **Tips:** This is best for older children who have had previous experiences in this type of "hands-off" museum; call for information about programs in progress for children.

◆ Fort Lauderdale Historical Society

219 SW Second Avenue, Fort Lauderdale 33301. (305) 463-4431. Tuesday through Saturday, 10 A.M.–4 P.M.; Sunday, 1–4 P.M. Adults, $2; students, $1; children age 6 and under, free. Memberships available.

Explore Fort Lauderdale and Broward County's history through exhibits that date from the Seminole Indians era through World War II. The building at 219 SW Second Avenue houses research and archive facilities. Temporary and traveling exhibits are also featured at the New River Inn, the King Cromartie House, and the Philomen Bryan House.

Field trips or group tours may be arranged for a small fee. Narrated, two-hour water tours of the New River can be scheduled through the museum; see listing in "By Land, Sea, and Air" for more information. An annual seafood festival is held the second Saturday in April. **Tips:** Plan to spend 30 to 40 minutes to tour. There are no picnic facilities.

◆ Graves Museum of Archaeology and Natural History

481 South Federal Highway, Dania 33304. (305) 925-7770. Tuesday through Saturday, 10 A.M.–4 P.M.; Sunday, 1–4 P.M. Adults, $5; students and children over 6, $3; children under 6, free. Annual memberships available.

Discover life among the Tequesta Indians 2,000 years ago, or imagine seeing the Ice-Age mammals whose bones are on display. The museum also exhibits pre-Columbian, African, and other cultural artifacts. A marine archaeological exhibit depicts shipwrecks. The "Sense of Egypt" room, a favorite with children, is set up to look like an Egyptian tomb. In 1992, the James W. Moseley exhibit was installed, displaying 170 pieces of pre-Columbian ceramics, fabrics, and metal objects from Dhimu, Moche, Chavin, Vicus, Chancay, and Ica. Another recent addition is an exhibit featuring *Touches of Culture: Vignettes from Greek, Roman, Indian, Chinese, Japanese and More.*

Classes for children are offered, as are monthly special exhibits and annual events. **Tips:** Plan to spend about an hour to tour. The museum closes for a period during the summer, so call before you go to be sure it's open. The museum moved from downtown Fort Lauderdale to its new home in Dania in late 1993.

◆ Hillsboro Lighthouse
Go east on Hillsboro Boulevard to Route A1A, then go south to Hillsboro Beach.

Designated a major historic landmark in 1907, this is one of the most powerful lighthouses in the United States.

◆ Himmarshee Village
Composed of an eight-block historical area in downtown Fort Lauderdale. Go north on First Avenue, turn left on SW Second Street, cross the railroad tracks, and turn left onto SW Second Avenue.

Renovations and reconstructions abound in this historical area. You'll find the Fort Lauderdale Historical Society complex that includes the New River Inn (Fort Lauderdale's first hotel), the King Cromartie House, the Philomen Bryan House, the Fort Lauderdale Historical Society Museum building (see listing in this section), antique shops, art galleries, and restaurants. Plans to develop Brickell Station, a 250,000-square-foot entertainment complex on Brickell Avenue and SW Second Avenue, are underway.

◆ Plantation Historical Museum
511 North Figtree Lane, Plantation 33322. (305) 797-2722. Tuesday through Thursday, 9 A.M.–noon, 1–4:30 P.M. Free admission.

Look at antiques that you might find in Granny's attic, artifacts from the Seminole and Tequesta tribes, the No. 1 Fire Engine, and other relics from the history of the town of Plantation. Exhibits change every few months. School and other groups should call ahead to make reservations for tours.

◆ Stranahan House

One Stranahan Place, 335 SE Sixth Avenue (one block south of Las Olas Boulevard above the Henry E. Kinney Tunnel), Fort Lauderdale 33301. (305) 524-4736. Wednesday, Friday and Saturday, 10 A.M.–3:30 P.M.; Sunday 1–3:30 P.M. Adults, $3; children, $2.

Built in 1901 by Florida pioneers Frank and Ivy Cromartie Stranahan, this is the oldest building in Broward County. Mr. Stranahan was a businessman, and he began trading with the Seminoles in 1892. His store served as an outpost on the road south to Lemon City (what is now North Miami), and later became their home. Ivy Stranahan earned $48 per month teaching the only nine pupils in the New River settlement called Fort Lauderdale. Their home is now a museum, furnished with antiques from that period.

The museum plays an active role in history education in the Broward schools, providing pre–field trip materials to get students ready for what they'll be seeing. The goal of the staff is to be a living museum, and "Trading Post Days," held in January, are one of the ways they accomplish that goal. For more information about this event, see listing in "Mark Your Calendar."

PALM BEACH COUNTY

◆ The Cason Cottage and Museum

Five NE First Street, Delray Beach 33483-0042. (407) 243-0223. Tuesday through Saturday, 10 A.M.–3 P.M. Free admission.

Cason Cottage houses a museum with art, artifacts, and records of Delray Beach. The house was built between 1915 and 1920 by Dr. and Mrs. John R. Cason, Sr., and the family played a major leadership role in the development of the area. A visit to the cottage will give children an idea of what South Florida was once like. Older children may enjoy listening to tape-recordings of pioneer oral histories available at the cottage. Special events and exhibits for children are also scheduled throughout the year.

◆ The Loxahatchee Historical Society and Museum

805 North U.S. 1 (in Burt Reynolds Park), Jupiter 33477. (407) 747-6639. Tuesday through Friday, 10 A.M.–4 P.M.; Saturday and Sunday, 1–4 P.M. Adults, $3; seniors, $2; children 6 to 18, $1. Call for information on memberships.

Nestled in a woodsy park by the water, this museum provides insight into "history shaped by nature" through permanent exhibits, a gallery for traveling exhibits, a research library, and many special events classes. They're designed to help you explore what was going on in the Jupiter area in 500 B.C., see how the arrival of Henry Flagler's railroad changed the area, and preserve the area's natural history.

A Seminole chickee in the back of the museum gives children an idea of how the Seminoles lived. The Dubois House, built on an ancient Indian mound in 1898, displays antique furniture and clothing that give children an idea of the lives of early South Floridian pioneers. The house is open to the public on Sundays from 1 to 4 P.M., weather permitting; tours can be arranged during the week by calling the museum staff. You can also arrange to participate in archaeological digs, sponsored by Florida Atlantic University, in the area around the museum.

When you're in Jupiter, be sure to tour the Jupiter Lighthouse, located just north of the museum. Built in 1860, it's still in use today. The lighthouse and the small museum located at its base are open to the public on Sunday from 1 to 4 P.M., weather permitting; the Historical Society staff can arrange special tours at other times. For more information, see listing for Dubois Park in "Under the Sun." For more information about the Seafare Festival held in May, see listing in "Mark Your Calendar."

♦ The Morikami Museum and Japanese Gardens

4000 Morikami Park Road, Delray Beach 33446. Take Linton Road exit off I-95 and head west about four miles. Go south on Carter Road, and then west on Morikami Park Road. (407) 499-0631 for recording or 495-0233. Museums: Tuesday through Sunday, 10 A.M.–5 P.M. Park: daily from sunrise to sunset. Closed Easter, Thanksgiving, Christmas, and New Year's Day. Adults, $4.25; seniors, $3.75; children age 6 to 18, $2. Memberships available.

George Sukeji Morikami, a winter vegetable and pineapple farmer, donated the land for what is now one of the most popular parks in Palm Beach County. Within the 200-acre park you'll find Yamato-Kan, the original museum that was inaugurated in 1977, housed in an imperial Japanese home on a man-made island. A new $5 million, 32,000-square-foot museum opened in January 1993 and includes an authentic Japanese Tea House, as well as a 225-seat theater, offices, and several classrooms. Explore the souvenir shop, library, and cafe (serving home-style Japanese food), and then tour the two-acre traditional Japanese garden. You'll have to take off your shoes outside and put on the paper ones provided at the door before you tour the Yamato-Kan.

A *chanoyu,* or traditional Japanese tea ceremony, is held in the tea ceremony room on the third Saturday of each month, from October through April. The ceremony is held hourly from 1 to 4 P.M. for $2 per

person, free for members. Japanese culture films for children are shown at
3 P.M. on Wednesdays and Fridays.

Wander down the one-mile nature trail through a wild area; explore
the gardens and climb to the observation deck (but please don't play in
the waterfalls!). Free garden tours are given at 2 P.M. on Wednesdays and
Fridays. Picnic facilities with covered pavilions and open tables are available, and there are large grassy areas around the lake where you can spread
out blankets.

Four traditional festivals are celebrated annually: *Bon* Festival (mid-
August); *Osho Gatsu* (New Year's in December and January); *Hatsume*
("First Bud," in February); and *Bunka-No-Hi* (Japanese Culture Days, in
November). Check local newspapers or call for information. Entrance fees
are charged at these festivals. **Tips:** Don't miss feeding the *koi* (large fish
in the pond); fish food is available on the boardwalk. For more information about the festivals, see listings in "Mark Your Calendar."

◆ Whitehall/Henry Morrison Flagler Museum

*Whitehall Way, Palm Beach. Take the Okeechobee Road East exit off I-95 or
the Florida Turnpike, continue east into Palm Beach to the first traffic light.
Turn left on Cocoanut Row, continue until the fourth light (Whitehall Way).
The museum is on the left. Mailing address is P.O. Box 969, Palm Beach
33480. (407) 655-2833. Tuesday through Saturday, 10 A.M.–5 P.M.;
Sunday, noon–5 P.M. Adults, $5; children 6 to 12, $2.*

The arrival of Henry Flagler's railroad in 1894, stretching from Jacksonville to Key West, was the catalyst for much growth in the Palm
Beach area and many other parts of South Florida. A founder of Standard
Oil Company (John D. Rockefeller was his partner), Flagler built beautiful hotels for wealthy visitors who arrived on his railroad. In 1901 he
spent $2.5 million to create Whitehall, a personal palace to enjoy with his
bride. His home has been restored and preserved as a museum that displays his collection of treasures from around the world. Children will
especially enjoy the playroom and dollhouses on the second floor, as well
as a trip outside to board "Rambler," Flagler's private railroad car.

The very popular "Open House" is held each February, with clowns,
magic shows, special exhibits, and other family activities. For more event
information, see listing in "Mark Your Calendar." **Tips:** Regular tours of
the museum last about 45 minutes and are too long for children under age
5. Special tours for children may be arranged by calling in advance. The
staff welcomes school groups and clubs throughout the year. Only a few
of the upper rooms are air conditioned, so plan the time of your visit accordingly.

MONROE COUNTY

♦ Audubon House and Tropical Gardens

205 Whitehead Street, Key West 33040. (305) 294-2116. Daily, 9:30 A.M.–5 P.M. Adults, $5; children ages 6 to 12, $1; children under 6, free. AE, MC, V accepted. Group rates available (15 people minimum, reservations required).

Completely restored, with the original furnishings intact, this house provides a glimpse of life in Key West in the mid-1850s. The home actually belonged to Captain John Geiger; the museum was opened to exhibit the work of John James Audubon. The engravings show many of the Keys' native birds. Bird lovers will also enjoy the exhibits of lifelike porcelain birds. The guided tour takes you through the rotating and permanent exhibits on the first floor of the home; you may explore the second and third floors on your own (children might be interested in the antique roller blades). Then walk through the acre of tropical gardens, stop to smell the herbs in the herb garden, and browse through the new gift shop. **Tips:** Guided walking tours and video show available. No wheelchair or stroller access inside house. No drinking fountains or eating facilities. Plan to spend about an hour to tour.

♦ Dry Tortugas National Park

Mailing address: Everglades National Park, P.O. Box 279, Homestead 33030. (305) 242-7700.

This national park is home to Fort Jefferson National Monument. It lies 69 nautical miles west of Key West in the Dry Tortugas and is accessible only by boat or seaplane. Built as a garrison for Federal troops during the Civil War, it later became a prison for Union deserters. Its most notable prisoner was Dr. Samuel Mudd, who, without realizing who he was treating, set John Wilkes Booth's leg after Booth assassinated President Abraham Lincoln. During outbreaks of yellow fever, Dr. Mudd treated so many prisoners that he was pardoned. In 1874 the fort was abandoned; it is now open for snorkeling, camping, swimming, and hiking. If you wish to use one of the park's 10 campsites (bathrooms are the only amenities), be sure to call first to make reservations and find out about local weather and wildlife conditions. You'll need to bring everything, including water, with you, and take everything, including your garbage, out. For transportation call one of the Key West outfitters, such as the Key West Seaplane Service, (305) 294-6978. For more information, see listing in "By Land, Sea, and Air." For more information about Dry Tortugas National Park, see listing in "Under the Sun."

◆ East Martello Museum and Art Gallery

3501 South Roosevelt Boulevard (adjacent to the airport), Key West 33040. (305) 296-3913. Daily, 9:30 A.M.–5 P.M.; closed Christmas. Adults, $3; children 7 to 12, $1; children under 7, free. Tours available.

This museum is housed in a former Civil War fortress. Today it exhibits many artifacts from Old Key West, as well as an interesting collection of some of Key West's oddest characters. For more information, see listing in "Adventures in the Arts."

◆ Ernest Hemingway Home and Museum

907 Whitehead Street, Key West 33040. (305) 294-1575. Daily, 9 A.M.– 5 P.M. Adults, $6; children 6 to 12, $1.50; children under 6, free.

The home of famed author Ernest Hemingway is now a National Historic Landmark. The furnishings are authentic, and the house, which is 140 years old, abounds with many descendants of Hemingway's famed six-toed cats. (Most children think the cats are the best part of this museum.)

◆ Fort Zachary Taylor State Historic Site

West end of Southard Street, Key West. Mailing address is P.O. Box 289, Key West 33041. (305) 292-6713. Daily, 8 A.M.–sunset; fort area closes at 5 P.M. Admission: $3.25 per vehicle; $.50 per passenger; $1.50 if you come in on foot, bike, moped, etc.

A stronghold for the Union during the Civil War, this site is also a National Historic Landmark. Built between 1845 and 1866 (progress was impeded by hurricanes, disease, and war), the fort was intended to protect the harbor at Key West. Take a look at the walls—they're eight feet thick. The largest collection of Civil War cannons was found here in recent excavations. A 40-minute guided tour begins at 2 P.M. daily, but you can explore on your own anytime. You'll also find one of the island's public beaches located here, as well as a picnic area with barbecue grills. Birthday parties can be held in this area, and Civil War Days events take place here each winter.

◆ Indian Key State Historic Site

P.O. Box 776, Long Key 33001. Located about three-quarters mile south of Lower Matecumbe Key, Mile Marker 78.5, oceanside. (305) 664-4815. Daily, 8 A.M.–sunset. Call for information about ranger-guided boat and walking tours.

This 12-acre key is accessible only by private or chartered boat. At one time a home to a community of wreckers, in 1840 Seminoles attacked this island, burning down most of the buildings. The island is overgrown with tropical plants once carefully cultivated by botanist Dr. Henry Perrine. You'll need to wear protective clothing if you take the self-guided tour of the island. On the key you'll find an observation tower, boat dock, and shelters. **Tips:** There are no restrooms. For information about the San Pedro Underwater Archaeological Preserve located just south of Indian Key, see listing in "Exploring Science and Nature."

◆ Key West Lighthouse and Military Museum

938 Whitehead Street, Key West 33040. (305) 294-0012. Daily, 9:30 A.M.–5 P.M. Adults, $5; children 7 to 13, $1; children under 7, free. MC and V accepted ($15 minimum).

Climb the 88 steps and get a sweeping view of Key West. Built in 1846, this lighthouse guided sailors until 1969. Handrails are installed all the way up the winding staircase, and safety bars enclose the lookout area, making the lighthouse safe for young visitors. Browse in the gift shop during your visit, too. The lightkeeper's quarters recently got a million-dollar makeover and displays military and other artifacts from the late 1800s and early 1900s.

◆ Perky Bat Tower

Near Mile Marker 17 on the bayside of U.S. 1, Sugarloaf Key.

Inspire your child's imagination with a visit to this tower, listed in the National Register of Historic Places. Clyde Perky built it in 1929 to attract bats that would eat mosquitoes that were attacking guests visiting his Sugarloaf Lodge. The bats never showed up, but the tower has outlasted several hurricanes, and young inventors or storytellers might like to stop and take a look at one man's attempt to solve a problem.

◆ Wreckers' Museum and Oldest House

322 Duval Street, Key West 33040. (305) 294-9502. Daily, 10 A.M.–4 P.M. Adults, $2; children 3 to 12, $.50.

This museum is located in the oldest house in Key West, originally built in 1829 on Duval Street. Some contend that the house on the corner of Angela and Margaret streets is the oldest, but whichever camp you side with, you'll find that the museum is filled with maritime history. This was the home of Captain Francis B. Watlington, a merchant seaman and wrecker (ask the staff to explain how wreckers got their name). The museum has a display of seagoing artifacts, model ships, documents, a small toy collection (including an elegant doll house), and many antiques.

Group tours may be arranged in advance. Thank the staff as you leave—
they are all volunteers! **Tips:** Tuesday is the best day for families to visit.
Plan to spend about 30 minutes to tour. Strollers are fine, but no wheelchair access on grounds.

ADVENTURES IN THE ARTS

South Florida is a wonderful place for children to learn about the arts. On almost every weekend of the year, there is an art, dance, music, or theater event for children happening somewhere. This section describes many of the area's fine arts organizations.

Universities, community colleges, and high schools often host low-cost or free exhibits and performances that are often close to home. These opportunities let children learn about and experience the arts in an informal environment. Commercial art galleries and those located on college campuses can provide a free education in the visual arts if you take the time to browse. Most welcome well-behaved children to exhibition openings, and children enjoy meeting the artists who created the works.

Don't overlook valuable and free community resources. Your local and regional libraries host a variety of dance and musical performances, puppet shows, ethnic art exhibitions, dramatic storytelling events, and film presentations. Ask your local librarian about bedtime storytelling hour, toy lending, "tell and touch," foreign language collections, Talking Books, Books-by-Mail, and "share box" (donate one of your books and pick another to take home).

Broward, Dade, Monroe, and Palm Beach counties have arts councils that can provide you with current information about cultural events. You can call or write to the following:

- **Broward Cultural Affairs Council,** 100 South Andrews Avenue, Fort Lauderdale 33301. (305) 357-7457. 24-Hour Arts and Entertainment Hotline: (305) 357-5700.
- **Metropolitan Dade County Cultural Affairs Council,** 111 NW First Street, Suite 625, Miami 33128-1964. (305) 375-4634 or 375-5024.
- **Monroe County Fine Arts Council,** 1435 Simonton Street, Key West 33040. (305) 296-5000.
- **Palm Beach County Council of the Arts,** 1555 Palm Beach Lakes Boulevard, Suite 206, West Palm Beach 33401-2371. Arts Line: (800) 882-ARTS (in Florida), (407) 471-2901.

The Children's Cultural Coalition of the Metropolitan Dade County Cultural Affairs Council provides up-to-date information about children's programs through their publication *Classroom Cultural Catalogue: A Resource Directory for Teachers: Cultural and Scientific In-School and Field-Trip Programs.* Call (305) 375-5024 for a free copy. The Broward Arts Council also publishes their *Cultural Directory,* a listing of hundreds of professional artists and cultural organizations. Call (305) 357-7457; the directory is available free of charge.

Your child will enjoy whatever cultural events you choose if you take time to explain what to expect in the program and what kind of behavior is appropriate for the event. The poem opposite, written by Peggy Simon Tractman of Maximillion Productions in New York, gives children a good picture of what they can see and do at the theater.

ART

Art museums are wonderful community resources, but don't forget that possibilities for learning about art can be found in festivals, galleries, neighborhoods (for works of architecture, exterior art, and decoration), corporate offices, and public places.

DADE COUNTY

◆ Bacardi Art Gallery
2100 Biscayne Boulevard, Miami 33137. (305) 573-8511. Monday through Friday, 9 A.M.–5 P.M. Free admission.

In 1963 Bacardi Imports established the gallery as a nonprofit community service in the visual arts. Exhibitions have included *Selections of Cuban Art, American Prints from Colonial Times to 1950, Urban Sculpture, 20th Century Mexican Masters,* and *German Neo-Expressionists.*

Group tours can be arranged by calling in advance. The gallery also works with the Dade County Public Schools to present an art education workshop for children to develop their creative skills through hands-on activities.

◆ Bass Museum of Art
2121 Park Avenue, Miami Beach 33139. (305) 673-7530. Tuesday through Saturday, 10 A.M.–5 P.M.; Sunday, 1–5 P.M. Adults, $5; students with I.D., $4; children 6 to 12, $2; children under 6, free. MC, V accepted.

Browse through this wonderful collection of paintings, sculptures, graphics, and textiles from the 14th through the 20th centuries. A $17

Matinee Manners

1. *The theatre is no place for lunch.*
Who can hear when you go
    "crunch?"

2. *We must wear our nicest clothes*
When we go to theatre shows.

3. *Do not talk to one another*
(that means friends or even mother)
When you go to see a show.
Otherwise you'll never know
What the play is all about
And you'll make the actors shout
Just to make themselves be heard.
So, be still—don't say a word
Unless an actor asks you to…
A thing they rarely ever do.

4. *A program has a special use*
So do not treat it with abuse!
Its purpose is to let us know
Exactly who is in the show—
It also tells us other facts
Of coming shows and future acts.
Programs make great souvenirs
Of fun we've had in bygone years.

5. *Keep your hands upon your lap*
But if you like something, you clap.
Actors like to hear applause
If there is cause for this applause.

6. *If a scene is bright and sunny*
And you think something is funny,
Laugh—performers love the
    laughter
But be quiet from thereafter.

7. *Don't kick chairs or pound your feet*
And do not stand up in your seat.
Never wander to and fro—
Just sit back and watch the show.

8. *And when the final curtain falls*
The actors take their "curtain
    calls."
That means they curtsy or they bow
And you applaud, which tells
    them how
You liked their work and liked
    the show.
Then, when the lights come on,
    you go
Back up the aisle and walk—
    don't run
Out to the lobby, everyone.

9. *The theatre is a special treat*
And not a place to talk or eat.
If you behave the proper way
You really will enjoy the play!

million, 50,000-square-foot expansion and renovation is scheduled for
completion in 1995. State-of-the-art improvements will provide additional exhibition space, educational facilities, and more. Special events and
classes for children are offered throughout the year; call for information.
Tip: Adult supervision is required.

◆   The Beck Museum of Judaica

*Beth David Congregation, 2625 SW Third Avenue, Miami 33129. (305)
854-3911.*

In 1989 Miami's oldest synagogue opened this museum to display
approximately 150 artifacts and artworks, including items rescued from
Czechoslovakian and other European synagogues destroyed by the Nazis.
Two large carvings made from Honduran mahogany depict the
Holocaust's suffering and death on one side and Israel's hope and life on
the other. **Tip:** The museum welcomes older supervised children. Call for
a tour appointment.

◆   Black Heritage Museum

*Mailing address is P.O. Box 50327, Miami 33255. (305) 252-3535.
Free admission; memberships available.*

Begun in 1987 to showcase positive aspects of black heritage around
the world, the museum's exhibitions are presented in various locations in
Dade County. A permanent display of paintings and traditional African
art from seven countries can be seen at the Minority Student Support
Services facilities at the University of Miami, on Dickenson Drive, Buildings 37B-C. Collections of dolls, art from Africa and Papua New Guinea,
and other works have been displayed at the Bacardi Art Gallery, the
Model City Cultural Arts Gallery, and at public libraries. Call for information concerning current exhibitions.

◆   The Center for the Fine Arts

*101 West Flagler Street (Metro-Dade Cultural Center), Miami 33130.
Take the Metrorail to Government Center, walk one block south and go up
the stairs. (305) 375-1700. Tuesday, Wednesday, Friday, and Saturday,
10 A.M.–5 P.M.; Thursday, 10 A.M.–9 P.M.; Sunday, noon–5 P.M. Adults,
$5; adult groups, $2.50 per person; children 6 to 12, $2; students with I.D.
and seniors, $2.50. Call (305) 375-1709 for group tour reservations;
discounts for groups of more than 10. Annual memberships available. MC
and V accepted.*

At least 12 to 15 new exhibitions each year keep this museum interesting for everyone, children included. You can call or send for a study

guide that will acquaint children with an exhibition before they actually see it. Children of members are welcome to attend openings.

"Family Saturday" takes place the third Saturday of every month and features studio workshops for several age groups: Art for Tots (for children 3 to 5), Young Artists (6 to 11), and Young Teen Artists (12 to 15). Art camps are offered during spring and summer vacations, and exhibition-related workshops, cultural festivals, and performances for children take place throughout the year. Call for more information on these and other special events. Some events require reservations. **Tips:** Plan on spending about an hour to tour. The staff recommends weekday afternoons as the best time to visit. If you drive, there is a parking garage west of the Metro-Dade Cultural Center; get your parking ticket validated in the museum to receive a parking discount. Joint tickets are available if you plan to visit the Historical Museum of Southern Florida on the same day. Picnic tables are located on the plaza in front of the museum. For more information about the Historical Museum of Southern Florida, see listing in "Tracing the Past."

◆ Cuban Museum of Arts and Culture

1300 SW 12th Avenue, Miami 33129. (305) 858-8006. Monday through Friday, 10 A.M.–5 P.M.; Saturday and Sunday, 1–5 P.M. Hours of operation may vary with exhibits. Admission charged for some exhibits.

Appropriate for older children. The exhibitions introduce viewers to Cuban and other Latin American artists.

◆ Florida Museum of Hispanic and Latin American Art

Hammond Antique & Art Center, Fourth Floor (in the Miami Design District), 191 NE 40th Street, Miami 33137. (305) 576-5171. Tuesday through Friday, 10 A.M.–5 P.M.; Saturday, 11 A.M.–5 P.M. Adults, $2; seniors and children 6 to 12, $1. Call for school and other group tours.

Founded in 1991, this unique museum features work by artists living throughout Latin America and Spain. A nonprofit organization, the museum offers tours to school groups, seminars, and other special events.

The museum is housed in the Hammond Antique & Art Center, where you can carefully browse through many art galleries and antique stores full of fascinating pieces of history.

◆ Gallery Antigua

5138 Biscayne Boulevard, Miami 33137. (305) 759-5355. Monday through Friday, 9 A.M.–5:30 P.M.; Saturday, 10 A.M.–6 P.M. Free admission. Major credit cards and personal checks accepted for art purchases. Family memberships available.

A trip to this gallery will provide children with an opportunity to learn about African, African-American, and Caribbean art. Quarterly exhibitions might feature a single artist, a group of artists, or art representing a geographic area. The gallery is unique in Florida for its commitment to exhibit fine art produced by artists of the African Diaspora. Ask for a copy of their quarterly newsletter, *The Scene,* which includes art reviews, exhibition information, poetry, and suggested readings for children and adults.

◆ The Jewish Museum of Florida

301 Washington Avenue, Miami Beach 33139. (305) 672-5044. Sunday through Friday, 10 A.M.–4 P.M. Admission charged.

Scheduled to open in late 1994, this $3.5 million museum houses photographs, artifacts, and other materials that depict Jewish life, traditions, and art. The Beth Jacob Synagogue building, where the museum will be housed, is on the National Register of Historic Buildings, and served as Miami Beach's first synagogue. Adults and children alike stand in awe of the stained glass windows. *MOSAIC: Jewish Life in Florida,* which started as a popular traveling exhibition, is now on permanent display here. Children will enjoy the exhibits and activities in the Children's Corner. Call for information about special programs and events for children.

◆ Lowe Art Museum

University of Miami, 1301 Stanford Drive, Coral Gables 33146. (305) 284-3536. Tuesday through Friday, noon–5 P.M.; Saturday, 10 A.M.–5 P.M.; Sunday, noon–5 P.M. Adults, $4; seniors and non-UM students, $2; members, children 16 and under and UM students, $1. Memberships available. AE, V accepted in gift shop.

Permanent displays are augmented by new exhibitions every eight weeks. Call or send for a calendar to decide in advance if the current exhibition is appropriate for your child. Art classes and camps for children 3 and up are offered during the summer and holidays. Call for information about special events, including children's activities at the Beaux Arts Festival. **Tips:** Plan to spend about 45 minutes to visit, and come early in the day. You can schedule group tours in the morning before the museum opens. There are lots of grassy areas for picnics on campus, or you can try out the cafeteria and other nearby eateries. For more information about the Beaux Arts Festival, see listing in "Mark Your Calendar."

◆ Metropolitan Dade County Art in Public Places

111 NW First Street, Sixth Floor, Miami 33128. The art can be seen throughout Dade County; many pieces are sited in or near Metrorail stations. (305) 375-5362.

Over 350 works of art (mostly contemporary art) can be seen throughout Dade County in parks, plazas, public libraries, hospitals, and transit facilities (including Miami International Airport). Since 1973 all kinds of art, including sculptures, paintings, photographs, mixed media, prints, ceramics, weavings, and fountains have been commissioned, sited, and maintained through this program. You'll also notice public-awareness campaigns that include artist-designed posters and billboards. A self-guided Metrorail art tour booklet will lead you to many of the works. The information office can tell you about field trips and community programs related to the Art in Public Places program, which form part of a new emphasis in public art to address social issues in the community. **Tips:** You may touch the artworks that are within reach. Don't tour more than three or four sites (five or six for older children), and take drinks or a picnic with you. There are several places near Metrorail stations suitable for picnics. Call for information about guidebooks and special Metrorail passes.

◆ North Miami Museum and Center of Contemporary Art

12340 NE Eighth Avenue, North Miami 33161. (305) 893-6211. Monday through Friday, 10 A.M.–4 P.M.; Saturday, 1–4 P.M. Free admission; memberships available.

This nonprofit fine-arts center showcases Florida artists. New exhibits are displayed every five weeks. Classes for children are available on Saturdays; group tours or field trips for children can be arranged. Call for information. **Tip:** Plan to spend up to an hour to tour.

◆ The Wolfsonian

1001 Washington Avenue, Miami Beach 33139. (305) 531-1001. Monday through Friday, 1–5 P.M. Admission, $1; seniors and children, $.50.

This is a wonderful treasure to find, but you won't get past the first floor exhibits until the formal opening of the museum, scheduled for late 1995. Founder Mitchell Wolfson, Jr., has been putting together his collection of over 60,000 pieces of political, decorative, and design arts for decades. Most of the objects are from the late 19th and early 20th centuries. Of special interest to children are the collections of toys, sculptures, posters, and postcards.

Established in 1986, the Wolfsonian Foundation provides research and exhibition centers in Miami Beach and Genoa, Italy. Exhibitions are held on the first, sixth, and seventh floors; collections management, conservation, and research occupy the others.

BROWARD COUNTY

◆ African-American Caribbean Cultural Center

1601 South Andrews Avenue (BancAtlantic Building), Second Floor (across from Broward General Medical Center), Fort Lauderdale 33301. (305) 467-4056. Tuesday through Saturday, 10 A.M.–6 P.M. Call before you go to confirm hours and exhibitions. Memberships available.

Founder Aina Olomo believed that Broward County needed a place to showcase black artists from around the world, and her vision has now become a reality. In the 4,500-square-foot center you'll find a variety of artistic expressions created by black artists from Africa, the Caribbean, and the Americas. Art education for children is an important component of the center, so call for information and schedules.

◆ Arts and Culture Center of Hollywood

1650 Harrison Street, Hollywood 33019. (305) 921-3274. Tuesday through Saturday, 10 A.M.–4 P.M.; Sunday, 1–4 P.M. Adults, $3; children, $2; children under age 12, free. Memberships available. Cash payment only.

This museum of contemporary paintings and sculptures annually sponsors several special events for children, including concerts and workshops and a summer program on Saturdays for children 4 to 12. Birthday parties and field trips are available by special arrangement. **Tips:** The museum staff suggests that children visit from 10 A.M. to 1 P.M. and that you collect all the brochures containing exhibit information when you arrive in order to take a self-guided tour.

◆ Broward Art Guild

207 South Andrews Avenue, Fort Lauderdale 33301. (305) 764-2005. Monday through Saturday, 10 A.M.–4 P.M.; Sunday, noon–4 P.M. Free admission; memberships available.

This nonprofit art guild mounts a new exhibition about every six weeks. Eight days following each opening (the following Saturday), children are invited to attend "Children's Opening-Night Day," a free event designed just for them, from noon to 2 P.M. The program includes a hands-on art activity, a gallery/exhibition tour, entertainment, refreshments, and balloons.

Art classes are available on Saturdays and after school for children ages 6 to 15 (younger children are admitted according to their ability). A summer art camp is also offered. Call for information. **Tip:** Wear clothes you won't mind getting dirty (or bring a painting smock) to the activities.

◆ Broward County Art in Public Places

Lee Wagener Gallery, Terminal 2, Fort Lauderdale–Hollywood International Airport. (305) 357-7457; 438-1525; 432-8611.

What better way to spend your time as you wait at the airport for out-of-town visitors to arrive. Call for information about the subjects and locations of current installations and exhibitions.

◆ Museum of Art

One East Las Olas Boulevard, Fort Lauderdale 33301. (305) 525-5500. Tuesday, 11 A.M.–9 P.M.; Wednesday through Saturday, 10 A.M.–5 P.M.; Sunday, noon–5 P.M.; closed on all national holidays. Adults, $4; seniors, $3; students, $2; children under 12 admitted free with adult. AE, MC, V, personal checks accepted.

The museum displays a fascinating collection of 20th-century contemporary American art. It also houses the largest collection of ethnographic art in South Florida, including pre-Columbian, Oceanic, American Indian, and West African material, and the world's foremost collection of CoBrA (the Copenhagen, Brussels, and Amsterdam movement) paintings. In 1986 the museum moved to its new home, which has a 262-seat auditorium, sculpture terrace, art library, and bookstore.

Delightful programs, including "Children's Openings" and "Family Days," happen throughout the year, usually on Saturday mornings, from 10 A.M. to noon. Free to the public, the openings use hands-on, mixed-media art activities, as well as an exhibition tour conducted by trained docents, to acquaint children from 3 to 10 with current exhibitions. Performances by dancers, musicians, and other entertainers, as well as refreshments and balloons, are usually included. Call for dates and to make reservations for these very popular events.

Field trips, workshops, after-school classes, and camps all keep the museum's education department busy throughout the year; call for schedules and other information. **Tip:** You can park in the Municipal Parking facility located on SE First Avenue, east of the museum.

◆ Young at Art Children's Museum

801 South University Drive (just south of Broward Boulevard), Building C, Suite 136A (on the south end of the Fountains Shoppes of Distinction),

*Plantation 33024. (305) 424-0085. Tuesday through Saturday, 11 A.M.–
5 P.M.; Sunday, noon–5 P.M. Adults and children, $2.50; children under 2,
free. Family memberships available. Cash payment only.*

Hands-on, interactive exhibitions make this museum an exciting
learning experience. Its goal is "to help children from infancy through
adolescence, understand and enjoy the complex world in which they live
through the arts." They do this using fascinating exhibits that teach about
line, color, shape, and texture within various cultural and historical con-
texts. For the toddlers in the family, a visit to the Playspace area is a must.
Two rooms are available for art classes and birthday parties; if you are a
museum member, you can host a special party there. A small gift shop
and recycle arts center are located near the front of the museum. Group
tours and field trips may be arranged in advance; call for more information. **Tips:** Visit during the week if possible, and plan to spend about two
hours to tour. Stroller access, wheelchair access, and changing area for
babies provided. No picnic facilities.

PALM BEACH COUNTY

◆ Ann Norton Sculpture Gardens

*253 Barcelona Road (a few blocks south of the Norton Gallery of Art), West
Palm Beach 33401. (407) 832-5328. Tuesday through Saturday, 10 A.M.–
4 P.M. Adults, $3; children under 12, free. Tours available by appointment.*

Large outdoor sculptures by Ann Norton are beautifully set in three
gardens. Stay on the paths as you explore, and if you're very quiet you'll
see lots of birds and wildlife. Try to count the 150 different varieties of
palm trees.

◆ The Boca Raton Museum of Art

*801 West Palmetto Park Road, Boca Raton 33432. (407) 392-2500.
Monday through Friday, 10 A.M.–4 P.M.; Saturday and Sunday, noon–
4 P.M. Free admission.*

This nonprofit cultural organization has served the community for
over 40 years. In addition to the collections and international exhibitions
found here, the museum sponsors classes for children in their Museum Art
School and hosts art tours, workshops, and other community events, such
as art fairs in shopping malls. Call for information about current classes
and activities for children.

◆ Cornell Museum of Art and History

*51 North Swinton Avenue (in Old School Square Cultural Arts Center, at
corner of Atlantic and Swinton), Delray Beach 33444. (407) 243-7922.*

Tuesday through Saturday, 11 A.M.– 4 P.M.; Sunday, 1–4 P.M. Donations suggested.

Part of the recently renovated Old School Square, this museum hosts a different traveling exhibit of art, sculpture, photography, and more every two to three months. After you browse though the exhibit downstairs, head upstairs to see the incredible multi-million-dollar collection of thousands of hand-painted tin and lead military miniatures, on permanent loan from Edwin S. Reynolds.

The collection spans almost 1,000 years of military history, from the Norman conquest right up to Norman Schwarzkopf and Desert Storm. Plan a visit on Wednesday or Saturday at 2 P.M. to get a guided tour from Mr. Reynolds. Displays change every six weeks, so plan on several visits a year if you have fans in the family. For more information about Old School Square, see listing below.

♦ Hibel Museum of Art

150 Royal Poinciana Plaza, Palm Beach 33480. (407) 833-6870. Tuesday through Saturday, 10 A.M.–5 P.M.; Sunday, 1–5 P.M. Closed for New Year's Day, Thanksgiving, and Christmas. Free admission.

Lithographs, drawings, etchings, paintings, and porcelains by artist Edna Hibel are displayed in this nonprofit museum. Call for information about the free concerts held on the second Sunday of each month, November through May.

♦ International Museum of Cartoon Art

Mizner Park, Boca Raton. Mailing address: P.O. Box 1643, Boca Raton 33429. (407) 391-2200.

Admit it. When you open the newspaper, you read the comics, right? It's the first part of the paper that your children learn to read. The National Family Opinion in Connecticut reports that 113 million people read the Sunday comics, 94% of all teenagers read the comics, and 55% of them say comics are their favorite part of the newspaper. Now you won't be so surprised to learn about a new and unique 50,000-square-foot museum devoted to collecting, displaying, and interpreting cartoon art. Formerly located in a historic castle in New York, the museum moved to Boca Raton in 1993. It houses a library of 10,000 books, hundreds of hours of cartoons on film and video, and over 100,000 original cartoon drawings. Over 25 major and smaller galleries display original art by format (comic strips, animation, etc.) and subject (sports cartoons, greeting cards, etc.). The museum's designers also created "magical environments" where visitors can explore Toon Town, the Prehistoric Cartoon Cave, the Cartoonist's Studio, and more.

Education programs for preschoolers through seniors are an important part of the museum's agenda. The Education Orientation Center for school children, a library and video center, classrooms, and research facilities are all available. Call for information about special programs and events, educational materials for teachers, school field trips, specialized tours, and literacy programs.

◆ Norton Gallery of Art

1451 South Olive Avenue (one-half mile south of Okeechobee Road on U.S. 1), West Palm Beach 33401. (407) 832-5194. Tuesday through Saturday, 10 A.M.–5 P.M.; Sunday, 1–5 P.M. Memberships available. $4 donation suggested. AE, MC, V accepted.

Steel magnate Ralph H. Norton founded this museum in 1941. Its permanent collection includes paintings by French impressionists and 20th-century artists (including Gauguin, Renoir, and Monet). An excellent library houses over 3,000 art books and periodicals.

Classes for children are offered occasionally throughout the year, and field trips or group tours may be arranged. Call for more information. **Tip:** The staff recommends visiting in the late morning or early afternoon to tour the museum when volunteers are available to answer questions.

◆ Old School Square Cultural Arts Center

51 North Swinton Avenue (at corner of Atlantic and Swinton), Delray Beach 33444. (407) 243-7922. Tuesday through Saturday, 11 A.M.– 4 P.M.; Sunday, 1–4 P.M.

Home to Delray Beach Elementary School (built in 1913) and High School (1925) until 1986, then abandoned to time, Old School Square has been beautifully restored and now serves as a cultural arts complex. The Cornell Museum of Art and History opened in 1990 in the elementary school building. The renovated 1926 gymnasium opened in 1991, followed by the Crest Theatre in 1993. The Delray Beach Historical Society also calls the center home. Call for a schedule of special events. For more information about the Cornell Museum of Art and History, see listing above.

◆ The Society of the Four Arts

Four Arts Plaza (off Royal Palm Way), Palm Beach 33480. Galleries and offices, (407) 655-7226. Library, (407) 655-2766. Galleries open December 3 to April 16: Monday through Saturday, 10 A.M.–5 P.M.; Sundays, 2–5 P.M. Library open November 1 to April 30: Monday through

Saturday, 10 A.M.–5 P.M. May 1 to October 31: Monday through Friday,
10 A.M.–5 P.M.

Incorporated in 1936 as a nonprofit organization, the Society of the
Four Arts provides programs for adults and children in art, music, drama,
and literature. The library here is the only public library on the island of
Palm Beach. Students from the Palm Beach County schools provide artworks for an annual children's exhibition presented in the gallery. The
library's children's room has over 7,000 books and is staffed by a full-time
children's librarian. During the summer, films for youngsters are presented in conjunction with the Department of Parks and Recreation.
There is a special collection of sea shells in the library and in the gallery
lobby. **Tips:** Picnics are not permitted in the Society's botanical gardens,
but this is a beautiful place for a supervised walk. Stay on the paths, and
please look but don't touch the flowers or the sculptures in the Philip
Hulitar Sculpture Garden.

MONROE COUNTY

In addition to the museums, there are several art galleries in Key West
that children may enjoy. Just remember that they are not places where
children are free to run around and pick up things!

◆ East Martello Museum and Art Gallery

3501 South Roosevelt, Key West 33040. Go north on A1A, the oceanside of
the island, just past the airport. (305) 296-3913. Daily, 9:30 A.M.–5 P.M.
Adults, $3; children 7 to 12, $1.

A Canadian welder named Stanley Papio moved to Key Largo in 1949
and started turning junk into sculptures in his yard. His neighbors called
the police several times to have the "eyesores" removed. Now his works
are collected here, and some people call him a genius along the lines of
Picasso, Dali, and Warhol. Other collections include painted wood carvings of Key West street scenes by Mario Sanchez, a local Cuban artist. The
museum is also home to the Key West Art and Historical Society, and it
displays artifacts from some of the islands famous and infamous citizens.
For more information, see listing in "Tracing the Past."

◆ Haitian Art Co.

600 Frances Street (corner of Southard Street), Key West 33040. (305)
296-8932. Daily, 10 A.M.–6 P.M. Major credit cards accepted.

A collection of over 200 artists working in Haiti is displayed in this
gallery. Oils and acrylics on canvas, wood sculptures, oil drum cutouts,

and painted cedar box cubes can be seen and purchased. Group tours and field trips can be arranged for children ages 3 and up.

DANCE

DADE COUNTY

◆ Ballet Concerto
3410 SW 22nd Street, Miami 33145. (305) 266-0050.

In-school performances, including classical ballets and informal concerts, are available for children in grades K through 12 in Dade County schools. Call for information about children's ballet performances open to the public.

◆ Ballet Flamenco La Rosa
1008 Lincoln Road, Miami Beach 33139. (305) 672-0552.

Children age 3 and up will enjoy performances of this lively Spanish dance form. The origins of flamenco and other forms of Spanish dance are discussed and demonstrated to students throughout Dade County in grades K through 12. Call for performance dates.

◆ Ballet Theatre of Miami
1809 Ponce de León, Coral Gables 33134. (305) 442-4840.

The Ballet Theatre of Miami is a nonprofit, professional ballet company that performs traditional classical and modern ballet. Performances of *The Nutcracker* are held every December at the Gusman Center for the Performing Arts. The company also performs special programs in elementary through high schools within Dade County. **Tip:** All public performances except *The Nutcracker* are appropriate only for older children (10 to 12) who have a basic understanding of ballet.

◆ Chiumba Imani Dance Theatre
c/o Model City Cultural Arts Center, 6161 NW 22nd Avenue, Miami 33142. (305) 638-6770.

Since 1978, director Chiku Ngozi and her dancers and drummers have presented East and West African dance, traditions, and culture through performances in various Dade County locations. They perform in the Model City Cultural Arts Center, Caleb Auditorium, at festivals, and local schools.

◆ Florene Nichols Inner-City Children's Touring Dance Company

4256 NW Seventh Avenue, Miami 33127. (305) 756-5595.

About 250 children, ages 2 1/2 to 17, are trained in dance in late afternoon and evening classes. The performing group includes students ages 8 to 16. They perform throughout Florida for social groups and community activities, such as the Miami Book Fair International.

Each summer Ms. Nichols organizes a group of students to travel to Dakar, Senegal, in West Africa, sponsored by the State of Florida Division of Cultural Exchange. Students learn dance, percussion, history, traditional medicine, hospitality, and cuisine. A summer performing camp in Miami is also offered. Call for information.

◆ Junior Ballet Company of the Cultural Arts Society of South Florida

77 NW 166th Street, Miami 33169. (305) 949-7200.

Founded in 1971 and dedicated to bringing free cultural programs to the community, the Cultural Arts Society of South Florida sponsors several free ballet performances throughout Dade County. Check newspaper announcements for performances at the Dade County Youth Fair, Vizcaya, and the Jackie Gleason Theatre of the Performing Arts. The Cultural Arts Society also sponsors a full two-hour program at the North Miami Beach City Hall Auditorium for families with older children. Laura Rose May serves as the artistic director. Call for performance information.

◆ Miami City Ballet

905 Lincoln Road, Miami Beach 33139. (305) 532-4880.

"Ballets for Young People," presented by the Miami City Ballet, provides an outstanding opportunity for children to learn about and enjoy child-size bites of ballet. Artistic director Edward Villela introduces and explains each segment of the performance. The ballet is followed by an activity designed to make the afternoon even more fun for the children. The "Ballet from the Balcony" program begins 45 minutes prior to the performance, with a chance to meet a ballerina and hear about the program. The subscription price is available for children ages 6 to 16 and their parents, and includes reserved balcony seats for four Sunday matinee performances. When you call for performance information (in Dade, Broward, and Palm Beach counties), ask about their annual spring Tea Dance as well as the Sugar Plum parties that follow performances of *The Nutcracker* in December.

In 1993, the Miami City Ballet opened the Dance Center. The goal of this classical ballet academy is to become a training ground for future dancers for the company.

◆ Miami Repertoire Ballet Company
8781 SW 134th Street, Miami 33176. West side of South Dixie Highway, just north of the Falls shopping area. (305) 252-9454.

Watch for special performances for children, such as *Snow White* and *Cinderella* in the spring and *The Nutcracker* in December. The company performs in public and private schools (contact your PTA to request a performance), at the annual Arti Gras in North Miami in March, in local shopping malls, and at festivals throughout the area. Ticket prices are very reasonable. Note that the number given in this listing for Miami Repertoire Ballet performance information is for the Ravich Ballet, the dance-school side of the organization.

 **BROWARD COUNTY**

◆ Children of the Caribbean Arts Center
3899 West Broward Boulevard, Plantation 33317. (305) 792-6778.

Art, music, theater, and dance from Caribbean, African, and Latin American countries are taught here and presented in student performances during the year. Call for information about classes and performances.

◆ Fort Lauderdale Children's Ballet Theatre
934 NE 62nd Street (Cypress Creek Road), Fort Lauderdale 33334. (305) 491-4668.

Each year two full-length ballets, such as *Sleeping Beauty* and *Coppelia*, are presented for children age 3 and up. Some performances feature children 5 and older chosen from auditions in Dade, Broward, and Palm Beach counties. The ballets can be seen at festivals, the main library in downtown Fort Lauderdale, and other sites throughout Broward County. Lecture demonstrations are presented in the schools. This theater also houses a performing arts school that offers dance, drama, and voice classes. Call for performance and school information. **Tip:** Performances last about 60 minutes, so plan ahead.

◆ Miami City Ballet
(305) 463-0109.

See listing under Dade County. Performances take place at the Broward Center for the Performing Arts.

PALM BEACH COUNTY

◆ Ballet Florida

West Palm Beach. (407) 659-1212.
A professional dance company and school, Ballet Florida presents ballets for children age 3 and up. Performances include *Sleeping Beauty, Coppelia,* and others, and take place at various sites, such as the Royal Poinciana Playhouse, public libraries, and the Dreher Park Zoo.

◆ The Florida Youth Ballet

337 First Street (in the Children's Gym), Jupiter 33458. (407) 626-9631 or (407) 747-3646.
Young dancers (11 to 14) from the Fiona Fairrie School of Ballet perform at festivals and other events throughout Palm Beach County. Call for information about upcoming performances or about the school.

◆ Miami City Ballet

Raymond F. Kravis Center for the Performing Arts, 701 Okeechobee Boulevard, West Palm Beach 33401. (407) 659-1328 or (800) 444-4622.
See listing under Dade County.

MUSIC

DADE COUNTY

◆ An Afternoon of Music for Children

Temple Beth Am Concert Series, Temple Beth Am, 5950 North Kendall Drive, Miami 33156. (305) 667-6667.
This concert series provides an excellent opportunity for children and families to learn music appreciation and concert etiquette. Past concerts include performances by the Florida Philharmonic Orchestra and the New World Symphony. Opera, jazz, classical, and other types of music are explored and performed for and by children. Concerts last about one hour, followed by light refreshments. Call for concert dates and ticket information. **Tip:** Recommended for children 6 and up.

◆ Florida Philharmonic Orchestra

Oakland Commerce Center, 3401 NW Ninth Avenue, Fort Lauderdale 33304. For concert and ticket information, call (305) 945-5180 in Dade, (305) 561-2997 in Broward, (407) 392-5443 in Boca Raton,

and (407) 659-0331 or (800) 226-1812 in West Palm Beach.
    See listing below in Broward County.

◆ Greater Miami Opera Association
1200 Coral Way, Miami 33145. (305) 854-1643. Monday through
Friday, 9 A.M.–5 P.M.

    The Greater Miami Opera Association sponsors two auxiliary groups,
the Young Patronesses of the Opera (YPO) and the Opera Guild, that
provide activities that help children learn to enjoy opera. The YPO funds
the "Opera Funtime" program and a program called "In-School Opera,"
which organizes performances in elementary schools in Dade, Broward,
and Palm Beach counties. The Opera Guild sponsors a similar program
for high schools. The Young Artist Program operas are free and open to
the public. Watch local newspapers or call for information.

    The YPO "Opera Funtime" program produces a series of outstanding
activity/coloring books that introduce children to a dozen different operas.
The books are available for a nominal fee through the Greater Miami
Opera office or in the gift store at the Center for the Fine Arts. For more
information about the Center for the Fine Arts, see listing in "Adventures
in the Arts."

◆ Miami Choral Society
536 Coral Way, Coral Gables 33134. (305) 443-7816.

    The Miami Choral Society is a nonprofit organization composed
of the Miami Youth Choir (for children 8 to 12), the Boy Choir (from
9 until the voice changes), and the Girl Choir (from 11 through high
school). Auditions are held yearly, and children enter a three-year program
to study music theory, voice, and ensemble participation. Public performances include annual concerts in May and December and appearances at
the Dade County Youth Fair, civic events, and festivals.

◆ The New World Symphony
Lincoln Theatre, 555 Lincoln Road, Miami Beach 33139. (305) 673-
3331. Tickets may be purchased at the theater or through TicketMaster.

    "Hands on Music" are family concerts that provide a great way for
children to get a taste of classical music in a fun but formal atmosphere.
"America's National Training Orchestra," led by artistic advisor Michael
Tilson Thomas, was founded in 1988 to provide young musicians (ages 21
to 30) with the opportunity to gain professional performance experience.
The New World Symphony is now known internationally and, in 1993,

released its first recording, *Tangazo,* on the Columbia label. During their October to April season, they present a series of concerts for families. Children 3 to 12 are invited to learn about and enjoy classical music. A delightful program guide describes the music, orchestra, instruments, and concert etiquette. **Tip:** Concerts last about one hour, with no intermission.

◆ Performing Arts for Community and Education (PACE)

Mailing address is P.O. Box 40, Miami 33168-0040. (305) 681-1470 in Dade; (305) 764-4270 in Broward.

PACE is a nonprofit organization that supports and promotes local artists by presenting "concerts on the beach, dance in the streets, theater in the malls, and music in the museums, hospitals, community centers, schools, and businesses." Artists include classical, jazz, reggae, country, and other musicians; puppeteers, mimes, and jugglers; and ballet, modern, and flamenco dancers. Check local newspapers for concert dates and locations, or call the PACE offices for information.

◆ South Florida Youth Symphony

555 NW 152nd Street, Miami 33169. (305) 238-2706.

Founded in 1963, the 70-member nonprofit South Florida Youth Symphony aims to "promote symphonic music among young people, encourage musical growth and appreciation in young people, enhance music appreciation in the community through quality public performances, and support the musical development of young musicians through a substantial scholarship fund." Free "Young People's Concerts" and "Family Day Concerts" are offered. Call or write for concert dates and locations; concerts are offered from Coral Springs to Homestead.

BROWARD COUNTY

◆ Broward Center for the Performing Arts

201 SW Fifth Avenue, Fort Lauderdale 33312. (305) 462-0222.

A walk from Stranahan House along the New River on the Riverwalk literally takes you from Fort Lauderdale's past to its future. You pass the Museum of Discovery and Science and end up at the new Broward Center for the Performing Arts. The center is very involved with arts education in Broward County, and on most school days you'll see busloads of students arriving to enjoy one of the many performances here. The Au-Rene Theater seats 2,688; the Amaturo Theater seats 595.

◆ Florida Philharmonic Orchestra

1430 North Federal Highway, Fort Lauderdale 33304. For concert and ticket information, call (305) 945-5180 in Dade, (305) 561-2997 in Broward, (407) 392-5443 in Boca Raton, and (407) 659-0331 or (800) 226-1812 in West Palm Beach.

Kinderkonzerts, which are geared for children from age 3 to 8, are presented in preschools, elementary schools, and at special events throughout Dade, Broward, and Palm Beach counties. Performances have included *Peter and the Wolf* and *The Circus Parade.*

"Music for Youth" concerts are presented in the public schools for children in grades 3 to 6, and feature special guest soloists chosen from local high schools. "Young People's Concerts" are presented at major auditoriums throughout Broward and Palm Beach counties. They are designed for children ages 6 to 12.

◆ Josephine S. Leiser Opera Center

333 SW Second Avenue, Fort Lauderdale 33312. (305) 728-9700.

The new (1993) home for the Fort Lauderdale Opera, Opera Guild, and Opera Society is another jewel in downtown Fort Lauderdale's cultural district. Equipped with state-of-the-art audio-visual systems, Riverview Theater is located on the second floor and seats 150. The theater space also serves as a rehearsal hall.

Each year "Viva Opera!" sponsors a delightful performance written especially for children. Operas have included *The Toy Shop, Hansel and Gretel, The Serpent Who Wanted to Sing,* and *Little Red Riding Hood.* Performances last about one hour and are appropriate for children ages 5 to 12. Check with the guild for concert dates, location, and other information.

☰ PALM BEACH COUNTY

◆ Florida Philharmonic Orchestra

Raymond F. Kravis Center for the Performing Arts, 701 Okeechobee Boulevard, West Palm Beach; Florida Atlantic Auditorium, Boca Raton. 500 East Spanish River Road, Suite #27, Boca Raton 33431. (407) 392-5443; (407) 659-0331 in Palm Beach.

See listing under Broward County.

◆ Greater Miami Opera Association

(305) 854-1643.

See listing under Dade County.

◆ Greater Palm Beach Symphony

Palm Beach, (407) 655-2657.

The symphony performs orchestral works and chamber music at various sites throughout Palm Beach County.

◆ Palm Beach Opera

Raymond F. Kravis Center for the Performing Arts, 701 Okeechobee Boulevard, West Palm Beach 33401. (407) 833-7888.

Older children will enjoy the grand opera performances by the Palm Beach Opera, directed by conductor Maestro Anton Guadango.

◆ Raymond F. Kravis Center for the Performing Arts

701 Okeechobee Boulevard, West Palm Beach 33401. Take exit I-95 at Okeechobee Boulevard; go east past Clear Lake, Tri-Rail tracks, and Connie Mack Field. The Tri-Rail station is only 200 yards from the Kravis Center. Call (800) 874-7245 for schedule information. Tickets may be purchased by phone or at the drive-through ticket windows. (407) 833-8300.

This outstanding $55-million multipurpose center includes 2,200-seat Dreyfoos Hall, which features Florida's largest stage (150 feet wide, 65 feet deep, and 100 feet to fly upwards), the 300-seat black-box Rinker Playhouse, and the 2,300-seat Gosman amphitheater outdoors. Home to groups such as the Florida Philharmonic Orchestra, the Palm Beach Opera, the Miami City Ballet, and the Ballet Opera, the center is busy day and night with performances for school groups and the public. Future arts center planners should note that Kravis stands above its surroundings—the center's architects saved $7 million in flood-control devices by building on the highest 5.4 acres of land in the area.

THEATER

DADE COUNTY

◆ Actors' Playhouse Children's Theatre

8851 SW 107th Avenue, Miami 33176. Located in the Kendall Mall. (305) 595-5515.

Four plays per year are presented for children ages 2 and up. Productions have included *The Magic Fishbone, The Emperor's New Clothes, The Stone-Age Cinderella,* and *Mr. Crinkle's Magic Spring.* The theater seats approximately 350, with separate stages for children and adult performances. Most shows last one hour, preceded by a brief presentation on theater etiquette and followed by a 15-minute question-and-answer session with the actor.

♦ Coconut Grove Children's Theatre

Mailing address: P.O. Box 33-1002, Coconut Grove 33133-1002. Classes and most performances take place at La Salle High School, 3601 South Miami Avenue (between Mercy Hospital and Vizcaya), Coconut Grove. (305) 442-0489.

Creative director Corky Dozier works to present "theatre by youth, for youth." The theater's workshops provide students with instruction in dance, singing, music, film and television, make-up, and drama, and are available for students in grades K through 12 in Dade and Broward counties. Watch your local papers or call for performance schedules by this innovative group.

♦ Fantasy Theatre Factory

Mailing address is P.O. Box 430280, Miami 33243. (305) 284-8800.

A professional touring company, this troupe calls themselves new vaudevillians and buskers (strolling entertainers). They are featured at, and often co-produce, festivals throughout South Florida, and appear regularly at the Miami Youth Museum. Their children's theater delights kids in grades K through 12. Workshops in creative movement, improvisation, mask-making, mime, clowning, circus skills, and creativity development are provided in the classroom. Call for information about performance schedules.

♦ Florida Shakespeare Festival

Coral Gables Playhouse, Carousel Theater, 235 Alcazar, Coral Gables 33146. (305) 446-1116. Discount tickets are available for children.

Innovative performances of classics, such as a '50s rock 'n' roll version of *Taming of the Shrew,* will entertain older children.

♦ The Genie's Workshop

Bonnie Kesling, (305) 829-7693.

Founded by Bonnie Kesling in May 1990 to encourage children of all ages to learn to express themselves, this singing and dancing troupe now performs throughout South Florida during the year. Most of the members are children with disabilities, and the Genie works wonders with them. Call for information about workshops.

♦ Kaleidoscope—A Young Show-Goers Series

Alper Jewish Community Center, 11155 SW 112nd Avenue, Miami 33176. (305) 271-9000.

Kaleidoscope brings the best nationally known children's performing groups to Miami. Productions usually appeal to children from ages 4 to 10, and they can accommodate groups of up to 1,000 children. Call for program and ticket information.

♦ Lighthouse Children's Theatre

Performances at 7 Seas Showroom of the Holiday Inn Newport Pier Resort, 16701 Collins Avenue, Miami Beach 33160. (305) 947-7654. Call for performance and ticket information. General admission is $5; group rates available.

Three unique adaptations of classic children's stories are performed each year by professional actors at the Lighthouse Playhouse. Prior to each performance, the children, from preschoolers to middle-school students, learn about theater etiquette. Following the play a short question-and-answer period lets children ask the actors and staff about what they've just seen.

♦ Locomotion Children's Theatre

Mailing address is P.O. Box 276326, Boca Raton 33427-6326. (407) 361-8318 (for Boca Raton and north Broward), or (800) 273-3765 for other Florida areas.

Locomotion Children's Theatre is a traveling theater that performs 12 different shows in parks, libraries, festivals, and other public places. Their original plays, which encourage audience participation and the use of imagination, are excellent for children from age 2 to 10. Some of their titles include *Alphabet Soup and Gobbledy-Goop, Dinosaur Eggs in My Lunchbox, Moon Voyager,* and *It's O.K. to Be Nice in Botswana.* Watch for performance information in your local newspapers, or give the theater a call.

♦ Model City Cultural Arts Center

6161 NW 22nd Avenue, Miami 33142. (305) 638-6770.

The center provides training for performing, visual, and media arts, trains and develops in-house performing groups, and provides performers for community events. A gallery features new exhibitions of local and noted African-American and minority artists every six weeks, and tours of the center are available.

Some of the programs offered through the center include "After School in the Arts" and "Saturday Creative Art Day Camp," which are open during the school year for children ages 5 to 15, and include classes in dance, drama, piano, guitar, drawing, and painting. Art day camps during spring break and summer are also offered.

"Magic City Monday Variety Show," at the Caleb Auditorium, takes place twice monthly on Monday evenings throughout the year. Perfor-

mances are appropriate for children ages 3 and up. The Cultural Arts
Center (CAC) Dance Troupe operates out of the Model City Cultural Arts
Center. June is Black Music Month, and a talent search and music festivals are held. In August the annual Youth Talent Show features performers from age 5 to 21.

◆ New Theatre's Theatre for Children

New Theatre, 65 Almeira, Coral Gables 33134. (305) 443-5909.
Performances on Saturdays at noon. Adults, $7; children, $5.

In the summer of 1988 the New Theatre began presenting special
plays based on classic stories for children. Recent performances have
included *Fabulous Fables, Stories Not So Grimm,* and *The Mark Twain
Storybook*. The plays use the "story theater" style, which combines narra-
tion, acting, and audience participation. The theater itself uses the "black
box" format, in which the stage and seats can be moved according to the
needs of the play. Call for information about performances and special
rates for parties and groups.

◆ The Puppet People

8705 SW 182nd Terrace, Miami 33157. (305) 253-3006.

Several full-length, professional puppet shows, 14 different shows for
holidays throughout the year, 7 different preschool programs, and puppet-
making workshops for teachers, recreation leaders, and students—all these
are available from the Puppet People. Excellent for children of all ages.
Call for more information.

◆ The South Florida Theatre of the Deaf

*(305) 373-7383; (800) 995-8770. Call for workshop and performance
information.*

This is the only deaf theater in Florida, and one of only 18 nationwide, to serve almost one million deaf or hearing-impaired Floridians.
Founder Robyn Brooks was born profoundly deaf. She organizes workshops to teach deaf children acting and movement skills that can help
them learn that their disability can't keep them from reaching their goals.

≡ BROWARD COUNTY

◆ Coral Springs Children's Theater/Children to Children

*Opus Playhouse, 3319 NW University Drive (in Coral Springs Mall), Coral
Springs 33067. (305) 753-7070. Performances on Saturday afternoons. Cost*

is $3, but may vary according to the play presented. Group rates are available.

This organization provides children interested in acting with an opportunity to learn as they rehearse for performances. Children from ages 8 to 14 perform in three children's theater productions each year at the Opus Playhouse. Performances include revues, musicals, and plays based on children's books. Auditions for children are held throughout South Florida, and performers are given drama instruction during the production. Drama classes are also available.

◆ Florida Playwright's Theatre

1936 Hollywood Boulevard, Hollywood 33019. (305) 952-8123.

Call for information about the original plays performed for and by children. Most performances take place on Saturdays at 11 A.M.

◆ Fort Lauderdale Children's Theater

640 North Andrews Avenue, Fort Lauderdale 33311. (305) 763-6882. Cost varies according to play; special rates are available for groups and schools.

This theater was founded in 1959 and continues to provide teaching and performance programs for children ages 3 to 18. Students produce and perform in the plays. The auditorium seats 140, and season tickets are available for the four plays presented each year. From November to May the young actors tour in schools throughout Broward; during the summer they go as far south as Key West and north to Palm Beach County.

Saturday workshops in special-effects makeup, voice, puppetry, and clowning are offered throughout the year. Drama classes are available for children ages 3 to 18. The Performing Arts Summer Camp teaches dance, drama, and music to children ages 5 and up.

◆ Hollywood Playhouse Children's Musical Theater

Hollywood Playhouse, 2640 Washington Street, Hollywood 33020. (305) 923-2623.

Performances are presented by children for children, and include singing, dancing, and acting, with an occasional puppet show thrown in. Musical theater workshops and acting classes for all ages are available.

◆ hyperACTive Children's Theatre

Majestic Glades Theatre, 7880 Wiles Road, Coral Springs 33065. (305) 346-7529.

Adaptations of classic stories for children, such as *Sleeping Beauty* and *Aesop's Fables,* are presented on Sundays. Call for information about performances.

◆ hyperACTive, TOO

Performances take place at the theater at the Center Court in Coral Square Mall (next to Burdines), 9133 West Atlantic Boulevard, Coral Springs. (305) 346-7529.

An offshoot of the previous listing, this troupe presents short performances (no more than 30 minutes) that encourage participation by toddlers in the audience.

◆ Lauderhill Arts and Cultural Committee

Lauderhill Community Center, 1176 NW 42nd Way, Lauderhill 33313. (305) 587-5720. Free admission.

Sponsored by the city of Lauderhill, this group has presented children's musical theater productions annually since 1979. All children ages 8 and up who are interested in participating will be included. Plays are performed at the Community Center and have been broadcast on local cable television.

◆ Lollipop Theater

Opus Playhouse, 3319 NW University Drive (in Coral Springs Mall), Coral Springs 33067. (305) 753-7070. Performances take place Saturday afternoons; call for schedule. Cost is $3.

Marionettes and puppets, plays, and other performances appropriate for children ages 3 to 8 are presented by professional actors. This is a wonderful and very inexpensive alternative to Saturday cartoons! See listing above for Coral Springs Children's Theater/Children to Children for more information about drama instruction.

◆ Story Theatre Productions

Mailing address is P.O. Box 4603, Fort Lauderdale 33338. Performances take place at Parker Playhouse, 707 NE Eighth Street, Fort Lauderdale. (305) 763-8813 in Broward, (305) 947-3790 in Dade.

These professional performances are excellent for mature 4-year-olds to 12th graders, depending on the play. Refreshments, autograph sessions with the actors, and other nice touches make this a very special event for children. When school groups make reservations, they are sent teacher's guides prior to the performance. Over 65,000 children enjoy these performances each year. **Tips:** Subscriptions are available; ask about special rates for groups of 10 or more.

◆ Theatre Company of Plantation

1871 North Pine Island Road (in Jacaranda Square), Plantation 33317. (305) 472-6873. Performances for children take place every Saturday morning at 11 A.M. Call for group rates.

New productions at this community theater begin every seven weeks and include original plays, classics, and musicals. Audience participation is a key ingredient here, so tell your children not to be shy. The company holds classes for children ages 4 to adult, and students can perform in the plays. The company also produces performances for teens and adults.

PALM BEACH COUNTY

♦ Gold Coast Mime Company

5151 Adams Road, Delray Beach 33445. (407) 495-1730.

This professional mime company offers performances, such as *Pirate Game,* that encourage audience participation. They also provide movement and theater training. Look for this group in libraries and parks throughout South Florida, or call for performance information. Recommended for children ages 4 and up.

♦ Little Palm Theatre for Young People (Florida Academy of Dramatic Arts)

137 SE First Street, Boca Raton 33429; (407) 394-0206. Freedom Hall, 128 East Ocean Avenue, Boynton Beach; (407) 738-7444. Performances in Boca Raton take place on Saturdays at 9 A.M. Adults and children, $6; group rates available. Call for information about performance and class schedules.

This nonprofit regional theater for young people has provided weekly Saturday morning performances since 1979. New and classic plays take place at the Royal Palm Dinner Theater in Boca Raton and Freedom Hall in Boynton Beach. Classes at Little Palm (the Florida Academy of Dramatic Arts) provide training in acting, directing, writing, teaching, arts management, building sets, costumes, and props. **Tips:** The Little Palm Theater Gift Shop recently opened in the Boynton Beach Mall (next to Burdines). Stop by to pick up Little Palm T-shirts and other souvenirs. This is a wonderful place for a Saturday morning birthday party.

♦ Quest Theatre Institute

West Palm Beach. (407) 832-9328.

Call for information about professional theater performances of original and classic works. The institute also holds classes in all areas of performing arts.

♦ Starmaker Family Theatre Company

In Mission Bay Plaza, corner of U.S. 441 and Glades Road (between Toys R Us and Albertsons) in Boca Raton. Mailing address is P.O. Box 1056,

Delray Beach 33445. (407) 487-3550. Call for performance information. Cost varies according to play.

A nonprofit children's theater company, Starmaker specializes in workshops that enhance children's self-confidence and self-esteem and provide instruction in singing, dancing, and acting. Starmaker's new facilities include a hands-on theater for children, with a lighting board, a scaled-down stage, and motivating decor. Performances take place every Saturday and Sunday, and are appropriate for all ages. Child performers, ages 4 and up, are chosen from auditions in Palm Beach, Broward, and Dade counties.

MONROE COUNTY

◆ Key West Players

Mailing address: P.O. Box 992, Key West 33041. Waterfront Playhouse, at entrance to Mallory Dock, Key West. (305) 292-3725.

Key West is a town full of actors, and the Key West Players is a community theater group that puts them to work. Their program includes two musical theater performances for children each year. Call for information about performances.

EXPLORING SCIENCE AND NATURE

Children are fascinated with the world around them. By studying the earth's natural beauty, as it is revealed in botanical gardens, bodies of water, and tropical hammocks, we can see how our ancestors once lived off the land and used its resources to survive. By exploring the world beyond us—the stars, planets, and weather conditions—we can tap a child's imagination and curiosity. By observing the creatures that share our globe—mammals, reptiles, amphibians—we can learn about ourselves. By delving into our world each and every day, whether through a walk in our backyards or an afternoon in a museum, we can help our children create dreams—and hopefully, someday, fulfill them.

 **DADE COUNTY**

♦ Environmental Center

Miami-Dade Community College South Campus, 11011 SW 104th Street (West Perimeter Road, opposite baseball diamond), Miami 33176. (305) 237-2600. Monday through Friday, 9 A.M.–4:30 P.M.

The Environmental Center was founded in 1977 in an effort to provide educational opportunities to the public. Hurricane Andrew damaged much of the center's vegetation, but restoration is in progress. The children's programs focus on small-critter care and hands-on science activities. Classes emphasize respect for the environment and are recommended for children ages 5 and up. A summer camp program is held annually and gives kids a chance to participate in nature-oriented activities in an outdoor suburban wilderness.

♦ Fairchild Tropical Gardens

10901 Old Cutler Road, Miami 33156. (305) 667-1651. Monday through Sunday, 9:30 A.M.–4:30 P.M.; closed Christmas. Adults, $7; children under 13 free when accompanied by an adult. Admission includes a 40-minute, narrated tram ride. Guided walking tours (not available in summer) are free. Annual memberships available; DISC, MC, V, local personal checks accepted.

Walking the grounds of this botanical paradise is a peaceful and educational way to spend a day. There are over 5,000 plants from around the world here, with the various species labeled for easy identification. The 83 acres make it the largest garden of its kind in the continental United States. The paved trail that winds around 11 lakes makes for a great stroller path. Children may touch the plants, feel the trees, and smell the flowers, but remind youngsters not to pick or collect them. Feeding of wildlife in the gardens is also prohibited.

Post-hurricane renovations are underway on the conservatory, food service facility, and other areas. A large plot of hurricane-damaged trees and plants has been left untouched, except to carve out a path with interpretive signs.

You may not bring food into the gardens, but Matheson Hammock Park is just next door, so take your picnic over there. The best time to visit is during the winter months, when the weather is beautiful and many of the tropical and subtropical plants are in bloom. The garden's annual Ramble, held the first weekend in December, is a must for nature-loving families. **Tips:** Management reminds us that the gardens are not a playground or park—please do not allow children to run freely without supervision. Wear sturdy walking shoes. The bookshop sells souvenirs and nature video cassettes. For information about Matheson Hammock Park, see listing in "Under the Sun." For more information on the Ramble, see listing in "Mark Your Calendar."

◆ Marjory Stoneman Douglas Biscayne Nature Center

North end of Crandon Park, 4000 Crandon Boulevard, Key Biscayne 33149. (305) 364-0150.

During a brief orientation under a chickee, children learn how to walk in the shallow water, how to drag the nets, and what to touch and what not to touch. The Center for Environmental Education, directed by the Environmental Studies Department of the Dade County Public Schools, hosts two-day field trips throughout the year. Field studies of sea grass, sand dunes, and coastal hammocks are complemented by laboratory experiences in the center. Call (305) 995-1989 for field trip information. **Tips:** Wear old sneakers or water shoes, long pants, and a long-sleeved shirt. You'll get wet up to your waist at least, and the clothes protect you from stings. Sunscreen is a must, too. For more information about Crandon Park, see listing in "Under the Sun."

◆ Miami Beach Garden and Conservatory

2000 Convention Center Drive, Miami Beach 33139. Take MacArthur Causeway; turn north on Alton Road, then right on 17th Street; turn left at Convention Center Drive; go north to 20th Street where you'll see the signs. (305) 673-7720. Daily, 10 A.M.–3:30 P.M. Free admission.

This is a small but beautiful collection of exotic earth and air plants (a plant that grows on another plant) found around South Florida. There is a 32-foot-high domed conservatory that always fascinates children, as does the authentic Japanese garden.

♦ Miami Museum of Science and Space Transit Planetarium

3280 South Miami Avenue, Miami 33129. Across from Vizcaya—take I-95 south to exit 1 and follow signs to Museum/Planetarium, or ride Metrorail to Vizcaya Station. (305) 854-4247; Cosmic Hotline, 854-2222. Daily, 10 A.M.–6 P.M.; closed Thanksgiving and Christmas. Museum: adults, $4; seniors and children 3 to 12, $2.50. Planetarium: adults, $6; seniors and children 3 to 12, $4; Thursday nights, free. Combination tickets: adults, $7; seniors and children 3 to 12, $4. Annual memberships available. AE, MC, V accepted in museum gift shop only.

Take a spin on the "Momentum Machine," yell into the "Echo Tube," learn about your own skeleton by watching Mr. Bones ride a bicycle, and try to find the queen in an active beehive. Within the museum, there are over 140 exhibits that focus on the ecology of South Florida, the structure and function of the human body, the patterns of light and sound, and natural history. Children will enjoy participating first-hand in these exhibits by pushing buttons, pulling strings, or turning dials, and then watching what happens. They'll also want to visit the exciting special exhibitions that are presented several times during the year.

The Collection Gallery is also interesting to kids. They can see petrified wood, butterfly species, ostrich eggs, and the skull of a killer whale. You can open one of the "pull-out" drawers to find a surprise!

The Wildlife Center, on an acre of land outside the museum, focuses on wildlife rehabilitation and environmental issues. You'll find 13 exhibits to study, including some that feature wood storks, lizards, snakes, and tortoises. Question-and-answer signs are posted throughout the area, making this a fun and educational adventure. The Birds of Prey Center, home to bald eagles, ospreys, hawks, owls, and more, is one of South Florida's major rehabilitative centers for injured birds, and includes a veterinary hospital on the premises.

The Planetarium is a 65-foot dome where learning about the night sky and space science is fun. View the heavens in 3-D and learn about the moon, planets, star clusters, and nebulae. Star-gazing on Thursday nights is free at the Planetarium.

Recent major additions to the facilities include a splendid overhead mural of famous scientists at the museum's main entrance and a wing of administrative offices.

There are plenty of reasons to visit the museum, so you may want to consider a family membership. Classes range from exploring computer labs to building simple electronic gadgets, as well as holiday, summer, and overnight camps, and are available for children from preschool to high school ages. Teachers throughout Florida and the nation also benefit from computer and science programs developed by museum staff. **Tips:** A hot dog stand, vending machines, and picnic tables are available. Gift shop sells film and unique science-related toys and games. Best times to visit are afternoons and holidays. Call for birthday party information.

◆ National Hurricane Center

1320 South Dixie Highway, Coral Gables 33146. (305) 666-4612. Call Monday through Friday, 8 A.M.–4:30 P.M., to schedule group visits between December 1 and May 30. Free admission.

Learn how to track hurricanes and see a film about these devastating storms at the National Hurricane Center. Recommended for children in grades six and up, your visit may include a talk about the activities at the center, a film or slide show about hurricanes, and a view of the operational area and satellite equipment. Visits usually last one hour and are geared for groups of 30 or less. Please note that tours may be canceled at the last minute due to inclement weather conditions. Plans are underway to move the center to new facilities at Florida International University, so check the address before you go.

◆ Naturalist Services

Metropolitan Dade County Park and Recreation Department, A.D. Barnes Park, 3701 SW 70th Avenue, Miami 33155. (305) 662-4124.

There are many opportunities for children to learn about nature and wildlife through the parks system. Call for information packets that tell about classes, workshops, nature walks, and more. Topics often include Florida's natural history, Indian culture, eco-systems, and marine life. You can also schedule customized programs at the facility at A.D. Barnes Park, at the nature center in Key Biscayne, or at your school or organization's site. A $6 annual subscription to *Tropical Trails* will keep you up to date on all the special events and programs in the parks.

◆ Pelican Harbor Sea Bird Station

1275 NE 79th Street Causeway, Miami Beach. Located behind the Florida Marine Patrol. (305) 751-9840. Free.

Rehabilitating and injured pelicans are resting at this new facility just off the causeway. If you happen to come during feeding time, you'll be treated to a show!

◆ Preston B. Bird and Mary Heinlein Fruit and Spice Park

14801 SW 187th Avenue, Homestead 33031. Thirty-five miles south of Miami; take Florida Turnpike or U.S. 1 to SW 248th Street and head west. (305) 247-5727. Daily, 10 A.M.–5 P.M. Adults, $1; children under 12, $.50. Tours on Saturdays and Sundays, 1 and 3 P.M.: adults, $1.50; children under 12, $1; minimum charge of $12 for weekday tours. Group tours are available by reservation only. Guidebook, $1.50.

The only park of its kind in the United States, the Fruit and Spice Park abounds with over 500 varieties of fruits, spices, herbs, vegetables, and nuts from around the world. Hurricane Andrew blew away 750 trees, and another 273 had to be propped up, but replanting is underway, and plans are in the works to make the park even better than before. They've already added an eight-foot-wide paved path through the park, which makes it wheelchair and stroller accessible, and restrooms are now handicapped accessible.

As you wander through the park, you'll see lots of fruit on the trees. You may not pick any, but you are welcome to eat any that have already fallen. Fruit cannot be removed from the park; if you'd like to identify a fallen sample before you eat it, ask park personnel for assistance. Adults can make special arrangements for collecting seeds and cuttings, or get advice on what to plant in the family garden.

Visit the Redland Fruit Store on your way into the park for interesting tips, or browse for a unique gift for Grandma, like canned fruits, jams and jellies, spices, or a special cookbook. While there, pick up a copy of *A Pioneer History of the Fruit and Spice Park,* which gives a detailed account of how this park came into existence (it's part of the Redland Historic District).

Tours of the 20-acre park are held on weekends or by special request during the week. School tours are available for preschoolers and older and can be specifically designed to coordinate with the students' courses. All tours include taste samples, as well as touching and smelling when appropriate. There is a nominal fee, so call for reservations and detailed information. Classes and workshops are also available.

Each January you'll want to visit the park during the Redlands Natural Arts Festival held there; it's fun for the entire family. **Tips:** Children should wear closed-toed shoes. Although there is an abundance of shade, remember the sunscreen. Visit any time of year, as there's always something "fruiting." Drinking fountains, picnic area, gift shop with souvenirs are available.

For more information on special events, see listing in "Mark Your Calendar."

◆ Southern Cross Astronomical Society

(305) 661-1375. Memberships available.

The Southern Cross Astronomical Society, founded in 1922, is one of the largest amateur astronomical organizations in the U.S. This society has free public telescope observations most Saturday evenings from 8 to 10 P.M. at the Bill Sadowski Park and Nature Center (take Old Cutler Road south to SW 176th Street, go west, and turn right at 79th Avenue; turn off your headlights as you drive in). The hammock area provides the darkest observing sky closest to downtown Miami, so you will be able to catch a glimpse of planets, constellations, and galaxies (weather permitting). Although telescopes are provided, you may want to bring your own, along with binoculars, lawn chairs, protective clothing, and bug repellant.

On Sundays from 10 A.M. to noon meet at the Metrozoo (12400 SW 152nd Street) to get a view of activity on the sun's surface. (You will be protected by special filters that screen out dangerous rays.) Call the hotline number above before 9:30 A.M. to confirm the viewing. For Metrozoo information, see listing in "On Safari in South Florida."

Call for more information about meetings, classes, and special events for children and adults. Southern Cross is a nonprofit organization. For more information and directions to the Bill Sadowski Park and Nature Center, see listing in "Under the Sun."

◆ Tropical Audubon Society

5530 Sunset Drive, South Miami 33143. (305) 666-5111. Open weekdays, 9 A.M.–1 P.M.

For many years the Audubon Society has given us an opportunity to learn about and appreciate the world around us by taking a closer look at nature and wildlife. Headquartered in the historic Arden Hayes "Doc" Thomas House in South Miami, this environmental education center has been designated a wildlife sanctuary. Presentations are offered periodically to bring the natural environment to the public.

Included in the center are an outdoor amphitheater for environmental programs, a campfire circle, a specialized library, an Indian chickee hut with picnic tables, a kitchen, barbecue facilities, and a restroom area. During the week the grounds are open to the public for picnicking, bird-watching, or touring the xeriscape areas. The facilities of the society can be rented for parties; call for information.

BROWARD COUNTY

◆ Buehler Planetarium

Broward Community College, Central Campus, 3501 SW Davie Road (one mile south of S.R. 85/I-595), Davie 33314. (305) 475-6680. Family show on Friday at 7:30 P.M. and Saturday at 1:30 and 7:30 P.M.; Sunday at 1:30 P.M. Call for other show times and prices. Telescope open following Friday and Saturday evening shows.

Located on the campus of Broward Community College, Buehler Planetarium was built in 1966. Renovations have added a modern star projector and a sophisticated, computerized automation system. You'll see this state-of-the-art equipment in action when you explore outer space from your seat in the "Cosmos Princess."

In addition to six public shows each week, the planetarium has programs geared for children from age 4 to 11, and school shows during the week for children in grades three and up. A mobile astronomy program that travels to schools and organizations provides young audiences (pre-kindergarten through second grade) a look at our universe. Reservations are a must, so call for details and cost information.

The public can also visit the observatory and use telescopes on Friday and Saturday evenings to gaze at the moon, stars, planets, galaxies, and other celestial objects. Be sure to stop by the Sky Theatre as well, where short multimedia presentations give you insight into astronomy and space-science topics. **Tips:** Shows last approximately one hour. Children under age 5 are not admitted to late evening laser shows. Stroller and wheelchair access provided.

◆ Spyke's Grove and Tropical Gardens

7250 Griffin Road (west of Davie Road), Davie 33314. Two miles west of U.S. 441, one-half mile east of University Drive. (305) 583-0426; (800) 327-9713. Daily (October through June), 9 A.M.–5:30 P.M. Closed July through September. Tours available. Admission is free.

Take a tram through working citrus groves and see such favorites as orange, grapefruit, tangelo, tangerine, lemon, and lime trees. Visit the alligators, goats, peacocks, and a Himalayan black bear. Spyke's, in business since 1945, ships fruits and gifts all over the country, so check out the gift shop for special things like jellies and candies. Free samples of fruits are available and a quarter buys you a cup of fresh-squeezed OJ. Then take a seat in the tropical garden for a nice rest! **Tips:** Plan to spend about 30 minutes to tour. Call ahead for the tram tour schedule.

PALM BEACH COUNTY

◆ Blood's Hammock Groves

4549 Linton Boulevard (look for signs on the south side of Linton Boulevard, about two miles west of I-95), Delray Beach 33447-2106. (407) 498-3400 or (800) 255-5188. Open November through April, Monday through Saturday, 8:30 A.M.–5 P.M.; closed Sunday.

Three generations of the Blood family have been in the fruit business, starting in 1949. Whether you're in the mood for some freshly squeezed OJ or want to impress your northern friends by sending them some of the best Florida citrus, Blood's is always a fun stop.

Over eight million pieces of fruit are packed by hand for shipping each year. Walk beyond the display room to an observation deck to see the 100 acres of citrus trees and watch the fruit come in from the field; they're washed, waxed, dried, polished, and graded here. At the gift store you can sample fresh varieties of fruit. There's also a vegetable and flower stand on the premises.

◆ Children's Science Explorium

Royal Palm Plaza (located in the corner of the plaza's first building as you enter the east parking lot), 131 Mizner Boulevard, Boca Raton. (407) 395-8401. Tuesday through Saturday, 10 A.M.–5 P.M.; Sunday, noon–5 P.M. Adults, $3.50; seniors and children, $3; children under 3, free. Memberships available.

The sign on the door you enter says "Explore, Investigate and Have Fun!" Science is a fascinating subject, and this museum has lots of hands-on ways to explore it. In addition to the permanent exhibits, the museum has a room full of computers for classes and special events and also hosts traveling exhibits. This is a fun place for birthday parties.

◆ Gumbo Limbo Nature Center

1801 North Ocean Boulevard (one mile north of Palmetto Park Road on Route A1A), Boca Raton 33432. (407) 338-1473. Monday through Saturday, 9 A.M.–4 P.M.; Sunday, 1–4 P.M. Call for information about tours. Free admission; donations accepted. Memberships available.

Named after a red, peeling-bark tree found in this area, the Gumbo Limbo Nature Center consists of 15 acres of well-preserved woods located in Red Reef Park, on a barrier island between the Atlantic Ocean and the Intracoastal Waterway. The land is similar to what the first pioneers encountered when they settled on the southeastern shores of Florida. A number of mammals, reptiles, birds, and fish can be found within the area's boundaries. Be on the lookout for sea turtles, osprey, manatees, and brown pelicans.

The nature center houses a display of sea turtles, snakes, birds, and other creatures. You'll also find a collection of shells, sponges, corals, and sea beans that can be found on our southern beaches. Call in May to reserve a space on a "Turtle Walk," held in June and July. See listing in "Mark Your Calendar" for more information about these events. **Tips:** Plan to spend one hour to tour. Drinking fountains, gift shop, and restrooms available.

◆ Loxahatchee National Wildlife Refuge

S.R. 7, Boynton Beach. The central entrance is approximately 13 miles north of Palm Beach/Broward county line. Mailing address is Route 1, Box 278, Boynton Beach 33437-9741. (407) 734-8303; concessionaire, 426-2474. Refuge: daily, 6 A.M.–sundown; Visitors' Center: weekdays, 9 A.M.–4 P.M.; weekends, 9 A.M.–4:30 P.M. Closed on Mondays and Tuesdays during the summer. Cars, $3; pedestrians, $1.

The Arthur R. Marshall Loxahatchee National Wildlife Refuge is a 146,000-acre segment of the Everglades. The park's boundaries create a haven for rare and endangered species, such as the Florida panther and the bald eagle. Over 250 species of birds have been identified here.

If you stop by the visitors' center you can request to see a short slide show about the area. There's also a display of animals, birds, and Everglades trivia. The concession area offers boat and fishing rentals and airboat rides. Note that picnicking is not encouraged on the refuge grounds.

◆ Marinelife Center of Juno Beach

1200 U.S. 1 (in Loggerhead Park), Juno Beach 33408. (407) 627-8280. Tuesday through Saturday, 10 A.M.–4 P.M.; Sunday, noon–3 P.M. Closed Monday. A suggested donation of $2 per person.

What a great find! This museum, inspired by Eleanor M. Fletcher (the Turtle Lady of Juno Beach), is devoted to the conservation of Florida nature and wildlife. The focus of the museum's work is on education, research, and rehabilitation of endangered sea turtles.

Located in Loggerhead Park, the museum was formerly known as the Children's Museum of Juno Beach. It includes exhibit rooms that house marine aquariums and hands-on table displays—an especially interesting exhibit shows the life stages of seashells! But perhaps the most unique feature of the museum awaits outside, where you can observe sea turtles of various sizes and ages as they swim in huge touch tanks. The baby turtles are fun to watch, while the older and larger ones show off their interesting shell and head features.

In the summer, "Turtle Watches" hosted by the center allow visitors to observe nesting habits. A nice resource library is found within the museum. Field trips to this destination are popular throughout the year. **Tips:** An underground tunnel goes to the beach—just a short walk from the museum. For Loggerhead Park information, see listing in "Under the Sun." For information about turtle walks, see listing in "Mark Your Calendar."

◆ Mounts Botanical Gardens

531 North Military Trail (between Southern Boulevard and Belvedere), West Palm Beach 33415-1395. (407) 233-1749. Monday through Saturday, 8:30 A.M.–5 P.M.; Sunday, 1–5 P.M. Guided tours by appointment on Saturday at 11 A.M. and Sunday at 2:30 P.M. Free admission.

A picturesque 15-acre botanical garden, Mounts features tropical and subtropical plants, a fern house, and a rain forest. Take a self-guided tour at your leisure, or join the staff for a Sunday afternoon walk. The poisonous plant area and herb garden will be interesting to young children. Please note that this is not a park facility. **Tips:** Gardens are accessible to strollers and wheelchairs. Picnic tables, drinking fountains, and restrooms available. Located across the street from an airport, so children will enjoy watching airplanes fly overhead.

◆ Palm Beach Groves

7149 Lawrence Road, Lantana 33462-5616. (407) 965-6699. Daily, 8:30 A.M.–5:30 P.M., October through May. Free admission.

Tour buses often fill the parking area at this popular destination. You'll see and smell and taste Florida citrus groves as you travel through them on a tram. The packing-plant tour lets you see how citrus is processed before being sent to kitchens all over the country. In addition to the native tropical trees, you'll also see many exotic trees. On the way home, ask your kids to try to remember how many different varieties of trees they saw.

◆ Pine Jog Environmental Education Center

6301 Summit Boulevard, West Palm Beach 33415. (407) 686-6600. Open to the public all year, Monday through Friday, 8 A.M.–5 P.M.; Saturday and Sunday, 1–4 P.M. Free admission.

Plan to spend at least a few hours exploring the native plants and creatures that inhabit the 150 acres of pinewood, flatland, and swamp areas here. Call ahead to arrange for a guided tour with one of the naturalists, or take a self-guiding tour. Pick up butterfly nets and magnifying glasses to better observe the insect life. This is a popular field trip destination; students also come for science camps during vacation. **Tips:** This is not a place for strollers, so don't forget the baby backpack. Bring drinks as well—exploring the outdoors is a thirsty business.

◆ South Florida Science Museum

4801 Dreher Trail North, West Palm Beach 33405. Adjacent to Dreher Park Zoo, off Summit Boulevard, east of I-95 between Forest Hill and Southern boulevards. (407) 832-1988. Gibson Observatory 24-hour STARLINE: (407) 832-1988, ext. *700. Daily, 10 A.M.–5 P.M.; Fridays, 10 A.M.–10 P.M. Planetarium show: weekdays, 3 P.M.; weekends, 1 and 3 P.M. Free admission for members; adults, $5; seniors, $4.50; children 4 to 12, $2; children under 4, free. Planetarium: $1; children under 4, free. Annual memberships available.

This museum contains permanent and temporary exhibits on natural history. Kids can participate in hands-on activities that give insight into the world of space and motion, study several South Florida aquaria (look for Kermit, a bright green and very long eel in one, as well as several species of sharks), take an adventure through a snake room, or try to outsmart a computer in a computer arcade. The Everglades display is popular and includes a small alligator, an aquatic-creature touch tank, and a native-plant learning center. The laser shows at the planetarium are always fun, and the Gibson Observatory welcomes visitors, so call the STARLINE for information. **Tips:** Best times to come for this 90-minute tour are in the afternoons, Friday evenings, or weekends. Be prompt for the planetarium shows. Picnic facilities available.

☰ MONROE COUNTY

◆ Captain Hook's Marina

Mile Marker 53, Marathon. Free.

This tackle shop has two large tanks stocked with neighborhood marine life, including sharks, tarpon, and turtles. Several times a day the employees feed the creatures, which provides an interesting show for youngsters.

◆ Key West Aquarium

*One Whitehead Street, Mallory Square, Key West 33040. (305) 296-2051.
Daily, 10 A.M.–7 P.M.; tours at 11 A.M., noon, 1, 2, 3, and 4:30 P.M.
Adults, $6; children 8 to 15, $3; children 7 and under, free. Private and
group tours available.*

You'll be able to view sea creatures up-close in over 40 aquariums of
different sizes and shapes. There's a 30,000-gallon aquarium that contains
barracuda, grouper, snapper, tarpon, and more. The touch tank has new
creatures daily; children are always interested in the starfish, conchs,
snails, and horseshoe crabs. Watch as the aquarium staff feed the stingray,
sea turtles, and sharks. If you dare, they'll let you pet a baby shark; then
pose outside with the 750-pound hammerhead shark, caught off the coast
of Key West. This museum has been entertaining visitors since 1932,
making it Key West's first tourist attraction.

◆ Lignumvitae Key State Botanical Site

*Mailing address is P.O. Box 1052, Islamorada 33036. Site is in Florida
Bay, off U.S. 1 near Islamorada. (305) 664-4815. Tour boat leaves
Thursday through Monday at 1:30 P.M. from the Indian Key Fill (Mile
Marker 78.5) on U.S. 1. Walking tours depart at 10:30 A.M., and 1 and
2:30 P.M. Boat tours: adults, $7; children under 12, $3. Reservations
required. Walking tours: adults, $1; children under 6, free.*

Lignumvitae Key lies southwest of Upper Matecumbe, about a 15-
minute trip by boat. Thousands of years ago, this 280-acre island started
out as a living coral reef; later it became a sacred burial ground for the
Calusa Indians. Now you can walk through tropical hammocks and mangroves and learn about the island's vegetation and formation. Once on the
island you may explore the Matheson home and yard. If you want to explore the woods you must take the ranger-guided two-hour walking tour,
so meet at the dock or the Matheson house. Be sure to wear proper shoes
and bring insect repellant. **Tips:** Call before you go to confirm whether
the tour boat is available—it occasionally goes out of service. If this is the
case, you must rent a boat or bring your own. No wheelchair access provided. For information about Indian Key State Historic Site, see listing in
"Tracing the Past."

◆ Looe Key National Marine Sanctuary

*Mile Marker 30, Big Pine Key. Mailing address is Route 1, Box 782, Big
Pine Key 33043. (305) 872-4039.*

Looe Key, located five miles offshore, was declared a National
Marine Sanctuary in 1981. Fishing, diving, snorkeling, and swimming

are popular because the water here is extremely clear and very shallow in areas. Brightly colored fish and other marine life inhabit the coral reefs, sea-grass beds, and sand flats. Of course you'll want to explore the remains of the HMS *Looe,* a British frigate that sank in 1744. **Tip:** Snorkeling equipment is available for rent.

♦ Museum of Natural History of the Florida Keys

Mile Marker 50.5 (bayside), Crane Point Hammock (in Marathon, across from K-Mart) 33050. (305) 743-9100. Monday through Saturday, 9 A.M.–5 P.M.; Sunday, noon–5 P.M. Adults, $3.50; seniors, $2; students, $1; children under 12, free.

Earth Day 1991 welcomed this wonderful 63-acre indoor-outdoor museum. Take the one-quarter-mile interpretive nature trail to explore a rare tropical palm hammock containing 210 native and exotic plants and 10 endangered animal species. An underwater cave with windows lets you get close to sharks, lobster, tropical fish, and turtles swimming in their 15,000-gallon saltwater lagoon. Learn about pre-Columbian Keys Indians and the ill-fated HMS *Looe.* Marine touch tanks and several other indoor exhibits give everyone in the family something to do. Special programs are presented at the Ronald McDonald Children's Charities Amphitheater. **Tip:** The admission price to the museum includes a visit to the Florida Keys Children's Museum, located behind the main museum building. For more information, see listing in "On Safari in South Florida."

♦ National Key Deer Refuge

Mile Marker 31.5, Big Pine Key 33043. Take Key Deer Boulevard to Watson Boulevard. (305) 872-2239. Daily, 8 A.M.–dusk.

Key deer, the smallest species of white-tailed deer in existence, make their home within the refuge. Considered an endangered species, only 250 of these deer exist in the world, and they all live here. When fully grown, the deer stand about two feet high at the shoulder and weigh 65 to 75 pounds.

Blue Hole, an old limestone quarry, is now a freshwater lake that provides water for the deer. Take the three-quarter-mile self-guiding nature trail that begins on Key Deer Boulevard just north of Blue Hole. If you go in early morning or late afternoon and you're very quiet, you may get to see deer as you explore the refuge. The refuge is open to the public and allows a unique opportunity to witness an endangered animal in its native habitat. **Tip:** Swimming with the alligators is strictly prohibited at Blue Hole—they can't tell the difference between people and dinner.

◆ Riggs Wildlife/Bird Refuge

Near International Airport and South Roosevelt Boulevard, Key West 33040.
(305) 294-2116, 294-3438, 269-3913.

Bird-watchers will find a variety of herons, egrets, ibis, and ospreys to observe here, as well as many types of fish. About 50 of the 470 acres that made up the Key West Salt Ponds during the 1830s are now a refuge area. An 80-foot observation deck offers a good view of the refuge.
Tip: If the gate is locked, please call one of the phone numbers above for the combination.

◆ *San Pedro* Underwater Archaeological Preserve

Loran coordinates: 14082.1 by 43320.6, about 1.25 miles south of Indian Key. (305) 664-4815.

In July 1733, a fleet of Spanish treasure ships left Cuba to deliver their cargo of gold and silver to Spain. On July 13, a hurricane sent the entire fleet to the bottom of the sea. You can explore one of those galleons, the *San Pedro,* with snorkeling or scuba equipment. Tie your boat to the mooring buoys. The ship is in 18 feet of water, and you'll find concrete cannons, an anchor, and other relics. Careful divers will see many tropical fish and other marine life, but no fishing of any kind is allowed.

◆ Windley Key Fossil Reef Geological Site

Windley Key, Mile Marker 85, bayside.

Fences surround three coral rock quarries that were mined for Henry Flagler's Overseas Railroad at the beginning of the century. What you see now are stone walls that show cross sections of fossilized coral reef. Volunteers are working to develop five trails for visitors to explore the quarries, so stop by to check on the progress.

UNDER THE SUN

The great outdoors is one of South Florida's primary attractions. Parks, nature centers, and beaches abound here, and you will see from the listings that follow that each has its own personality. There are theme parks and recreational parks; parks just for kids and parks that have something for each member of the family; large regional parks and cozy neighborhood parks; garden parks and beach parks. But they all have one thing in common—they're ours to enjoy.

Many of the parks in South Florida are designated as wildlife or historic preserves. They provide wonderful places to teach young children respect and compassion for our environment, its wildlife, and its rich history.

You'll find that the Florida Keys are somewhat of a playground of their own! This tropical paradise is a haven for those who like to boat, fish, and snorkel. Keep in mind that there aren't too many sandy beaches for children to just swim and play. Strong currents keep the sand from building up at the shoreline. Encourage children to cautiously explore marine life in the shallow water of the reefs, examine the formations of rocks and coral, and view the wildlife native to the area—and they will be enriched by their visit to the Keys.

Here are a few hints to keep in mind when visiting outdoor areas in South Florida, particularly parks and beaches:

- Never forget the power of the Florida sun. You must consider its strength and be aware of its potential harm. Please take care of yourself and your children, especially infants and toddlers, by using a sun block, not only at the beach, but any time you are outdoors. Purchase a reliable brand that gives a Sun Protection Factor of at least 15 and protects against UVB and UVA rays. Avoid direct sunlight especially during the hours of 11 A.M. and 3 P.M., when ultraviolet rays peak. Even in the winter months the sun's rays can produce severe burns and long-term side effects.
- Bring along plenty of water and avoid lengthy mid-day outdoor activities.

- When visiting beaches, always swim near a lifeguard and check out the water's condition. In the spring you may find the ocean waves to be rough, and the undertow may be too strong for children. Weather conditions can cause dangerous riptides. Lifeguards are helpful and can give good advice on swimming conditions. If you see red or yellow flags posted on the beach, avoid swimming there.
- Drowning is the number one cause of death for children from age 1 to 4. Consider swimming lessons for your child from a certified instructor. Call local parks, community centers, and country clubs to learn about swimming lessons and aquatic programs offered in your neighborhood.
- Remind children to never touch jellyfish and to be cautious around other sea creatures.
- Sea lice are pesky little critters often found in beach water. If you've been a victim, you'll know by the itchy red welts that appear on your skin (particularly under the bathing suit) after swimming in the ocean. Most common from April through July, their bites can be treated with a freshwater bath after you remove your bathing suit. Cortisone creams and Benedryl seem to alleviate the itch.
- South Florida weather is unpredictable—if you see lightning or a storm approaching, always find shelter.
- Watch out for biting insects. Mosquitoes are year-round pests but are especially prevalent in the summer months. Keep insect repellant handy. Effective and inexpensive repellents include vinegar, yeast tablets, and, believe it or not, Avon's Skin-So-Soft bath oil. Calamine lotion or half-percent hydrocortisone cream are also effective. Bug-proof netting is great when camping and for placing over baby playpens and carriages. On the ground, look out for fire ants—their bites can be extremely bothersome, and some people have terrible allergic reactions. It's a good idea to carry ammonia dabbers (available in pharmacies) to get the sting out of bug bites. Meat tenderizer is another quick-relief method for bites and stings.
- If you visit parks often you may want to keep a box of outdoor toys in your car for those unplanned trips.
- National parks do not have trash bins available. Upon entering these parks, visitors may be given a plastic trash bag to use while picnicking. Please be considerate and follow guidelines for each park.
- Always check out the condition of playground equipment before your children begin to play. For guidelines on minimum safety standards and playground equipment that has been recalled, contact the Consumer Products Safety Commission at (800) 638-CPSC.

There are many wonderful national, state, county, city, and neighbor-hood parks that have programs for all interests. Observe the safety rules and regulations at each of the places you visit. Also, many parks change their hours and admission prices during the summer months, so be sure to call ahead for up-to-date information. Concessions and rental policies may also fluctuate with the seasons. For information and literature regarding the following listings, write or call:

- **State Parks, Department of Natural Resources,** Office of Recreation and Parks, Mall Station 525, 3900 Commonwealth Boulevard, Tallahassee 32399-3000; (904) 488-9872.
- **Dade County Parks and Recreation,** 50 SW 32nd Row, Miami 33129; (305) 857-6868. Leisure Access Services, (305) 372-7733.
- **Dade County Interpretive Services,** 3701 SW 70th Avenue, Miami 33155; (305) 662-4124.
- **City of Miami Parks and Recreation Department,** (305) 575-5256.
- **Broward County Parks and Recreation Division,** 950 NW 38th Street, Oakland Park 33309-5982; (305) 357-8100.
- **Broward County Special Events Hotline,** available 24-hours, (305) 563-PARK.
- **Palm Beach County Parks and Recreation,** (407) 964-4420. Special Events, (407) 966-6623; Special Populations, (407) 964-4822.
- **Beach conditions in Palm Beach County:** North Palm Beach County, (407) 624-0065; South Palm Beach County, (407) 276-3990.

DADE COUNTY

♦ A.D. Barnes Park

3701 SW 72nd Avenue, Miami 33155. Look for the tall trees on Bird Road! Mailing address is 3701 SW 70th Avenue, Miami 33155. Park and pool, (305) 665-1626; naturalist services, (305) 662-4124. Park: daily, sunrise to sunset; free admission. Pool: daily, 12:30–5 P.M.; adults, $1.75; children, $1.

There's something here for everyone to enjoy. From the "tot lot" play area to a wheelchair-accessible "tree house," you'll have a fun outdoors experience in this nature area tucked away from the busy city. Within the 62-acre park you'll find picnic facilities, a jogging and biking path, and a solar-heated swimming pool. The pool has a hydraulic floor that is raised and lowered to accommodate wheelchairs. The tree-house facility is actually a 200-foot ramp that extends about 12 feet above ground into a cluster of trees.

Children will enjoy the Sense of Wonder Nature Center and Trail, offering hands-on activities and animal exhibits. Call to find out when the center is open. Field trips can be arranged, and families can enjoy Saturday morning nature walks during the school year. The unique trail is made up of outdoor exhibits that teach children how to use their five senses to learn about the wonders of nature. One stop on the trail focuses on the Seminole and Miccosukee Indian cultures—touch and smell the dried palm fronds that make up an Indian home. At the pond, listen to a waterfall as it splashes on the rocks, or watch fish and turtles as they are fed. Smell different fragrances in a herb garden and watch as beautiful butterflies dance around the plants. The trail is wheelchair-accessible.

Previously called Bird Drive Park, A.D. Barnes Park (named for Doug Barnes, the first director of the Dade County parks system) often hosts special-needs camps and programs. Call for information about their annual camps for asthmatic and ventilator-dependent children.

◆ Alice Wainwright Park

2845 Brickell Avenue, Miami. From Bayshore Drive turn east on side street north of entrance to Vizcaya. Follow around until it becomes Brickell Avenue (you can't get there directly on Brickell Avenue south from downtown); park on street near entrance. Daily, sunrise to sunset. Free admission.

This native hardwood hammock has shady picnic sites and a view of Biscayne Bay that make it especially peaceful. (A hammock is a fertile land area made up of densely grown hardwood trees.) You'll need a watchful eye for young children here, as there is no barrier at the water's edge. Two playground areas and a nature trail through the hammock are located within the park. **Tip:** Restrooms are near entrance.

◆ Amelia Earhart Park

401 East 65th Street (NW 119th Street and LeJeune Road), Hialeah 33013. (305) 769-2693. Daily, 9 A.M.–sunset. Admission, $3 per vehicle.

Bill Graham's Farm Village at Amelia Earhart Park is a hit with children. From the authentic red barn (complete with goats, chickens, horses, and sheep) to the farm-type play equipment, they'll never be bored. Plus, mom can browse in the General Store or enjoy an ice cream cone! Pony rides and hayrides are offered for a nominal fee, and children can also feed the animals for $.50.

Not all of the 515 acres are developed at Amelia Earhart, but already you can find bike paths, picnic facilities, a playground, and a jogging trail. If water's your preference, try out the beach or rental items, such as boats and canoes, on the weekends. The Tom Sawyer Play Island can be reached by a suspension bridge and has plenty of play equipment for children. Young children should be supervised on the island—rock structures for climbing and easy access to water can make this area a bit dangerous for adventurous children.

♦ Arch Creek Park

1855 NE 135th Street, North Miami 33181. (305) 944-6111. Daily, 9 A.M.–5 P.M. Park admission is free, small fee for naturalist group activities.

This historical park offers a unique opportunity to study history, archaeology, and nature. There is a museum on the grounds modeled after a pioneer home, and in it you'll find a treasury of artifacts from the Ice Age, as well as relics from the prehistoric Tequesta Indians and early pioneers. Shell tools, vertebrae fossils, and pottery are housed in the museum.

Many children are introduced to Arch Creek Park through school field trips; however, families can participate together in archaeological digs that are held periodically throughout the year. The digs take about three hours, and participants just might find Tequesta Indian artifacts from 3,000 years ago.

Teachers may inquire about classes visiting the site during the week. A very popular field trip is called "Indian Powwow," where children become Indians for a day and trace the history of the Seminole and Tequesta tribes by walking the nature trail, studying edible plants, and digging for artifacts. A popular summer camp program is offered here each year. Birthday parties can be held at the park upon request. **Tips:** Children should wear old clothes when participating in the programs. Make reservations for special programs. Bring your own drinks and food treats. Trails are not accessible to strollers or wheelchairs. Restrooms, drinking fountains, and picnic areas are available. Self-guided tours run 45 minutes to one hour—best time to visit is afternoons or on Saturdays at 1 P.M. for a free nature walk.

♦ Bill Baggs/Cape Florida State Recreation Area

1200 South Crandon Boulevard, Key Biscayne 33149. Located south of downtown Miami off the Rickenbacker Causeway. (305) 361-5811. Park: daily, 8 A.M.–sunset. Admission: $3.25 per vehicle, plus $.50 per person; $1.50 for walk-ins or bikers. Rickenbacker Causeway toll: $1.

The 400-acre park that sits at the tip of famous Key Biscayne was virtually flattened by Hurricane Andrew in August 1992. With an ambitious restoration plan underway, Cape Florida is making a comeback!

About 90 percent of the park's original trees were destroyed in the hurricane, so many new plantings have taken place and include coconut palms, sea grapes, and native species. Park personnel have imported seeds from plants on the outer islands to ensure native plantings. New parking areas and freshwater ponds are in the works. The park is a major migratory route for warblers making their way back north from the West Indies. New freshwater marshes will provide drinking water for these birds and other wildlife. The new plantings and improvements will transform the park into a historically correct setting.

Within the park is the Cape Florida Lighthouse, built in 1825. It is the oldest structure built in South Florida. The lightkeeper's house is open for tours, but the lighthouse itself will be reopened in 1995.

The concession stand offers rental bikes, lounges, umbrellas, windbreakers, and fishing equipment. Take a few moments to sit on the seawall at the tip of the island to watch the sunset and the many boats finding their way back to port. **Tips:** Outside showers are available. For more information, see listing for Cape Florida Lighthouse in "Tracing the Past."

◆ Bill Sadowski Park and Nature Center

17555 SW 79th Avenue (half mile west of Old Cutler Road on SW 176th Street), Miami 33157. (305) 255-4767. Daily, 9 A.M.–5 P.M. Free admission.

In 1992 this park and nature center was renamed in memory of Bill Sadowski, a public servant and "shepherd of growth management," who was killed in a plane crash earlier that year. The park was formerly called Old Cutler Hammock Nature Center. Hidden among trees, this park is excellent for young children. The play area, with swings and equipment, is good to visit on weekday mornings, when you can have the whole playground to yourselves. If children bring their own fishing poles, they can try their luck in the canal located off the trails. The interpretive center houses snakes, turtles, and other reptiles.

A very active nature program for children and adults is offered, with Saturday morning classes, campfire circles, and summer camps. On Saturday nights you can go star-gazing here from 8 to 10 P.M., with the help of the Southern Cross Astronomical Society. It's free! For more information, call (305) 361-2502, or see listing in "Exploring Science and Nature."

◆ Biscayne National Park

9700 SW 328th Street, Homestead 33030. Located nine miles east of Homestead at Convoy Point. From the Florida Turnpike Homestead/Key West Extension take Tallahassee Road (SW 137th Avenue) south to North Canal Drive (SW 328th Street) and head east. Mailing address is P.O. Box 1369, Homestead 33090-1369. Visitors' Center: (305) 247-7275. Daily, 8 A.M.– 6 P.M. (hours may vary with seasons). Free admission. Boat rentals and tours, (305) 247-2400. Reef Rover IV Glass-bottom Boat Tour: daily, 10 A.M.;

adults, $16.50; children under 12, $8. Snorkeling tours: daily, 1:30 P.M.; adults, $27.50; children under 12, $13.75. DIS, MC, and V accepted.

America's largest national aquatic park comprises 181,500 acres of islands, mangrove forests, water, and reefs, providing a picture of what South Florida looked like hundreds of years ago. Approximately 44 small keys, including Elliott Key and Sands Key, are within the park's boundaries and are accessible only by boat. Ninety-six percent of the park is water and contains the northernmost living coral reef in the United States. Tales of ancient shipwrecks and fascinating islands make it a legendary place.

The park's headquarters and information area are located on the mainland at Convoy Point. A new visitors' center was constructed in 1993 after Hurricane Andrew left its mark here. The new center contains dioramas and a video aquarium. The purpose of the displays, said one ranger, is "to wet people's appetites and have them visit the reefs personally." Schedules of park activities are posted in the visitors' center. Inquire about Ranger Choice programs, given upon request.

Picnic areas have tables, grills, and restrooms nearby. Following a short trail offers a view of the marine life and birds of Biscayne Bay. Swimming and shoreline snorkeling can be enjoyed here, with rental equipment available for canoeing, snorkeling, and scuba diving.

A very popular, three-hour trip on the Reef Rover IV, a glass-bottom boat, gives you a first-hand look at the scenic underwater reefs. Remind or inform your young companions that a coral reef, although it appears lifeless, is actually a colony of small animals called polyps. Call ahead for departure times and reservations, which must be made one day in advance. An off-shore snorkeling trip departs from the park's headquarters daily and lasts approximately four hours; rental equipment is included in the ticket price. In addition, three marinas make the park accessible for visitors with their own water crafts. When boating, remember to anchor in sandy areas, not reefs. **Tips:** There are no lifeguards on duty. Some of the Keys have recreation facilities, but Elliott Key is the only one with drinking water. The park puts out a wonderful map and information guide—write or call for a copy. For more information on the Reef Rover IV, see listing in "By Land, Sea, and Air."

♦ Castellow Hammock

22301 SW 162nd Avenue, Goulds 33170. From the Florida Turnpike take Quail Roost Drive (starts as 186th Street and becomes 200th Street) west to SW 162nd Avenue, then turn left. (305) 257-0904. Daily, 9 A.M.–5 P.M. Free admission.

This 60-acre tropical hammock suffered damage by Hurricane Andrew. The interpretive building that once stood on the property will be
rebuilt—a bigger and better version—during the next few years. Keep
this on your list of best bird-watching parks, and call for information
about interpretive programs.

◆ Crandon Park

*4000 Crandon Boulevard, Key Biscayne 33149. (305) 361-5421. Marjory
Stoneman Douglas Biscayne Nature Center: 364-0150. Daily, sunrise to
sunset. Cost is $3 per car; $6 per bus. Rickenbacker Causeway toll, $1.*

Key Biscayne and Crandon Park have been popular with tourists and
locals for decades. The park has undertaken major negotiations for expansion. Proposed ideas include a large tennis facility, increased landscaping,
an improved garden area, a sea turtle hatchery, and more. You'll have to
visit the park just to see what was accepted from the proposal to the
county. The three-mile beach is very popular, and visitors can find cabana
rentals, picnic areas, lifeguards on duty, restrooms, grills, and concessions.
Snorkeling is popular at the Bear Cut area north of the park. Discover a
unique black mangrove fossil reef here—one of only two such reefs in the
world.

Within Crandon Park is Calusa Park (across the street next to the fire
station). This unusual play area has climbing equipment, a hippo for children to crawl through, and a giant turtle to sit on. For more information
about the Marjory Stoneman Douglas Biscayne Nature Center, located
within the park, see listing in "Exploring Science and Nature."

◆ Douglas Park

*2755 SW 37th Avenue, Miami 33145. (305) 442-0374. Daily, 8 A.M.–
sunset. Free admission.*

This city park, with its "Friendship Playground" or "Parque de la
Amistad," is a wonderful find for anyone with imaginative children. You
and your children will be enchanted by the wooden castle, built by the
Kiwanis Club of Little Havana (with assistance from the Frito-Lay Corporation). There is a fenced-in section for toddlers that allows them to climb
around and peek through the windows of their own castle. The play area's
floor is gravel, not sand—so while you won't have to worry about Junior's
shoes being filled with sand, you may want to enforce the "no-eating-the-
gravel" rule. There is a large multipurpose field and a small picnic area;
food is not allowed in the castle area. Birthday parties are popular here on
the weekends, so come on weekday mornings or other non-peak periods.
Tip: The park's playing surface is gravel, so be sure to wear appropriate
shoes.

◆ Everglades National Park

There's no place like it in the world. It has a mixture of 1.4 million acres of land and water and is the second largest national park in the United States, outside of Alaska. It's made up of pine forests, dense subtropical hammocks, tree islands, mangroves, sawgrass prairies, and swamp. It's the Everglades, with a beauty all its own, home to 11 endangered wildlife species and more mosquitoes than possibly anywhere else in the world.

Everglades National Park was established in 1947. Twenty-five native mammals, over 300 bird species, and 60 reptiles (including 23 snake varieties) live within the Everglades' boundaries. They roam here naturally and freely. Feeding them is dangerous and is prohibited by law. Possibly the most noted creature in this part of Florida is the alligator, a quick and unpredictable fellow. He can move with amazing speed, so remind your children to keep their distance.

From mid-December to mid-April, all the visitor centers are busy and crowded. In the summer (when it's hot, humid, and extremely buggy), weather is very unpredictable, with heavy rains and lightning storms forming very quickly. Be a sky-watcher and carry an umbrella in your car. Whenever you visit, come with a full tank of gas, drinks, and suitable wading clothes (loose-fitting, long-sleeved shirts and long pants) that will also protect you from the biting bugs.

Swimming in the Everglades is not encouraged. Fresh water ponds have alligators and poisonous snakes living in them, while salt water areas are often shallow, muddy, and home to many sharks and barracudas.

Always call ahead when planning your trip. If you call weeks in advance, ask for a newsletter or park brochure to be mailed to you. There's some very good information at the park's offices. Open year-round, the Everglades' peak visiting season is from mid-December through mid-April. Here is a list of visitors' centers and places of interest within Everglades National Park.

Main Park Headquarters and Visitors' Center

Mailing address is P.O. Box 279, Homestead 33030. Located approximately 10 miles southwest of Florida City and Homestead on State Road 9336. (305) 242-7700. Daily, 8 A.M.–5 P.M. Private motor vehicles (car, van, motorcycle), $5; commercial vehicles (bus), pedestrians, or bikes, $3 (for visitors ages 16 or older). Golden Access, Golden Age, and Golden Eagle passes accepted. Admission is valid for seven days.

Stop by this visitors' center for an orientation film, displays, and a schedule of activities and events. There's a nice bookstore here with excellent reference material for children and adults. Inside this entrance, you will find the Royal Palm area.

Royal Palm

Inside park, take first left at S.R. 9336 Extension. Visitors' Center, (305) 242-7700. Daily, 8 A.M.– 4:30 P.M.

Wet or dry hikes, three-hour walking tours that take you through the various landscapes of the Everglades, are planned periodically. The popular Anhinga Trail, made out of Timbrex, a combination of recycled wood and plastic, lets you see alligators, snakes, birds, and fish in the Taylor Slough from a boardwalk. Adjacent to the Anhinga Trail is the Gumbo Limbo Trail, a one-half-mile junglelike trail. Wear shoes, long pants, and mosquito repellant! Call ahead—there's a limit to the number of people who can participate.

A 45-minute campfire program with a park ranger is fun for everyone. Topics include wildlife, plants, and ecology. Call for a schedule.

Flamingo

Thirty-eight miles southwest of the main entrance at the end of the road on Florida Bay. Mailing address for Flamingo Lodge, Marina and Outpost Resort is P.O. Box 428, Flamingo 33030. (305) 253-2241. Daily, 7 A.M.–7 P.M.

This is the southernmost point of the park that is accessible by car. A motel, swimming pool, restaurant, gift shop, store, gasoline, cruises, tram tours, campsites, canoe rentals, fishing boats, and houseboats are all available.

In the Visitors' Center you'll find exhibits of the flora, fauna, and natural history of the area. Check the bulletin board for special weekly naturalist programs. A ranger-led program, "The Naturalist's Backpack," is an excellent hands-on experience for kids. They'll see alligator skulls, a manatee rib, and flamingo feathers for a start. Check for times.

One of only two camping places in the Everglades, Flamingo has 300 sites for trailers and tents and an additional 4 sites for large groups. There is a shower facility, marina store, and amphitheater meeting place. Stargazing at night might interest your youngsters. There is no light pollution here—you are definitely in the wilderness! Bring your binoculars and celestial maps, and search for Orion, Scorpio, and other constellations.

Walking tours, led by rangers, leave from Eco Pond periodically. You'll see ibis, alligators, and roseate spoonbills.

A half-day wilderness canoe trip leaves Fridays at 8:30 A.M. The trip is for children 6 and older, and previous canoeing experience is required. Please bring a packed lunch and beverage, as well as insect repellant. Reservations are needed; call (813) 695-3101. A shorter canoeing adventure is held on Sunday and Tuesday afternoons. The same rules apply as for the half-day trip.

Shark Valley

Tamiami Trail (U.S. 41), about 35 miles west of downtown Miami.
(305) 242-7700; tram tour reservations, 221-8455. Daily, 24 hours.
Visitors' Center: daily, 8:30 A.M.–5:15 P.M. Cars, $4; admission is valid for
seven days. Tram rides run at 9:30 and 11 A.M. and 1 and 3:30 P.M.
Adults, $7.30; seniors, $6.50; children under 12, $3.65. Cash only.

A tram tour of the area, a two-hour trip that takes you to the heart of
the Everglades, is available daily. Call ahead to confirm the schedule and
to check weather conditions. You'll get off to stretch your legs at a 65-
foot observation tower, where you'll be provided with a spectacular view
of the Everglades, and you'll probably see dozens of alligators nearby.

On weekends Shark Valley rangers sponsor a three and one half hour,
15-mile bike tour, through sawgrass prairies and hammocks, that may be
okay for durable children! Bring your own bikes and drinks, along with
your own baby carrier if needed. Rental bikes are available on a first-come,
first-serve basis. Don't forget your binoculars!

Meet a park ranger for a stroll along the Bobcat Trail—it lasts about
a half-hour and you never know what you'll see! There is a tape cassette
trail guide available. Ask at the information center for times.

West of Shark Valley you'll be glad you found the Loop Road Interpretive Center. The drive is scenic and the reward is great! Children will
enjoy a library set up just for them and learn lots from the displays about
the Everglades. There's a nature trail through a hardwood hammock here,
too.

For more information about tram rides, see listing in "By Land, Sea,
and Air." Late afternoon is often the best time for bird-watching. Park
your car outside the gate if you plan to be there after 6 P.M., or it will be
locked in until morning. Law requires that you have a flashlight or bike
light after dark.

Chekika Ranger Station

24200 SW 160th Street, Homestead. Take Krome Avenue to SW 168th
Street (Richmond Drive), go west to SW 237th Avenue. Turn right to
entrance. Signs are posted. Mailing address is P.O. Box 1313, Homestead
33030. (305) 242-7700.

These 640-acres (there are plans to expand) are named after Chekika,
an Indian chief of the early 1800s who played a major role in the Second
Seminole War. While walking the nature trail here (about a 20-minute
walk), you can almost visualize the Indians behind the trees. The trail will
give you a feel for a true tropical hammock—signs posted along the way
tell brief, interesting stories about the vegetation and hammock characteristics. Rangers give guided tours upon request, if staffing allows.

From the parking lot, walk along a boardwalk to the picnic and swimming areas. You may see a number of alligators along the way—remember that these are dangerous reptiles and must be treated with caution. Never approach or try to feed them.

There's a small sandy beach at the swimming hole, which once was a natural depression in the hammock. The swimming area was built by diking and directing artesian water into the depression from a nearby well, discovered in 1943 when prospectors were trying to strike oil.

Campsites are located within the park, along with a primitive camp for youths available by reservation.

Everglades City

Across U.S. 41 and five miles south on S.R. 29 (causeway to Chokoloskee Island); 80 miles west of downtown Miami; 40 miles southeast of Naples. Daily, 8:30 A.M.–5 P.M. (305) 242-7700. Cruises: (800) 445-7724. Cruises: adults, $10; children 6 to 12, $5. Tours leave on the hour from 9:30 A.M. to 4:30 P.M.

This area of the Everglades can only be explored by boat, and the Gulf Coast Ranger Station boat-tour concession schedules several daily tours through the Ten Thousand Islands. You'll see herons, ospreys, pelicans, cormorants, alligators, dolphins, and more. Canoe rentals are available, and during the winter and spring (the rangers don't want to be out in the summer and fall heat and bugs, either), rangers lead canoe trips on the Turner River. You can explore the mangroves along Florida Bay on a narrated boat cruise. The Visitors' Center has displays, slide shows, maps, and other useful information.

◆ Greynolds Park

17530 West Dixie Highway, Miami 33160. Park: (305) 945-3425. Interpretive services: (305) 662-4124. Daily, sunrise to sunset. Parking on weekends and holidays: cars, $1.50; RV, van, or bus, $6.

You'll almost believe you're out in the country when you enter Greynolds Park. The lush tropical landscaping and rolling hills are a welcome site in an otherwise busy part of town. This 160-acre park is a good place to picnic in the shade and have the children close by in a playground. (Try the Mahogany picnic area past the golf course, around the corner on your left.) There's a castle on a hill for young children to play in and around—it may be dangerous for toddlers, as the path leading up to it is rocky and steep, but sure-footed and imaginative kids will love playing in this storybook dwelling.

Greynolds is famous for its bird rookery (a bird colony or breeding place), home to almost 3,000 long-legged wading birds. Every Thursday evening there is a free bird-watching program. Call for times, as they vary throughout the year. "Owl Prowls" are offered on the first Wednesday of every month (winter only) at 7:30 P.M. Reservations are suggested.

The park also has bike paths, several nature trails, and a coral rock boathouse that is now a concession area renting rowboats and paddleboats on the weekends for $3 for 30 minutes. A summer camp program offered here is very well attended. **Tip:** Another concession area at the park's golf course is open seven days a week.

♦ Homestead Bayfront Park

9698 North Canal Drive, Homestead 33030. Located next to Biscayne National Park. (305) 247-1543. Daily, 7 A.M.–sundown. Cars, $2; boats, $5.

You don't have to be on Miami Beach to get close to the water! The beach here is a favorite for young and old alike. All the ingredients—an ocean view, clean sand, and nice playground equipment—make this a good family stop. Restrooms, showers, and concessions are available.

♦ Island Park

Take MacArthur Causeway (I-395) to Palm Island entrance. Go through the 24-hour manned security gates. Open daily, 8 A.M.–dusk.

This is a tiny treasure in the middle of Biscayne Bay that most people don't know about, and you'll be glad you found it. Dedicated in 1975, it measures only 300 feet by 300 feet, but offers swings, a covered picnic table, three tennis courts, and a regulation basketball court.

♦ Kendall Indian Hammocks Park

11395 SW 79th Street, Miami 33173. (305) 596-9324. Daily, 7 A.M.– sunset. Free admission.

This large neighborhood park is especially nice, with lots of shade and land. You'll be amazed at the open space, picnic areas, and play equipment that you will find at the end of the winding road that leads you into the park.

There are lots of ways to picnic here: tables, shelters, barbecue pits, a chickee hut, and a picnic "platform" set among the trees provide all the options you need. After lunch, visit the play area. Two kinds of slides, a swinging bridge, and a tire swing make the wooden climbing apparatus a fun spot for kids. (The little ones will want to play in the sandy area underneath!) This is a good place to meet other parents and children. **Tips:** Shelter rentals available for parties. Inquire about summer camp programs for children ages 7 to 10.

◆ Larry and Penny Thompson Park

12451 SW 184th Street, Miami 33177. (305) 232-1049. Park open daily, 7 A.M.–sunset. Call for hours of waterslide and beach. Park admission is free; beach: $1 per person; children under age 3, free; waterslide (must be over 42"): weekdays, $3; weekends, $4.

Located south of the Metrozoo, this park offers a peaceful country setting for a picnic. A swimming lagoon with a waterslide (under repair at press time) is a sure way to cool off. Lifeguards are on duty daily from 9 A.M. to 5 P.M. Canoe, paddleboat, and sailboat rentals are available in the summer months.

Also within these 200 acres is a campground for RVs, trailers, and tents. The camping area is accessible for handicapped travelers. If you bring your own horse, you'll find a quiet bridle path to explore.

◆ Matheson Hammock Park

9610 Old Cutler Road, Miami 33156. (305) 666-6979. Daily, 6 A.M.– sunset. Cars, $3; boats, $5.

The swimming lagoon has relatively calm, shallow water and is quite ideal for small children. Plant life is abundant in the water. There is a lifeguard on duty from early morning to near closing seven days a week. Showers, dressing areas, concessions, picnic shelters, and tables are all near the beach.

A marina is situated within the park, and a nature trail winds through the hammock. The land was donated to the county in 1930 by the late William Matheson, a philanthropist and conservationist of the south Dade area.

◆ North Shore State Recreation Area

Located east of Collins Avenue, from 79th to 87th streets, Miami Beach. Mailing address is 3400 NE 163rd Street, North Miami Beach 33160. (305) 940-7439. Daily, 8 A.M.–sunset. Admission: $3.25 per vehicle, plus $.50 per person; $1.50 for walk-ins or bikers.

This 40-acre park has wooden boardwalks along a stretch of beach, which provide a nice place to walk. Showers, pavilions, snack stands, restrooms, and lifeguards make this a convenient place for parents with young children. A bike trail is also located in the park.

◆ Oleta River State Recreation Area

3400 NE 163rd Street, North Miami Beach 33160. (305) 947-6357. Daily, 8 A.M.–sunset. Admission: $3.25 per vehicle, plus $.50 per person; $1.50 for walk-ins or bikers.

Here's an 840-acre oasis in the middle of the bustle of North Miami Beach. Located on the Oleta River and the Intracoastal Waterway, this park's main attraction is the man-made, sandy white beach. A large population of birds and mammals can be seen around the forests of the area, and porpoises and manatees frequent the waterways. Primitive camping facilities are a big draw for scouts and other youth groups (reservations required). A 90-foot fishing pier provides a place to cast-off. Boats and bikes (trails available) can be rented here.

◆ South Pointe Park

1 Washington Avenue, Miami Beach 33139. (305) 673-7730. Free admission; parking, $3.

At the tip of Miami Beach, this 17-acre park overlooks Government Cut and the water activity near the Port of Miami. A 300-foot fishing pier, playground, two observation towers, and picnic area are found here.

◆ Tamiami Park

11201 SW 24th Street, Miami. (305) 223-7070. Recreation building: 8 A.M.–5 P.M. Park: 8 A.M.–11 P.M. Free admission.

The park's solar-heated swimming pool (wheelchair accessible with a lift) may be the largest of its kind in the U.S., so you might guess that this is a popular spot for kids when the temperatures soar. There's also baseball, football, soccer, tennis courts, and multipurpose playing fields to give children plenty of opportunities to get involved in some kind of a game. Many events are held throughout the year at this busy 265-acre park, including RV shows, dog shows, circuses, and the Dade County Youth Fair in March. For more Youth Fair information, see listing in "Mark Your Calendar."

◆ Tropical Park

7900 SW 40th Street (Bird Road), Miami 33155. (305) 226-8315. Daily, 7 A.M.–10 P.M. Free admission.

Over two million people a year visit this busy county park, where there is an array of activities to choose from, including tennis, racquetball, baseball, boxing, swimming, soccer, and basketball, to name only a few. There are four lakes for sailing, paddleboating, and fishing during the summer. Children enjoy the two large play areas located within the park.

At one time a popular racetrack, the park is now equipped with an equestrian center, an 8,400-seat stadium for sporting events, and a vita course (for exercise!). For information about the equestrian center call (305) 554-7334. In December, the east side of the park becomes Santa's

Enchanted Forest, a magically lighted paradise for children. For more Enchanted Forest information, see listing in "Mark Your Calendar."

BROWARD COUNTY

◆ Brian Piccolo Park

9501 Sheridan Street, Cooper City 33024. (305) 437-2600. Daily, 8 A.M.–sunset. Velodrome: Saturday, Sundays, and holidays, $3 per 1-hour session; weekdays, $3 per 2-hour session.

This park opened in late 1989 and is named for the late football legend Brian Piccolo, who spent his childhood years in the area. The 180-acre park currently has playing fields, batting cages, a tennis and racquetball complex, a canoe/kayak course, two playgrounds, and a jogging/bike path. Picnicking and fishing are popular here. Paddleboats and canoes can be rented through the park office. The launch area is located at the north end of the park.

In 1993 the park celebrated the opening of the Broward County velodrome—the first in the state and only the 19th in the country. ("Velo" is short for the French word "velocipede," which was the original name given to the bicycle.) The velodrome features two sloped-oval tracks: one for training and competition, the other for in-line skaters, slower cyclists, bike-safety classes, and wheelchair races. An underground tunnel makes the track accessible to wheelchairs. Track bikes and helmets can be rented for $5 each session; safety equipment is mandatory. Call for a schedule of races and events, either for your participation or to watch. If you are planning to watch an event, be aware that there are no permanent seats.

◆ C.B. Smith Park

900 North Flamingo Road (just north of Hollywood Boulevard), Pembroke Pines 33028. (305) 437-2650. Daily, 8 A.M.–sundown. Weekends and holidays: driver, $1; passengers, $.75; children 5 and under, free. Daily beach admission: adults, $1; children 4–12, $.50; children 3 and under, free with parent. Waterslide and other attractions extra.

If your family enjoys water sports, they'll enjoy this 320-acre park situated around an 80-acre lake. You might start your day at the beach, where paddleboats, canoes, and aquacycles can be rented to provide exercise and fun. Try out the 700-foot waterslide (you can't miss it!) and tube ride that provides a new challenge around every turn. A children's playground is located at the beach. Next, move on to the 2.5-mile bike and skate trail, where rentals are also available. (Some of the bikes have baby seats!) You might even be game for 18 holes of miniature golf.

Picnic shelters are available in three sizes—small, medium, and large—to match the size of your group. There is also a meeting cabin that will accommodate over 300 people. RV and tent campsites are situated near the lake. For a breezy ride, try the nine-station tram route that runs through the park. There are 11 restrooms and 15 drinking fountains available!

◆ Colohatchee Natural Park

1975 NE 15th Avenue, Wilton Manors 33305. (305) 390-2130. Daily, 9 A.M.–5 P.M.; closed Tuesdays. Free admission.

Named for William C. Collier, the first white settler of the area, this natural park is a peaceful find in a relatively busy area. Just off the main street you will walk along a boardwalk nestled among mangrove trees (tropical trees with spreading branches and thick roots) that are very interesting to look at; they're even eerie at certain times of the day. Small children should be confined to strollers, as wiggly toddlers may find it too tempting to stray from the trail (it's not solidly fenced on either side). At the end of the trail there is a fenced-in area with play equipment, a basketball court, and a sand pit for volleyball or castle-building. There's a nice picnic pavilion with a stone fireplace in the center. Restrooms and soda machines are available, and a boat ramp is across the street. Groups of 25 or more need a permit to use the park facilities.

◆ Cypress Park

1300 Coral Springs Drive, Coral Springs 33071. South of Sample Road at Lakeview Drive. Park extends east and west of Coral Springs Drive. (305) 345-2100. Daily, 7:30 A.M.–10 P.M.; hours for pool vary. Free admission to park; fees for tennis and swimming.

This 42-acre recreational facility straddles both sides of Coral Springs Drive. To the west, visitors will find a swimming pool, clubhouse (a real beauty!), tennis courts, nature trail, and picnic area. A tot lot, multipurpose fields, and basketball courts can be found on the east side of the park.

◆ Deerfield Island Park

1 Deerfield Island, Deerfield Beach 33441. Go east on Hillsboro Boulevard. Turn left (north) across traffic onto Riverview Road just before Intracoastal Waterway bridge. Mailing address is P.O. Box 966, Deerfield Beach 33443. (305) 360-1320. Open daily at 8 A.M.; closing hours vary. Nature tours on Wednesdays and Saturdays at 8:30 A.M. Free admission.

This heavily wooded island serves as home to many animals, including gray foxes, raccoons, gopher tortoises, and armadillos. It is also the roosting and feeding place for many sea birds. It's hard to believe the hustle and bustle of city life is just moments away from this unique place.

Accessible only by boat, visitors must leave their cars at Sullivan Park, located off Hillsboro Boulevard at Riverview Road. Call for a schedule of activities, so you can plan when to catch the free boat over to the island. Nature walks are usually available Wednesdays and Saturdays at 8:30 A.M.—you can check in at the park office for these walks. They last about 90 minutes. A 1,500-foot boardwalk leads through winding mangroves, while another trail gives you a view of the Intracoastal Waterway. A children's playground is located just beyond the park office. A special event, "Show and Tell," teaches about the care and feeding of park animals. It is usually scheduled on the first Wednesday of every month, but call for information and reservations. **Tips:** Be sure to bring a picnic lunch; there is a shelter on the island that accommodates 60 people. Vending machines and restrooms are located near the picnic and playground area. Transportation to the island is free; parking is available near the shuffleboard courts.

◆ Easterlin Park

1000 NW 38th Street, Oakland Park 33309. From I-95 take Oakland Park Boulevard east to NW Ninth Avenue (Powerline Road). Turn north on NW Ninth Avenue to NW 38th Street, then go west across railroad tracks. Park entrance is on the left. (305) 938-0610. Daily, 8 A.M.–sunset. Weekends and holidays only: driver, $1; passengers, $.75; children 5 and under, free.

This 46-acre park is a nice setting for a picnic lunch in the shade. There are two children's playgrounds located north and south of a lake where ducks and other wildlife gather. Some of the cypress trees here are 250 years old and 100 feet tall.

◆ Everglades Holiday Park and Campground

21940 Griffin Road, Fort Lauderdale 33332. Exit I-95 at Griffin Road west. Eastern entrance to the Everglades, west of U.S. 27, 30 to 45 minutes west of Fort Lauderdale. (305) 434-8111. Park open 24 hours a day; airboats run daily, 9 A.M.–5 P.M. Park admission is free. Airboat rides (alligator wrestling included): adults, $12.50 plus tax; children 4 to 11, $6.25 plus tax; children under 3, free. Group rates and private airboat tours available. MC and V accepted.

You'll feel like you're on a safari in this 750,000-acre portion of the Everglades. Freshwater fishing from a pier, RV camping, picnicking, and bird-watching can all be enjoyed in the park. Visitors can even tour the area by airboat. When you buy an airboat ticket, you also get the chance to see alligator wrestling. Boat rentals and guided fishing tours are available. (They say that more fishing licenses are sold here than anywhere else in South Florida!)

Chickee huts are available for picnicking. There are no grills, but if you bring your own you will be charged $.50 per person. If you get hungry and you didn't come prepared for a picnic, try some barbecue cooked fresh daily at the restaurant. **Tips:** Don't forget your mosquito repellant. For more information about tours, see listing in "By Land, Sea, and Air."

◆ Fern Forest Nature Center

201 Lyons Road South (half block south of Atlantic Boulevard), Pompano Beach 33068. (305) 970-0150. Daily, 8:30 A.M.–6 P.M. Free admission.

Fern Forest has three nature trails that wind through a scenic woods—on weekend afternoons you can join a park naturalist for free guided walks that will delight young and old alike. The half-mile Cypress Creek Trail has a raised boardwalk accessible for wheelchairs and strollers. The one-mile Prairie Overlook Trail explores an open prairie and boasts a 20-foot-high observation platform. The Maple Walk, the shortest of the three trails, winds through a red-maple swamp.

Be sure to stop in the interpretive building; a covered amphitheater, which seats 125 people, is on one side of the building, and an assembly hall with displays and exhibits is on the other. It is available for rent and is complete with a full buffet counter and kitchen. A nice facility for a special function! **Tips:** Restrooms are in the building. There are a few tables north of the parking lot available for picnickers.

◆ Fort Lauderdale Beach

Stretches along A1A from East Sunrise Boulevard to East Las Olas Boulevard. (305) 523-1407.

Once the spot for the spring-break crowd, this beach now appeals more to young families. Lifeguards are on duty from 9:30 A.M. to 5:15 P.M. Restrooms, picnic tables, and metered parking are nearby. (Restroom facilities are also available across the street at Burger King and McDonald's, and a parking lot is available near the Sheraton Yankee Clipper Hotel for $3.) Forget your beach chair? You can rent one here! Look across the street to find the International Swimming Hall of Fame; for more information on this attraction, see listing in "On Safari in South Florida."

◆ Hampton Pines Park

*7800 Hamptons Boulevard, North Lauderdale. (305) 726-0274. Daily,
10 A.M.–5 P.M. Weekends and holidays only: adults, $1; children 3 to 12,
$.75.*

Hampton Pines is a 32-acre park with nature trails, a nature center,
playground, and bike paths. On weekends and holidays you can rent
paddleboats, rowboats, canoes, and bikes.

◆ Hollywood North Beach Park

*3501 North Ocean Drive, Hollywood 33019. Located at the intersection of
A1A and Sheridan Street, across the Intracoastal Waterway from West Lake
Park. (305) 926-2444. Daily, 8 A.M.–sunset. Parking fee only; walk-in
admission is free.*

At this facility you will have access to the city of Hollywood's public
beach, as well as the park's food concessions, picnic area (with tables and
grills), and 2.2-mile boardwalk, used for walking, skating, biking, and
jogging. There is a 60-foot-high tower, which you can enter for free and
observe what's happening in the area.

There is also a sea turtle hatchery and holding tank area for this endangered creature. During the summer months (nesting season) you may
want to take part in one of the educational programs about the sea turtles
offered here. **Tips:** Metered parking is available on the Intracoastal side of
Route A1A. Lifeguards are on duty along the beach; play areas are located
within the park.

◆ Hugh Taylor Birch State Recreation Area

*3109 East Sunrise Boulevard (north side of Sunrise Boulevard, west of A1A
and east of the Intracoastal Waterway), Fort Lauderdale 33304. (305)
564-4521. Daily, 8 A.M.–sunset. Admission: $3.25 per vehicle, plus $.50
per passenger; $1.50 for walk-ins and bikes.*

This 180-acre park, located on a barrier island, comprises a beach,
hammock, freshwater lagoons, and mangroves. Lots of shade can be found
throughout the park, except at the children's play area. Picnic areas, ball
fields, hiking, and biking can all be enjoyed here. This is a popular canoeing spot as well. Call ahead to see if the concessions are open for canoes
and other rental equipment and to get a schedule of nature walks. Children will enjoy walking through the tunnel to Fort Lauderdale Beach.

◆ John U. Lloyd Beach State Recreation Area

*6503 North Ocean Drive, Dania 33004. East of Dania Beach Boulevard on
Route A1A. From I-95, take Sheridan Street east to Route A1A; go north on*

Route A1A to entrance. (305) 923-2833. Daily, 8 A.M.–sunset. Admission:
$3.25 per vehicle, plus $.50 per passenger; $1.50 for walk-ins and bikes.

This 244-acre park has over 300 picnic tables, 60 grills, and lots of
shade. The beach (Atlantic Ocean side) has plenty of dunes to climb and a
lifeguard on duty every day. Canoeing (rentals available), kite-flying, and
fishing can be enjoyed here. A boat ramp is located on the Intracoastal
Waterway, where on warm winter mornings manatees can often be spotted (and even petted) near the concession area. Turtle walks are scheduled
in the summer on Wednesday and Friday evenings, but call months in
advance to assure a reservation. **Tip:** There is wheelchair access to the
fishing jetties.

♦ Markham Park and Target Range

16001 West S.R. 84, Sunrise 33326. Park, (305) 389-2000; target range,
(305) 389-2005. Park: daily, 8 A.M.–sunset. Range: hours vary, call for an
update. Weekends and holidays only: driver, $1; passengers, $.75; children 5
and under, free. Annual pass available.

One of the largest parks in Broward County, Markham encompasses
665 acres. Located on the edge of the Everglades Conservation Area, it
offers a wide variety of activities—everything from a target range to a
model airplane field. A new 56-acre island complex offers swimming,
boating, and picnicking facilities, as well as racquetball and tennis courts.
Bicycles (some with baby seats) and boats can be rented on the island.
Children under 14 must be accompanied by an adult. Children's swimming lessons are offered at the park. Call for information.

Just north of the park office you will find the Fox Observatory, which
is open to the public for star-gazing on the second and fourth Saturdays of
each month. Call for more information, or stop by the park office during
your next outing.

The regional target range is the park's most unique feature. (Juniors,
ages 10 through 17, must be accompanied by an adult at the range.) It is
equipped with rifles, pistols, skeets, and traps. There are a number of
classes available, including one on home protection techniques taught by
the National Rifle Association. A complete set of rules and regulations is
available through the park office. A model airplane field is also located
within the park and serves as the gathering place for regularly scheduled
meets.

♦ Plantation Heritage Park

1100 South Fig Tree Lane, Plantation 33317. Located west of the Florida
Turnpike, just north of Peters Road (Davie Boulevard turns into Peters

Road). (305) 791-1025. Daily, 8 A.M.–7:30 P.M. Weekends and holidays: drivers, $1; passengers, $.75; children 5 and under, free.

There are four children's playgrounds in this 90-acre park, which was once the University of Florida's agricultural experimentation farm. The flowering trees that abound here give a brief hint of the park's past. There's also lots of open, grassy areas for organized (and unorganized!) play. Stop in the park office for permission to pick fruit in designated areas.

While touring the park, be on the lookout for *Baldwin's Mountain*, a metal sculpture by international artist John Henry.

Bicycles, tandems, funcycles, paddleboats, and three-wheelers are available to rent on weekends and holidays at the park office. Children under 12 must be accompanied by an adult. Be sure to take a rest at the gazebo, located across Peters Road to the south of the park, and enjoy the view of the duck pond. **Tips:** Free field trips by reservation. Picnic areas are scattered throughout the park; shelters can be reserved and a deposit is needed.

◆ Quiet Waters Park

6601 North Powerline Road, Pompano Beach 33073. (305) 360-1315. Ski information, 429-0215. Daily, 8 A.M.–sunset. Weekends and holidays: driver, $1; passengers, $.75; children 5 and under, free. Annual pass available.

Quiet Waters Park is known for its many activities in, on, and around the water. In the summer a freshwater swimming beach with lifeguard staff is always a nice place to cool off. If you like a bit more action, try cable water-skiing or kneeboarding (popular with 10-to-12 year olds!). At the far northwest end of the park is a marina with canoe, johnboat, and paddleboat rentals. Fishing is permitted in the various lakes, and you'll find that bass, bream, and catfish are plentiful.

Also located within Quiet Waters is a children's play area (look for the clown!), an 18-hole miniature golf course, picnicking and camping facilities, and over two miles of bike paths (rentals are available). Special events are a constant at this park. For instance, a free campfire and hayride program is offered to campers the first Saturday of every month. It includes a marshmallow roast, refreshments, and a sing-a-long. **Tips:** Best time to visit is weekends after 10 A.M. "Rent-a-Camp" equipment, a complete, preassembled camping package, is available for both novice and experienced campers. Ask for details when you register. Bring firewood, insect repellant, and quiet games for children. Rainchecks are available on boat and bike rentals and miniature golf.

◆ Secret Woods Nature Center

2701 West S.R. 84, Fort Lauderdale 33312. Located one-half mile west of I-95 on the north side of S.R. 84. (305) 791-1030. Weekdays, 8:30 A.M.– 5 P.M.; weekends and holidays, 8 A.M.–5 P.M. Free admission. Field trips by reservation.

Secret Woods Nature Center is an educational and relaxing recreation area. Its nature conservatory contains an active beehive exhibit, as well as displays on the park's flora and fauna. Its 3,200-foot New River Trail, wheelchair and stroller accessible, helps visitors explore the different environments within the park. A self-guiding tour book is available for a small fee.

A wide variety of topics are covered in nature-oriented programs. Call for a reservation for your group or school. Weekly nature walks are offered from September to June, and special events are held periodically throughout the year.

◆ Snyder Park

3299 SW Fourth Avenue, Fort Lauderdale. Located south of S.R. 84. (305) 468-1585. Monday through Friday, 9 A.M.–5 P.M.; Saturday and Sunday, 9 A.M.–7 P.M. Weekdays: adults, $1.25; seniors, $.75; children, $1. Weekends and holidays: adults, $1.75; seniors, $1; children, $1.25.

This neighborhood park has something to offer every member of the family: picnicking, freshwater swimming, bass fishing, biking and boating (rentals available), and hiking. Nature activities are offered periodically.

◆ Topeekeegee Yugnee (T.Y.) Park

3300 North Park Road (west off I-95 at Sheridan Street), Hollywood 33021. (305) 985-1980. Daily, sunrise to sunset. Weekends and holidays only: driver, $1; passengers, $.75; children 5 and under, free. Beach: adults, $1; children, $.75.

T.Y. Park's name comes from the Seminole language and means "meeting or gathering place." So what better way to meet or gather than by having a picnic near beautiful oak trees and a 40-acre lake! Shelters and tables can be found throughout the 150-acre park, with food and snacks available near the marina area and the beach. This is one of the most popular picnic spots in South Florida.

A swimming lagoon has been designed so that children can swim in a shallow area and play on a sandy white beach. Waterslide and flume rides were in the midst of repair at press time. Call to see if these are in working order.

Sailboats, paddleboats, canoes, and bicycles are available for rent. Camping is another popular family activity at T.Y.

◆ Tradewinds Park

3600 West Sample Road, Coconut Creek 33073. Park, lake, and Butterfly World on south side of Sample Road; farm, train rides, and stables on north side. Park, (305) 968-3880. Daily, 8 A.M.–sunset. Weekends and holidays only: driver, $1; passengers, $.75; children 5 and under, free. Annual pass available. Butterfly World, (305) 977-4400. Tradewinds Stables, (305) 973-3220. Pony rides for children 8 and under (or less than 52" tall), daily, 11 A.M.–3:30 P.M. $1 once around ring, $2.50 three times around ring. Guided trail rides offered weekends only at 10 and 11:30 A.M. and 1 and 2:30 P.M. for children 9 and up (52" height requirement) at $12.50/hour.

There's so much to do at Tradewinds that you'll need a whole day to tour and explore. This enormous park is home to the famous Butterfly World, where thousands of exotic and domestic butterflies live in an 8,000-square-foot screened-in tropical rain forest. There is a separate entrance fee for this attraction, which you'll find by turning into the south section of the park. Also located in the same area is an 18-hole miniature golf course, picnic shelters, bicycle rental station (for use on a 1.75-mile path), and playing fields. If you enjoy water sports, try renting a paddleboat, canoe, or rowboat at the concession area near the lake.

Venture to the north end of the park for a fun photo opportunity in front of Tradewinds' water-pumping windmill. Or have your children pose with "Kimberly," a 700-pound pig who calls the park's farm complex home.

At the farm complex, inquire about trail rides, pony rides, English riding lessons, horses and the handicapped programs, and special equestrian events. The stables are usually open on weekends and holidays. Call ahead to plan your trip.

On the third full weekend of the month, model steam railroad rides are offered free to the public by the Florida Live Steamers and Railroaders. There is a picnic area near the train area. **Tips:** When horseback riding, wear long pants and shoes with closed toes and heels. The park's four concession areas are open weekends and holidays only. For more information about Butterfly World, see listing in "On Safari in South Florida." For details about Tradewinds Stables, see listing in "On Your Mark, Get Set, Go!"

◆ Tree Tops Park

3900 SW 100th Avenue, Davie 33328. Take University Drive to Orange Drive, across the canal from Griffin Road. Go west 1.6 miles to SW 100th Avenue. Turn right and go one-half mile to park entrance on right. (305)

370-3750. Daily, 8 A.M.–sunset; pavilions close at 6:30 P.M. Weekends and holidays only: driver, $1; passengers, $.75; children 5 and under, free. Annual pass available.

Tree Tops' history has been traced to the time of the Tequesta Indians (circa 1565), and evidence shows that a Seminole Indian village and garden existed here almost 200 years ago.

Before venturing out on one of the three nature trails within the park, stop by the Tree Tops Center, a beautiful wood building available for rental. The center, located to the rear of the park, has brochures and literature about special events.

The 1,000-foot Sensory Awareness Trail offers everyone an opportunity to explore the park. The hard-surfaced path was donated by the Davie Kiwanis Club and is wheelchair accessible. Signs posted along the way are written in braille and explain the characteristics of the woodlands surrounding the trail. Live Oak Trail and Seminole Trail are a bit longer and have wood-chip surfaces. At the entrance of Live Oak Trail you can climb a 28-foot observation tower for a "tree tops" view.

Picnic areas and playgrounds are available here, as well as a boat rental and concession area near the lake.

♦ West Lake Park

1200 Sheridan Street, Hollywood 33019. (305) 926-2410. Daily, 8 A.M.– sunset. Weekends and holidays only: driver, $1; passengers, $.75; children 5 and under, free. Annual pass available.

This park has a long future ahead of it, with only a portion of its 1,400 acres developed at this time. The park is home to many threatened and endangered plant and animal species. The Anne Kolb Nature Center is being built as a world-class facility, focusing on environmental concerns through educational programs and exhibits. Nature trails, observation towers, canoeing trails, and bicycle paths are in the works. A children's playground, racquetball and tennis courts, picnic shelters, and a vita course are among the facilities now open to enjoy.

≡ PALM BEACH COUNTY

♦ Caloosa Park

1300 SW 35th Avenue, Boynton Beach 33435. (407) 964-4420. Daily, sunrise to sunset. Free admission.

Here is a large, 66-acre, district-level facility with plenty of lighted ball fields for all types of sports, tennis and racquetball courts, bike paths, and walking and wheelcourse trails. After you play, enjoy a picnic, or cast-off in the lake, where hatchery-raised catfish are abundant.

◆ Coral Cove Park

19450 S.R. 707, Tequesta 33458. (407) 964-4420. Daily, sunrise to sunset. Free admission.

Coral Cove is a tranquil beachfront park with picnic facilities, a playground, and a nature trail. It's also a popular spot for snorkeling and fishing. Check out the rock formations.

◆ Dubois Park

19075 Dubois Road, Jupiter 33458. (407) 964-4420. Daily, sunrise to sunset. Free admission. Dubois House Museum, (407) 747-6639. Sundays, 1 P.M.–4 P.M. Closed holidays.

Toddlers can play in the water and swim in the inlet while adults prepare a picnic (a popular spot for this!). On Sunday afternoons the Dubois House is open for tours. The home, built on an ancient Indian mound in 1898, demonstrates the lifestyle of early pioneers through its furnishings and exhibits. For more information about the Loxahatchee Historical Museum, see listing in "Tracing the Past."

◆ John D. MacArthur Beach State Park

10900 S.R. 703 (A1A), North Palm Beach 33408. Located 2.8 miles south of U.S. 1 and PGA Boulevard on Singer Island. (407) 624-6950. Admission: $3.25 per vehicle, plus $.50 per passenger; $1.50 for walkers and bikes. Park: 8 A.M.–sunset. William T. Kirby Nature Center: (407) 624-6952. Wednesday through Sunday, 9 A.M.–5 P.M. Guided nature walks: Wednesday through Sunday, 10 A.M.

On a scale of one to ten, this state park is a ten-plus! Whether you want to hike, swim, study nature, collect shells, snorkel, or picnic, you'll find your niche here.

Your trip to the park might start by visiting the new William T. Kirby Nature Center. Outside this enormous wooden structure, you will find an elaborate birdhouse, a butterfly garden, and a kiosk providing such information as current weather and tide conditions. The center contains numerous aquariums and nature displays to the right after entering. A Loggerhead Turtle display is outstanding. Pick up a "measuring stick" to see if your child is as big as one of the local turtles. The mangrove and estuary display is a favorite. Walk back around to the other side of the center and enter the theater area where a 15-minute video informs visitors about the sea turtles that nest on the beaches. Nature awareness walks, geared to children ages 4 to 6, are offered Saturday mornings at 10 A.M. Groups can meet at the wooden amphitheater, located just outside the center, for discussion, regrouping, or snacking! (Vending machines are nearby!)

Pick up a brochure and map about the plants in the park, and take a hike around the property to discover the various species—wild coffee, nickerbean, and moonflower! Another brochure gives you details about the butterfly garden. Note that a local high-school group was instrumental in designing and planting the unique garden.

Take the 1,600-foot boardwalk that spans Lake Worth Cove to the dunes that lead to the Atlantic. Enjoy the surprises of the mangroves as you reach the other side of the cove.

Turtle walks are offered during June and July on Monday and Thursday evenings at 9 P.M. Call to make a reservation. **Tips:** A tram to the beach runs throughout the day, ending at 4 P.M. It would be worthwhile to take the tram if you have toddlers or a lot of beach equipment. Snack and soda machines, a telephone, and drinking fountains are located near the restrooms (large and clean) across from the exhibit area. If you are looking for a bite to eat after leaving the park, continue north on U.S. 1 and you'll find a McDonald's and Burger King together on the west side of the road. Both have tremendous play areas for the children. Groups may request speakers or video or slide programs to fit subjects they're studying.

◆ John Prince Park

2700 Sixth Avenue, Lake Worth 33461. (407) 964-4420; campground, 582-7992. Daily, sunrise to sunset. Concessions, 795-3610; Wednesday through Friday, 11:30 A.M.–4:30 P.M.; Saturday and Sunday, 9 A.M.– 5 P.M. Free admission.

For a lakeside view, visit this 600-acre county park, complete with picnic facilities, softball fields, tennis courts, cycling routes, nature trails, wheelcourse, and fishing areas. There's even a model airplane ramp. A concession area handles boat rentals ($5–$15), including canoes, kayaks, paddleboats, and rowboats. With over 250 campsites here, each with water and electric hookups, many groups find this a prime meeting spot.

◆ Lake Ida Park

West entrance: 2929 Lake Ida Road; south entrance: 950 Ninth Street; east entrance: 13369 Lake Drive, Delray Beach. (407) 964-4420. Daily, sunrise to sunset. Free admission.

Two children's playgrounds are found at this park, situated on a 300-acre lake. Biking, fishing, picnicking, boating, and hiking are common interests shared by its visitors. Football, soccer, and rugby fields are used by local children throughout the year.

◆ Lake Lytal

3645 Gun Club Road, West Palm Beach 33406. Take I-95 to Southern Boulevard, west to Congress Avenue; turn left on Congress Avenue, and right at the first stop light on Gun Club Road. The pool is located on the north side of the road. (407) 983-4436. Daily, sunrise to sunset. Free admission to park.

Lake Lytal is home to a therapeutic day camp called "Little Bit of Leisure," a recreational program of games, arts and crafts, and storytelling open to children ages 2 1/2 to 5. A playground, multipurpose playing fields, and picnic areas dominate the rest of the park. Call for information about pool activities and lessons available to the public.

◆ Lake Worth Municipal Beach

Enter the beach from Ocean Boulevard and Lake Avenue, Lake Worth.

Lifeguards are on duty at this developed beach area. A pool, picnic area with grills, fishing pier, and restaurant are all conveniently located.

◆ Loggerhead Park

1200 U.S. 1, Juno Beach 33408. (407) 964-4420. Daily, sunrise to sunset. Free admission.

This beachfront park is an especially nice place to visit. First, let the children run through the sand dunes and nature trails just beyond the playground area. An observation tower is fun to climb and sit in. Two tennis courts and a picnic area are situated to the north of the park, with an amphitheater-like structure for meetings or tennis viewing. Walk across A1A to the beach.

When you need a break from the sun and sand, make your way to the buildings at the south end of the park. Here you will find the Marinelife Center of Juno Beach. This is a wonderful little place to learn about marine life, especially sea turtles. Ask for a turtle walk schedule. **Tips:** No lifeguards on duty. For more information on the Marinelife Center of Juno Beach, see listing in "Exploring Science and Nature."

◆ Meadows Park

1300 NW Eighth Street, Boca Raton 33486. Park: (407) 393-7806; pool: (407) 393-7851. Pool open daily, noon–5:45 P.M. Free admission.

A major renovation of the pool in 1989 made this facility like new. Summer camp, classes, and special swimming-related activities are provided to the public. The pool has a modern wheelchair lift that assists people into the water. Also within the park are lighted little-league baseball fields, a children's playground, and tennis courts.

◆ Morikami Park

4000 Morikami Park Road, Delray Beach 33446. Located just west of Carter-Jog Road between Clint Moore Road and Linton Boulevard. (407) 495-0233. Free admission to park. Daily, sunrise to sunset. Museum: adults, $4.25; seniors, $3.75; children 6 to 18, $2. Tuesday through Sunday, 10 A.M.–5 P.M. Group rates available. Museum closed major holidays.

Morikami Park encompasses 200 acres and is the proud home of The Morikami Museum and Japanese Gardens. The park offers a peaceful setting amid tall pine trees and lakes. Nature trails run throughout the park, and picnic areas are plentiful. For more information about the museum, see listing in "Tracing the Past." To learn more about the annual events held at the park, see listings for *Hatsume* Fair (February), *Bon* Festival (August), and the *Osho Gatsu* (Japanese New Year in December/January) in "Mark Your Calendar."

◆ Ocean Inlet Park

6900 North Ocean Boulevard, Oceanridge 33435. Located south of Inlet. (407) 964-4420. Daily, sunrise to sunset. Free admission.

This beach has a shallow area for children to enjoy, plus a tot-lot for some exercise. Bring a picnic to enjoy, or order from the snack bar.

◆ Okeeheelee Park

7715 Forest Hill Boulevard, West Palm Beach 33463. Located about one mile west of Jog Road. (407) 964-4420. Daily, sunrise to sunset. Free admission. Nature Center mailing address: 2700 Sixth Avenue South, Lake Worth 33461. Nature center: (407) 233-1400. Tuesday through Friday, 1–5 P.M.; Saturday, 8 A.M.–5 P.M.

A beautiful view and plenty of fun activities await you at Okeeheelee. The serene 200-acre lake is available for boating and fishing (catfish are plentiful!). A fine waterskiing course is located here and draws many fine skiers from around South Florida. The American Red Cross offers sailing lessons for children ages 9 and older. Call for schedules.

Picnic facilities, baseball and multipurpose playing fields, nature trails, and concessions are all located within the park. A popular BMX racing track is available for children and adults. Call for practice and racing schedules and fees.

The Okeeheelee Nature Center opened in late 1992 and contains displays of animals and other nature-related exhibits. Two miles of nature

trails (there are two trails, only one is accessible to strollers and wheelchairs) meander from the center and take hikers to a deer overlook area.
Seminars are offered for adults and older youngsters on such topics as
birds, trees, butterflies, exotic plants, and animals. Nature walks are also
hosted periodically. **Tips:** Wanted: nature treasures for display at the
Okeeheelee Nature Center—bring those unusual bugs and rocks to share
with the center. For more information about the sailing program, see
listing in "On Your Mark, Get Set, Go!"

♦ Patch Reef Park
*2000 NW 51st Street (Yamato Road, just west of Military Trail), Boca
Raton 33431. (407) 997-0791. Park: Monday through Saturday, 7 A.M.–
11 P.M.; Sunday, 7 A.M.–sunset. Community Center: Monday through
Friday, 8 A.M.–10:30 P.M.; Saturday, 8 A.M.–5 P.M. Free admission.*

A city park with fields galore! Try any sport and you'll find the
facilities you need at Patch Reef! A tennis facility with 16 courts (plus
a pro court, pro shop, and lockers) is available for tennis lessons and
leagues. Softball, baseball, soccer, basketball, and football are played here
during all seasons. Restrooms and concession facilities are conveniently
located. The community center within the park offers a variety of classes
(ballet, cooking, karate), activities, and special events.

♦ Red Reef Park
*1400 North Route A1A, Boca Raton 33431. (407) 393-7815. Daily,
8 A.M.–sunset. Weekdays, $8 per car; weekends, $10 per car. Resident stickers
available.*

An ocean boardwalk and pavilion, as well as grills, picnic facilities,
restrooms, showers, and lifeguards are available at this 80-acre park. This
is a delightful beach park for family outings.

♦ Spanish River Park
*3001 North Route A1A, Boca Raton 33431. (407) 393-7815. Daily,
8 A.M.–sunset. Weekdays, $8 per car; weekends, $10 per car. Resident stickers
available.*

A wonderful beach and picnic park, encompassing 46 acres of land
and 1,850 feet of ocean frontage, Spanish River is a delight! Shady picnic
areas are equipped with grills and tables, and a children's playground is
nestled in the trees. A nearby nature trail, tunnels to the beach (with
wheelchair access), and a 40-foot observation tower give you lots of
choices for activities. For boaters, there's a lagoon boat dock near the
tower. Lifeguards are on the beach from 9 A.M. to 5 P.M.

 **MONROE COUNTY**

◆ Astro City Park

Across from Higgs Memorial Beach, Reynolds and White streets, Key West.

This popular kiddie park boasts a giant rocket ship that will certainly catch your children's eye! The fenced-in play area has extra-nice climbing equipment and the picnic area is equipped with chickee huts and plenty of shade! The beach is close by.

◆ Bahia Honda State Park

Mile Marker 38, Big Pine Key 33043. Located 12 miles south of Marathon. Mailing address is Route 1, Box 782, Big Pine Key 33043. (305) 872-2353. Daily, 8 A.M.–sunset. Admission: $3.25 per vehicle, plus $.50 per passenger; $1.50 per walker and bikes. Individual and family passes available.

Bahia Honda, or "deep bay" in English, is an ancient coral reef now covered by beaches, dunes, hammocks, and mangroves. You'll find a variety of bird life (great white heron, reddish egret, and brown pelican), as well as rare plant species (satinwood tree, spiny catesbaea, and dwarf morning glory) within the park.

One of the best beach areas in the Keys, Bahia Honda's own Sandspur Beach lets you swim in the Atlantic Ocean to the south and in Florida Bay to the north. Many other water sports are offered here, such as snorkeling, fishing, and boating. Windsurfing lessons are provided, and rental equipment for all activities is available.

Camping facilities, including cabins, can be reserved for a special family outing. Regular campfire programs and guided nature walks are offered, but reservations should be made in advance. Snacks and some grocery items are available at the concession area. **Tips:** Best time to visit is from September through November. If the park gets extremely busy, it may close briefly at times to accommodate the crowds. Shade is limited, so bring sunscreen. Men-of-war can be spotted in the water and on the beaches year-round. Ramp access to beach and bathhouse is available.

◆ Dry Tortugas National Park

Located 68 miles west of Key West. For information call or write: Everglades National Park, P.O. Box 279, Homestead 33030; (305) 242-7700.

The Dry Tortugas, made up of seven isles at the western end of the Florida Keys, is accessible by seaplane or boat only. The massive Fort Jefferson National Monument is the main attraction here, but the history of the islands is also quite interesting. First discovered by Ponce de León in 1513, the area provided the explorer and his crews with meat from sea turtles ("tortugas"), but they were hardpressed to find drinkable water, as the islands were "dry." Thus, the name the isles acquired!

Snorkeling, scuba diving, and fishing are popular in the surrounding waters, and camping is available at a primitive site. Please note that no water, food, or supplies are available at the monument.

Chartered boats and seaplanes are granted permission from the National Park Service to go to the island. For information on tours, see listings in "By Land, Sea, and Air." For more information about Fort Jefferson National Monument, see listing for Dry Tortugas National Park in "Tracing the Past."

◆ Fort Zachary Taylor State Historic Site

West end of Southard Street, Truman Annex, Key West 33040. Follow the small signs! Mailing address is P.O. Box 289, Key West 33030. (305) 292-6713. Daily, 8 A.M.–sunset. Admission: $3.25 per vehicle, plus $.50 per passenger; $1.50 for walkers and bikes.

Travel back to the mid-1800s as you visit a Civil War–era brick fort. Over the past 20 years, excavations here have uncovered the largest collection of Civil War cannons. If weather and staffing permit, take a free daily tour at noon or 2 P.M. A museum and beach are also available to ticketholders! Picnicking (grills, tables, and showers are available) is popular here. For more information, see listing in "Tracing the Past."

◆ Harry Harris County Park

Mile Marker 92.5, Beach and East Beach roads, Tavernier. Daily, sunrise to sunset. Free on weekdays; weekends and holidays only, $2 per car.

A popular swimming spot, with a rare white beach! The swimming lagoon is great for small children, and the play equipment on the beach makes watching the kids extra fun. Snorkeling is enjoyed here as well. Softball fields, boating and picnicking facilities, hiking trails, and basketball courts make this a fun-filled park.

◆ Higgs Memorial Beach

Reynolds and White streets, Key West. Daily, sunrise–11 P.M. Free admission.

A lovely beach for the whole family, Higgs provides picnicking facilities, swimming and fishing areas, and tennis and racquetball courts. The playground area on the beach offers a view of the Atlantic Ocean. **Tips:** Restrooms and a small fast-food restaurant are right on the beach. There's also plenty of parking for RVs.

◆ John Pennekamp Coral Reef State Park

Mile Marker 102.5, Key Largo. Mailing address is P.O. Box 487, Key
Largo 33037. (305) 451-1202. Daily, 8 A.M.–sunset. Admission: $3.25
per vehicle, plus $.50 per passenger; $1.50 for walkers and bikes. Concessions:
(305) 451-6325 or (800) 272-4148. Camping: (305) 451-1202. Glass-
bottom boat: (305) 451-1621; daily, 9:15 A.M., 12:15, and 3 P.M. Adults,
$14; children under 12, $9. MC and V accepted.

This park was named for John Pennekamp, an associate editor of the
Miami Herald, who played an influential role in the establishment of Everglades National Park. Nearly 70 nautical square miles, the park is the first
underwater state park in the United States and is known for its coral reefs
located five miles offshore. Snorkeling is an excellent adventure here. The
reefs can be reached by glass-bottom boats that depart from the concession
area three times daily. Reservations are strongly recommended. You'll get
a once-in-a-lifetime view of brightly colored corals and fish, as you head
out to Molasses Reef. Once there, gaze into the water to find coral formations in the shapes of tunnels and towers. Another key spot, especially for
divers, is Dry Rocks. This is the location of "Christ of the Deep," a famous
statue resting in 25 feet of water.

A concession area offers snorkeling tours, scuba lessons, canoeing,
sailboat, and motor boat rentals. In addition to its water activities, the
park offers 47 campsites, fishing, hiking along two nature trails, and
picnicking.

An excellent nature museum in the visitors' center contains a huge
(30,000-gallon) saltwater aquarium filled with dozens of species of sea
creatures. Touch tanks also allow visitors a closer look at the underwater
world. **Tips:** Accessible areas include boardwalk trails and visitor center.
For more information about the glass-bottom boat tour, see listing in "By
Land, Sea, and Air."

◆ Long Key State Recreation Area

Mile Marker 67.5, between Conch and Lower Matecumbe Keys. Mailing
address is P.O. Box 776, Long Key 33001. (305) 664-4815. Daily,
8 A.M.–sundown. Admission: $3.25 per vehicle, plus $.50 per passenger;
$1.50 per walker and bikes.

Long Key was an important depot during the railroad days, before it
was destroyed by the "Hurricane of 1935." Nowadays, its nature and
campfire programs, offered on Fridays, the Wednesday morning guided
tours, as well as canoeing and swimming are popular with visitors. Reservations are suggested for the various programs. Canoes can be rented for

$2 per hour (a $10 deposit is required) and must be used within the park's canoe trail. Picnic facilities are on the key, as is an observation tower that gives you a spectacular view. A nature trail at the base of the tower takes you along the beach and over a mangrove-lined lagoon. Be sure to look for the interpretive signs along the way.

◆ Smathers Beach
Along South Roosevelt Boulevard, Key West. Free.

Here's a nice shady beach with equipment rentals. The water along this stretch is nice, but be careful of the rocky bottom when wading here. Vendors park along the beach and sell food and beverages. There are public restrooms, and plenty of parking is available on the beach side of the road.

Across the street is an indigenous park. Stroll among native tropical plants and trees that are marked with identification tags.

◆ Sombrero Beach Park
Mile Marker 50, Sombrero Beach Road, Marathon. Head east on S.R. 931. Free.

Sombrero has that rare white sandy beach you might be looking for in the keys. The park's Atlantic waters prove to be a great spot to snorkel. Facilities include picnic areas, playground equipment, and restrooms. A grassy area provides a good place for children to run and play. At the end of the day, before you pack up the car and head to your home or hotel, look out at the large boats making their way back to the Boot Key Harbor, where Marathon's commercial fishing fleet originates.

ON YOUR MARK, GET SET, GO!

EXTRA! EXTRA! Read all about it! The South Florida sports scene has gone through a growth spurt in the early 1990s. Sports fans can now see football (the regular game and the new arena type), baseball, basketball, soccer, ice hockey, rodeos, polo, and horse racing to name a few.

Here's a re-cap:

- **Baseball.** 1993 was the inaugural season for the Florida Marlins, the first professional major league baseball team in Florida, even though 20 of the 28 major-league baseball teams hold spring training camps in the state. We have only listed the teams that practice in South Florida, but many others are just a day-trip away. There is a terrific following of the major league clubs that flocks to the state for spring training camps. The Florida State League (Class A minor league) plays and trains at the same ballparks as the pros, but during the summer months. Tickets run about $3. College-level teams also provide the area with plenty of spectator opportunities.

- **Basketball.** Always a favorite, fast-moving game, professional basketball made its debut in Miami in 1988-89, when the Miami Heat burned its way into the heart of South Florida. Basketball is a fun family adventure. Try taking the Metrorail downtown for a Miami Heat or University of Miami game and enjoy the festivities.

- **Football.** The Miami Dolphins and the University of Miami Hurricanes have huge followings in South Florida. The Dolphins play at world-class Joe Robbie Stadium, while the Hurricanes host teams in the classic Orange Bowl Stadium. The new kids on the block are the Miami Hooters, the newly formed arena football franchise that plays its games at the Miami Arena.

- **Hockey.** Late-breaking news from book-writing central was the addition of South Florida's first-ever professional ice hockey team, the Florida Panthers. Ice hockey and South Florida are sure to be a "cool" match.

- **Horses.** Polo is a great family sport to watch. Not only will you see great athletic competition, you'll be fascinated with the grace and skill of the polo horses. When it comes to horse racing, South Florida is tops—Calder, Gulfstream, and Hialeah form a winning trifecta! Keep in mind that a 1988 state law granted permission for children under 18 years of age to attend parimutuel events when accompanied by an adult.

- **Soccer.** One of the most popular games for kids, soccer is not only fun to play but also fun to watch. With so many youngsters playing in youth leagues, watching professional soccer games is a great way to help them understand the game and see professionals demonstrate their techniques.
- **Other sports.** In addition to seasonal sports, children may also enjoy annual sporting events such as the Doral/Ryder Open golf tournament, the Miami Grand Prix automobile racing extravaganza, and the Orange Bowl Classic football game. For more information, see listings in "Mark Your Calendar."

Recreational opportunities are endless in South Florida. All year long, youngsters and their adult companions can enjoy their favorite recreational activities. From bowling to biking, horseback riding to fishing, swimming to skating—South Florida has it all!

Sports events are not only exciting to watch and healthy to participate in, but are usually affordable as well. Whether you buy season tickets to your favorite professional or college team, or attend local high-school games, the only thing that matters is that you're having fun and you're doing it with someone special.

To give your child an idea of how many different kinds of sports South Florida has to offer, and to help him or her select one that may be of special interest, collect a few sports pages from local newspapers and magazines and cut out photographs and headlines. Sort and categorize the clippings and then make a collage or sports notebook. If your child has a favorite team, perhaps he or she could write a letter to the team to request information and players' autographs. Then, when you attend a game in the area, you'll all be more knowledgeable. So—on your mark, get set, go! Have some fun!

The state produces a few brochures for people with special sports interests. Write for your copy of the following:

- *Bicycles Are Vehicles: Florida's Bicycle Laws...and Some Safety Tips,* State Bicycle Program, Florida Department of Transportation, 605 Suwannee Street, M.S. 19, Tallahassee 32301-8064; (904) 488-4640. (You can also request a list of bicycle clubs and trails in the state.)
- *Canoe Trails,* Florida Recreational Trails Systems, Department of Natural Resources, Division of Recreation and Parks, 3900 Commonwealth Boulevard, Tallahassee 32399-3000; (904) 487-4784.

- *Major League Baseball Spring Training Schedule,* Sports Development Office, 455 Collins Building, Department of Commerce, Tallahassee 32399-6528.
- *Major League Baseball,* 350 Park Avenue, New York, NY 10022.
- *Who Needs a Florida Saltwater Fishing License & Why Florida Requires One,* Department of Natural Resources, Division of Recreation and Parks, 3900 Commonwealth Boulevard, Tallahassee 32399-3000.
- The Florida Sports Foundation has lots of literature and information about every type of sport imaginable. Call or write: 107 West Gaines Street, Tallahassee 32399-2000; (904) 488-8347.

SPECTATOR SPORTS *(in all South Florida counties)*

◆ Atlanta Braves

Municipal Stadium, 715 Hank Aaron Drive (at Palm Beach Lakes Boulevard and Congress Avenue), West Palm Beach 33401. (407) 683-6100. Ticket prices range from $5 to $10.

You can watch the Braves' games and practice sessions during March and early April at the West Palm Beach Municipal Stadium. This is also home to the West Palm Beach Expos summer baseball league. The Montreal Expos share the stadium with the Braves.

◆ Calder Race Course

21001 NW 27th Avenue, Miami 33055. Located just north of Joe Robbie Stadium. (305) 625-1311. Open for spring/summer and fall/winter racing seasons; call for exact dates.

Watch thoroughbred racing at its best at this ever-popular racing facility. Calder opened in 1971 and has two racing seasons a year on the all-weather synthetic track. The dates change yearly, so be sure to call or watch the newspaper for announcements. This glass-enclosed, air-conditioned facility is one of the largest of its kind in the South. During racing seasons, Sundays are designated family days at the track, with a petting zoo, bounce house, and carnival rides available for children.

◆ Davie Rodeo Arena

Davie Arena, 6591 SW 45th Street (Orange Drive), Davie 33314. (305) 797-1145. Cost varies with event.

Every Wednesday evening at 7:30 P.M., the Davie Rodeo Arena hosts a "Jackpot Rodeo." Bucking broncos, steer wrestling, calf roping, and bareback riding give visitors a first-hand look at true rodeo action. Tickets are $4 for adults and $2 for children 12 and under. "Five-Star" rodeos are held once a month, when cowboys compete to increase points toward their national ratings. This event is $7 for adults and $4 for children.

◆ Florida Marlins

P.O. Box 030196, Fort Lauderdale 33303-0196. (305) 779-7070. Games at Joe Robbie Stadium: 2269 NW 199th Street, Miami 33056. (305) 623-6100 or 620-5000. Tickets start at $1.50 for children 12 and under. Call (800) 944-HITS. Parking: $4–$8.

With the Marlins' inaugural season in 1993, the long-awaited dream of South Floridians was fulfilled. The Marlins were one of two National League expansion teams in 1992, and they now play home games at the 48,000-seat Joe Robbie Stadium. Not only is the baseball action great, but those hot dogs at the concession stand are almost as entertaining for some children. Typical ballpark fare is served: hot dogs, popcorn, peanuts, and more.

For ticket information and to order by mail, write to Florida Marlins Ticket Office, 100 NE Third Avenue, Third Floor, Fort Lauderdale 33301.

Once you've been bitten by Marlin fever, you'll want to plan a trip to the team's new spring training facilities in Brevard County, just north of Melbourne. Take I-95 to exit 73, about 190 miles from Miami. At the exit turn west at Lake Andrew Drive. Turn north to St. John Street, then west to Stadium Parkway and go north. The stadium complex is on the west side. **Tip:** No strollers are admitted to Joe Robbie Stadium.

◆ Florida Panthers

100 NE Third Avenue, Tenth Floor, Fort Lauderdale 33301. (305) 768-1900. Call for ticket and schedule information.

South Florida now has its own National Hockey League team! The Florida Panthers dropped their first puck of the regular season in October 1993. Look for future games against their state rivals—the Tampa Bay Lightning.

The team has a commitment to assist its namesake, the Florida panther. It is the most endangered mammal on earth. Throughout the year, the team holds fund raisers and special events to boost public awareness and support for the *real* panthers.

◆ Fort Lauderdale Strikers

Lockhart Stadium, 5301 NW 12th Avenue, Fort Lauderdale 33309. Located one-half mile west of I-95. Mailing address is 2200 West Commercial Boulevard, Suite 305, Fort Lauderdale 33309. (305) 771-5677.

Season runs April through August. General admission: adults, $8; children, $4. Family of four: $20.

The Strikers, members of the American Soccer League, play about 12 home games, including exhibitions, at Lockhart Stadium. Tailgating parties, entertainment, and special events at the games are fun for children and adults.

◆ Gulfstream Park

901 South Federal Highway (U.S. 1 and Hallandale Beach Boulevard), Hallandale 33009. (305) 454-7000. Grandstand, $2; clubhouse, $4; children under 18 admitted free with adult.

For over 50 years Gulfstream has been one of the most famous horse racing tracks in the country. In 1989 it was host to the Breeder's Cup, horse racing's top event, and throughout the year it entertains the most famous of horses. Two annual events, Family Day in January and the Florida Derby in March, are always exciting for adults and children. Polo matches are also played on the grounds. **Tips:** Children are not permitted near betting area. For more event information, see listings in "Mark Your Calendar."

◆ Hialeah Park

Corner of East Fourth Avenue and 79th Street, Hialeah 33011. (Metrorail Hialeah stop puts you right outside the gates.) (305) 885-8000; (800) 423-3504 (in Florida). Off season: daily, 9:30 A.M.–4:30 P.M. for sightseeing. Free admission. Racing season: April and May. Cost varies according to seat selection; children 17 and under admitted to races free with adult.

Hialeah horse racing has been an exciting tradition since 1925. It's always a thrill to see a horse speed down the stretch of a close race. The historic building here is a charmer, with an antique fire engine and vine-covered walls. Sight-seeing tours of this 220-acre park are available when the horses aren't running.

If you are an early rising family on weekends, "Breakfast at Hialeah" is a fun adventure. Arrive at the track at 7:30 A.M. (plan to spend two hours), watch the horses work out, and chat with famous jockeys and trainers. Watching is free; breakfast (a nice treat) is $4 for adults and $2.50 for children. If the children get restless, have them try counting the flamingos (there are over 600 of the salmon-colored birds here!) or any of the other 100 species of birds that make Hialeah Park their home. Watch the sports page for dates and information regarding this popular family event. **Tips:** If the elevator at the Hialeah Metrorail station is working, you can go right down to ground level; if not, be prepared to walk up and down two flights of stairs. A free Metrorail return ticket is available from the gift shop or information booth. Call for updated information on the park's Flamingo Fest concert series for families. For more information about the park, see listing in "Tracing the Past."

◆ Miami Dolphins

Joe Robbie Stadium, 2269 NW 199th Street, Miami 33056. Sixteen miles northwest of downtown Miami; one mile south of Broward County line. From the north, take I-595 west to the Florida Turnpike south. Take the turnpike south nine miles to exit 2 (NW 199th Street/Honey Hill Road). Take exit to 199th Street and turn right. Enter Parking Gate 4. From the airport: take I-95 north to Ives Dairy Road. Head west five miles (name of road changes to 199th Street), and the stadium will be on right. (305) 620-5000. Call the box office at (305) 620-2578 for ticket information.

In 1989, Miami's first professional franchise hosted Super Bowl XXIII in what is considered the best stadium in the country—Joe Robbie Stadium. The $115 million complex is considered "South Florida's Major League Facility," so you can only imagine how exciting a big league football game can be there. Watch for announcements about Family Day (in the summer), where the public is invited to a scrimmage, and season ticket holders can select their seats for upcoming games. When ordering tickets, consider asking for the Family Section or the Family Section/No Alcohol. Tickets for these sections run $20 each.

◆ Miami Heat Basketball

Miami Arena, 721 NW First Avenue, Miami 33136. (305) 577-4328. Tickets range from $12 to $25.

See Miami's entry in the National Basketball Association play against the best in an atmosphere second to none. A new arena and a new team made for an exciting first season in 1988-89. NBA stars come alive here during basketball season. Children can anticipate all kinds of excitement at the games, including bands, cheerleaders, and prize giveaways.

Teachers should be aware of the Heat's Corporate Education Program, which rewards "at-risk" students for academic improvements, as well as a number of other programs designed as incentives for students at all levels. Summer basketball day camps are offered; call for information.

◆ Miami Hooters Arena Football

2977 McFarlane Road, Coconut Grove 33133. (305) 461-8665 or (800) 289-4587. Tickets start at $7.50.

The Hooters made their debut in 1993, with the Miami Arena as home, playing against teams like upstate rival Tampa Bay Storm. Arena football is just a few years young in the state of Florida, and fans will enjoy the fast-paced action, indoor fireworks, entertaining half-time shows, and prize give-aways. If you happen to see a ball coming your way, catch it—it's yours to keep!

When not attending home games, fans can occasionally watch the Hooters on ESPN, Sportschannel, or the Sunshine Network.

◆ Montreal Expos

Municipal Stadium, 715 Hank Aaron Drive (at Palm Beach Lakes Boulevard and Congress Avenue), West Palm Beach 33401. Mailing address is P.O. Box 3566, West Palm Beach 33402. (407) 684-6801. Ticket prices range from $5 to $10.

The Expos play about 15 exhibition home games from mid-March to mid-April in the West Palm Beach Municipal Stadium. Remember, the Expos share the stadium with the Atlanta Braves.

◆ Moroso Motorsports Park

17047 Beeline Highway, Palm Beach Gardens 33410. From the south take I-95 to PGA Boulevard (exit 57B) or Florida Turnpike (exit 109) west to S.R. 710 and turn right, go 8.2 miles. Track is on the right. From the north take I-95 to S.R. 706 (exit 59B) west to Beeline Highway. (407) 622-1400.

Hot rod, drag racing, high school racing programs, and many championship races are run here.

◆ New York Yankees

Fort Lauderdale "Yankee" Stadium, 5301 NW 12th Avenue, Fort Lauderdale 33309. (305) 776-1921. Ticket prices range from $6 to $9. No credit cards.

The famed Bronx Bombers play about 15 to 17 games at Fort Lauderdale Stadium in March. February practice sessions are open to the public as well.

◆ Palm Beach Polo and Country Club

13198 Forest Hill Boulevard, West Palm Beach 33414. (407) 793-1440. Winter season only. Adult general admission, $5; reserved, $10; box seats, $14 and $17; children under 12 admitted free for general admission; reserved and box seats, regular price. Call for season ticket information. AE, MC, V accepted.

Enjoy polo matches from January through April at this world-famous facility. Sunday matches begin at 3 P.M. and feature top players from around the world, including Prince Charles of Wales. Occasionally there will be special entertainment before the Sunday afternoon matches, so call ahead to see what's planned. If you'd rather not sit in the grandstands, try a picnic on the sidelines. Just drive your car to a designated area 10 yards from the action and tailgate for a leisurely afternoon. The cost for a prime space is $20 for the driver and $5 for each additional passenger.

If you are polo fans, plan on attending the annual Winter Equestrian Festival, which runs for about three weeks in February and March. This event is held at the Palm Beach Equestrian Club and features Olympic and world-class riders. On Wednesdays through Saturdays during this time you can attend the events for free. There is an admission charge on Sundays. **Tips:** Rainchecks available for Sunday polo matches played during the same season. Wheelchair and stroller access in general admission and reserved seating only. Tours can be scheduled. Gift shop with souvenirs open during season. Drinking fountains and restrooms available. For information on the Winter Equestrian Festival, see listing in "Mark Your Calendar."

◆ Pompano Harness Track

1800 SW Third Street, Pompano Beach 33069. (305) 972-2000. Grandstand, $1; clubhouse, $2; children under 18 admitted free to grandstand with adult.

Harness racing is fun for kids to watch. For more than 25 years Pompano Track has provided exciting racing seasons to local residents and tourists. Call during the season to see if barn tours are being conducted on Saturday mornings.

◆ Royal Palm Polo Sports Club

6300 Clint Moore Road, Boca Raton 33496. (407) 994-1876. Summer: 5:30 P.M. matches on Wednesday, Friday, and Sunday; Winter: 1 and 3 P.M. matches Wednesday, Friday, and Sunday. Adults, $5; children under 17, $2.

This 160-acre club hosts international competitions on Wednesdays, Fridays, and Sundays during the summer and winter seasons (exact dates vary from year to year). In the summer, there is only an admission fee if the match is a charity event. Tailgating is a fun way to watch the matches, or try brunch at the club's restaurant, and then head out to the polo grounds. Watch for special half-time events, celebrity week, Octoberfest, rodeos, and arts festivals. A summer sports camp is also held at the club.

◆ University of Miami Hurricanes

Hecht Athletic Center, 5821 San Amaro Drive, Coral Gables 33146. (305) 284-3822; ticket information, (800) GO-CANES.

Baseball, football, basketball, and more! The Hurricanes are always competitive and exciting to watch no matter what sport!

An afternoon or evening of college baseball at Mark Light Stadium on the university's Coral Gables campus can be truly entertaining for youngsters. In 1982 and 1985, the 'Canes were NCAA champions and have been in the College World Series 11 out of the last 16 years. Besides watching superb baseball, fans are also entertained by some of the most creative promotions. You might see the Hurricane mascot, the Miami Maniac, drop from a helicopter, or you might be picked for a "Dash for Cash."

The Hurricanes recently joined the prestigious Big East basketball conference, enabling fans to see such competitors as Syracuse, Boston College, Connecticut, and Georgetown at the downtown Miami Arena.

The fall brings the best in collegiate football to the Orange Bowl, where the three-time national champion Miami Hurricanes play a strong schedule. The 'Canes were the most successful college team of the 1980s.
Tips: You can see other great collegiate sports events hosted by UM, including the Doral Park Intercollegiate Golf Tournament, the Ryder Collegiate Tennis Tournament, the West Palm Beach Basketball Tournament, and the Burger King Women's Basketball Classic.

RECREATIONAL ACTIVITIES

There are many opportunities for children to participate in team sports like T-Ball, flag football, volleyball, softball, and soccer. Call your neighborhood community centers or parks and recreation departments for information. Here are just a few suggestions for other recreational activities and unusual facilities for specialized sports.

FAMILY ACTIVITIES

The indoor playground arrived on the scene in full force in the early 90s. Look for many more locations to pop up around South Florida in the months to come.

◆ Blockbuster Golf and Games

151 NW 136 Avenue, Sunrise. Located at the corner of I-595 West and 136th Avenue. (305) 846-0030. Sunday through Thursday, 9 A.M.– 11 P.M.; Friday and Saturday, 9 A.M.–midnight. Driving range balls: $4– $6; batting cages: $2/20 balls; bull pen: $1.50/20 balls; 36-hole miniature golf: adults, $5; children, $4; bumper boats: $4/four minutes.

The Blockbuster name is synonymous with family entertainment—in more ways than just movie rentals. Wayne Huizenga, Blockbuster's father of invention, has big plans for families, offering sports entertainment centers such as Golf and Games, and, of course, with many of South Florida's professional teams under his wings, Huizenga is a name to watch in the 1990s.

Families visiting this location will have golf and baseball activities to choose from: an 80-tee driving range, 36-holes of miniature golf, state-of-the-art "golf analyzing" computers, 17 batting cages, and a bull pen. Motorized bumper boats offer rides in a lagoon-like setting (beware of gas fumes) for up to three passengers.

A 20,000-square-foot games arena features Virtual Reality games, arcade games, restaurant, party rooms, and a soft play area (Kidsport) for the children. Groups may reserve a special room for party use.

◆ Discovery Zone

730 Riverside Drive, Coral Springs; (305) 345-7500. 6832 Forest Hill Boulevard, Green Acres; (407) 641-KIDS. 13700 SW 84th Street, Kendall; (305) 383-4321. 15520 NW 77th Court, Miami Lakes; (305) 827-5555. 801 South University Drive, Plantation; (305) 452-9010. Cost: $4 for two hours. Memberships available.

Crawl, jump, pounce, leap, roll, stretch, and slide at this fun indoor fitness and play area. There's a place for children under 12, and one just for toddlers, where slides and a moon walk are set up, giving the little ones there own space. Remember to bring your socks! Free coffee will be served to tired parents! **Tips:** The Green Acres (West Palm Beach) location has a "quiet zone" just for adults. Birthday parties are popular here.

◆ Explorations

23078 Sandalfoot Plaza, Boca Raton. Located at the corner of 18th Street and S.R. 441. (407) 451-3511. $4.99 for two hours; $1.49 for each hour thereafter. Memberships available.

This two-story play area is in the configuration of a ship—the USS *Explorer* to be exact! A total of 40 activities can be enjoyed here. Swim or sink in a pile of plastic balls, slide down tubes, and climb a rope to avoid walking the plank! Toddlers will enjoy their own area. Have a question or request? Ask one of the sailors walking around—they're employees in disguise! An arcade, kiddie rides, video lounge, and full-service restaurant are all within the facility. (This place honors competitors coupons!) Birthday parties are offered here.

◆ Fun Fair

4545 N. Pine Island Road, Sunrise. Located between Commercial and Oakland Park Boulevard in the Old Florida Plaza. (305) 748-3520.

Sunday through Thursday, 10 A.M.–10 P.M.; Friday and Saturday,
10 A.M.–midnight. Free admission; pay as you play. Playrobics: $4.95 per
child per hour.

This center is 30,000 square feet of batting cages, pitching machines,
basketball courts, air hockey, ping pong tables, and carnival booths. The
children's "playrobics" arena has mazes, ball baths, and a fireman's pole to
slide down and attempt to climb up. A toddler area is separate. Parties for
up to 300 people are permitted here with advance arrangements. The
concession area serves family favorites like pizza and mom-and-dad favorites like gourmet coffee. Look for more locations around South Florida in
the future; plans are also in the works for the taping of a children's television show at one of the locations.

◆ Funtastics

The Shops at Broward, 8160 West Broward Boulevard, Plantation 33324.
(305) 370-5009.

Like many of the new indoor play areas, Funtastics has its share of
slides and ball pits, but this place also offers a summer camp that includes
arts and crafts among other creative opportunities. This is another popular
birthday spot.

◆ Grand Prix Race-o-Rama

1801 NW First Street (between Griffin and Stirling roads on I-95), Dania
33004. (305) 921-1411. Game room open 24 hours a day; go-karts open
Sunday through Thursday, 10 A.M.–11 P.M.; Friday and Saturday, 10
A.M.–1 A.M. Park admission is free; costs vary for activities.

Buy tickets to drive go-karts around this large and sophisticated race
track, just like the great racing stars. Almost a mile around, the track has
curves and graded banks that will give kids a thrill. The bumper cars are
also exciting to drive. Birthday parties are fun here, and you'll be able to
take advantage of group rates. There's also an arcade with more than 400
games for everyone. **Tip:** Children 15 and under must be accompanied by
an adult.

◆ Malibu Grand Prix

7775 NW Eighth Street, Miami 33126. West of the Palmetto Expressway,
just north of the Mall of the Americas. (305) 266-2100. Monday through
Thursday, 11 A.M.–11 P.M.; Friday and Saturday, 10 A.M.–2 A.M.;
Sunday, 10 A.M.–midnight.

This castle fun-house was remodeled in 1989 and has plenty of
amusements for kids of all ages. Kiddie rides (for children 6 and older),
miniature golf, 9 batting cages, 160 video games, and 2 new go-kart

racetracks can be found here. This place is known for its entertaining birthday parties.

◆ Play City
Lower level of Miracle Center, 3301 Coral Way, Miami 33134. (305) 441-2021. Monday through Thursday, noon–9 P.M.; Friday and Saturday, 10 A.M.–10 P.M.; Sunday, 10 A.M.–9 P.M. $5.31 per child (no time limit).

Come play around at this indoor play area. Groups are welcome with advance reservations. A giant indoor maze is the center of attention, plus you'll find an arcade and skill games. Socks are required to be worn in the play areas. Teens might enjoy playing laser tag. **Tips:** Mommy and Me classes are offered here. Children 12 and under must be shorter than 52". Parties can be planned here.

◆ Rapids Water Park
6566 North Military Trail (between 45th Street and Blue Heron Boulevard), West Palm Beach 33407. (407) 842-8756. Group rates: (407) 848-6272. Daily, 10 A.M.–sunset (weather permitting). $13.50 per person; children under 2, free.

Rapids has grown and expanded during the past few years. From just a miniature golf course with a waterslide to South Florida's only water park! Features at the park include a quarter-mile action river, wave channel, waterfalls and waterslides, water-shooting cannons atop a pirate's wreck, and a tadpole area just for toddlers. Call to see what special offer is running. (Surf & Turf is one of the specials that includes golf, water activities, and a meal all for a reasonable price.)

◆ Telesis
6900 Okeechobee Boulevard, West Palm Beach 33411. Located one mile west of the Florida Turnpike. (407) 687-2055. Monday through Thursday, 5–10 P.M.; Friday, 5 P.M.–midnight; Saturday, 10 A.M.–midnight; Sunday, 11 A.M.–10 P.M. Free admission; purchase tokens for each activity.

Just think, 25,000 square feet of fun for the family! Carnival rides (some with height requirements), skee ball, air hockey, 150 token-takin' games, and pinball are all part of the fun. A snack bar is on the premises.

BASEBALL

◆ Bucky Dent's Baseball School
490 Dotterel Road, Delray Beach 33444. (407) 265-0280.

For baseball players ages 8 to 23 who want to improve their knowledge and ability, this school teaches proper skills and playing habits through an organized and disciplined program. There's a special program for kids ages 12 and under—instructors work closely with these young-sters and give each student personalized attention.

◆ Red Berry's Baseball World
7455 SW 125th Avenue, Miami 33183. (305) 279-2668.

For over 20 years, Coach Red Berry has hosted baseball camps for boys and girls. With an emphasis on fun and player development, Berry and his staff run various programs throughout the year at this terrific facility, including summer vacation camps, spring and fall instructional leagues, boy's baseball, and girl's softball. Try this place for your child's next birthday party!

BIKING

This is a fun way to spend time with your family. Small children can ride in seats attached to the backs of bicycles or in a "trailer" that attaches behind adult bikes. Older children can usually pedal a long way before tiring. Parks are good places to ride, and some have special trails for bikers. Call (904) 488-7950 for a handy free publication from the state called *Florida Bicycle Trails*. Also available through many bike stores is an important reference called *Bicycles Are Vehicles: Florida's Bicycle Laws*. Backpacks and canteens are great to bring on bike outings, and always remember to wear safety helmets. Below is a short list of places that rent bicycles for adults and children. Please check for additional listings in the yellow pages of your telephone directory.

◆ The Bicycle Center
523 Truman Avenue, Key West 33040. (305) 294-4556. Daily, 9 A.M.–6 P.M. $4/day. All major credit cards accepted; bring an I.D.

The Bicycle Center offers children's 20" bikes and adult bikes with attached carriers (which will transport children weighing 40 pounds or less). Helmets are for sale in the store.

◆ Dade Cycle
3216 Grand Avenue, Coconut Grove 32133. (305) 443-6075. Monday through Saturday, 9 A.M.–6 P.M.; Sunday, 10:30 A.M.–6 P.M. Adult bikes: $3/hour, $15/24 hours, $46/week. Children's bikes: $2/hour. Baby seats: $1.50/day. MC, V, personal checks accepted.

Guaranteed to reverse your aging process, try renting a bike here for a ride through the Grove. BMX (racing bikes), baby seats, helmets, and in-line skates are available.

◆ Equipment Locker Sport and Cycle

11518 Overseas Highway, Marathon 33050. (305) 289-1670. Weekdays, 9 A.M.–6 P.M.; Saturdays, 9 A.M.–5 P.M.; closed Sundays during the summer, call for winter hours. Hourly, daily, and weekly rates. AE, MC, V, personal checks accepted with I.D.

All sizes of bikes can be rented here. Baby seat attachments can be rented; helmets are for sale. Call for current rates. Sporting goods are for sale on one side of the shop, bikes on the other.

◆ Gary's Megacycle

18151 NE 19th Avenue, North Miami Beach 33162; (305) 940-2912. 1260 Washington Avenue, Miami Beach 33139; (305) 534-3306. 15422 NW 77th Court, Miami Lakes 33014; (305) 824-0120. Monday through Friday, 9:30 A.M.–8 P.M.; Saturday, 9 A.M.–6 P.M.; Sunday, 10 A.M.–4 P.M. Cost begins at $10/day. MC, V, personal checks accepted.

Rent a trailer that connects to adult bikes and carries children. Most of your biking needs can be found here, plus trails are near each of the rental locations.

◆ Key Largo Bikes

Mile Marker 99.5, Key Largo 33037. (305) 451-1910. Monday through Saturday, 9:30 A.M.–6 P.M. Closed Sundays and some Mondays. Summer and winter hours vary. $20 deposit required. $8/day, $35/week, $10/baby seats. AE, MC, V, personal checks accepted.

Adult bikes, 16" and 20" children's bikes, and seat attachments are available at this Key Largo shop. Ask if helmets for children are available.

◆ Mangrove Bicycle (Key Biscayne Bicycle Shop)

260 Crandon Boulevard (middle of the village of Key Biscayne), Key Biscayne 33149. (305) 361-5555. Daily, 10 A.M.–6 P.M., closed Mondays. $7/2 hours, $10/day. AE, MC, V, personal checks accepted; I.D. required.

Since 1973, this has been a popular rental stop for people exploring Key Biscayne. This store is close to Crandon Park and Bill Baggs/Cape Florida State Recreation Area. Adult bikes with seat attachments and 12" and 16" bikes for small children are available. Free baskets are provided with the bikes to carry your picnic lunch!

◆ Palm Beach Bicycle Trail Shop

223 Sunrise Avenue (in the Palm Beach Hotel), Palm Beach 33480. (407) 659-4583. Daily, 9 A.M.–5 P.M. Deposit required; $6/hour, $15/half day, $20/day, $45/week. AE, MC, V, local personal checks accepted.

The Palm Beach Bicycle Trail Shop can satisfy all your bicycle needs, from training wheels to adult bikes. Locks come with all bikes; helmets are available to buy. The shop provides bikers with a map of area trails, most of which run along the Intracoastal Waterway. The famous Palm Beach Bicycle Trail is just seconds away. In-line skates are also available for rental.

BOATING

With over 1 million boats in the state of Florida, it is well worth your time and energy to inquire about boating laws in your local waters. Safety is the primary factor when going out on the waters. And by the way, be on the lookout for friendly manatees that often visit marinas and warm water areas. These lovable creatures call Florida home and are extremely vulnerable to boats and other water craft.

For information on rules and regulations, obtain a free copy of the *Florida Boaters Guide* from the Florida Marine Patrol, Division of Law Enforcement, Douglas Building, 3900 Commonwealth Boulevard, Tallahassee 32399, or call (904) 488-5757.

A nifty little brochure called *Who Can Make Your Kids Wear Their Life Jackets?* includes a chart to help parents discern what type of life jacket their child must wear when boating. Ask for a copy when you write to the Florida Marine Patrol.

Here are a few listings to get you thinking.

◆ American Red Cross Sailing

Offered at Okeeheelee Park, 7715 Forest Hill Boulevard, West Palm Beach 33463. Call (407) 964-4420 and request information.

Your 9 year old (or older) can learn how to sail a 12-foot mini-fish sailboat during these highly regarded lessons offered by the American Red Cross. Participants will learn basic seamanship, safety, and how to rig the vessel. A swim test will be given upon enrollment. Call for course fees and information. For more information about the park, see listing in "Under the Sun."

◆ Coconut Grove Sailing Club

2990 South Bayshore Drive, Coconut Grove 33133. (305) 444-4571. Monday through Friday, 10 A.M.–3 P.M. Booklet, $2.50; classes are free.

A junior pram program for children ages 9 to 13 offers beginner lessons for kids who live in Miami. The week-long summer sessions teach children the essentials of sailing: tacking, water safety, general handling of the boat, basic seamanship, and rigging and unrigging. Sign up in mid-March to secure a spot in this popular summer class. If you don't get in, however, don't lose heart—this same beginners' class is available on weekends during the school year or during spring break.

BOWLING

There are many bowling alleys in South Florida, so inquire about children's leagues and bumper bowling at your favorite location.

◆ Don Carter's Lanes
Locations throughout South Florida. See yellow pages for listings. Open 24 hours a day.

Bumper Bowling is the latest fad for 18-month-olds! This Saturday morning bowling league is especially for young children. Youngsters up to age 5 have the advantage of the gutters being blocked with plastic inserts called bumpers. This helps them build confidence and gives them a better chance at knocking down the pins. Coaches work with the children and parents are encouraged to watch. (Children ages 6 and up bowl without the bumpers!) Winter leagues run 30 weeks, summer leagues are about 10 weeks long. Birthday parties are popular at all locations.

CAMPING

For a current list of camping facilities in the state, write for the *Florida Camping Directory,* Florida Campground Association, 1638 N. Plaza Drive, Tallahassee 32308-5364; (904) 656-8878. Also, many parks offer camping. Call your county parks department for more information.

FISHING

South Florida is a fisherman's paradise, offering the best in salt and freshwater fishing. Islamorada, for instance, calls itself the "sportfishing capital of the world." As a matter of fact, recreational fishing is a $5-billion-a-year industry for the state of Florida. Many area parks, beaches, rivers, canals, and bridges permit fishing, but it is important to know the rules and regulations of the spot you've picked out to show your child the "ropes"…'er "lines." If this is your hobby, contact the parks in your area for information. Remember that fishing licenses are required for residents and non-residents. For information, call your local park district or write:

• **Florida Game and Fresh Water Fish Commission,** Farris Bryant Building, Tallahassee 32301; for saltwater fishing, **Florida Marine**

Patrol, Majory Stoneman Douglas Building, 3900 Commonwealth Boulevard, Tallahassee 32303.

- **Florida Department of Natural Resources,** (904) 488-7326.
- **Florida Marine Patrol,** (407) 626-9995.
- **The *Official State Information and Visitor Guide to Florida Fishing and Boating*** can be obtained by writing the Florida Sports Authority, 107 West Gaines Street, Tallahassee 32399-2000; (904) 488-8347.
- Palm Beach County offers ***Fish Finder Kit,*** a booklet describing essential information on tides, ramps, rules, and tips. Write: WPB Fishing Club, P.O. Box 468, West Palm Beach 33402.
- **The Florida Keys Fishing Hotline,** (800) 54-FISH9

◆ Anglin's Pier

2 East Commercial Boulevard, Lauderdale-by-the-Sea. (305) 491-9403. Open 24 hours. Adults, $2.75; children 12 and under, $1.75; sightseeing, $1.

There is a fishing fee. Bait and tackle are available at this illuminated 875-foot pier. Anglin's hosts monthly fishing contests, so ask about upcoming events when you sign in. Metered parking is ample, with restaurants and an ice cream shop nearby.

◆ Black Point Marina

24777 SW 87th Avenue, Miami. Take Old Cutler Road to SW 87th Avenue and head east. (305) 258-3500.

This bait and tackle shop is situated near Biscayne Bay. Trout and snapper are plentiful, and you'll see plenty of manatees, as this protected area attracts the friendly aquatic mammals. Fishing equipment and boats are available for rent, but call for prices and times of operation. A dockside restaurant is located here.

◆ Dania Beach Pier

300 North Beach Road, Dania. (305) 925-2861. Open 24 hours. Adults and children 5 and over, $2; children under 5, free.

Catch it all here—you'll find snook, grouper, mackerel, and more in these waters. Rental equipment includes rods and bait. A restaurant and a picnic area are available.

◆ Deerfield Beach International Pier

200 NE 21st Avenue, Deerfield Beach. (305) 426-9206. Open 24 hours. Adults, $1.75; children 5 to 17, $.75; children under 5, free.

Here's a popular snapper and barracuda spot. Rod rentals, bait, and tackle are available, and a restaurant is nearby. The pier is 840 feet long!

◆ Haulover Pier

10501 Collins Avenue, North Miami Beach. (305) 947-6767. Open 24 hours. Adults, $2; children under 16, $1; spectators, $1. Parking, $2.

This is a busy 1,103-foot pier, offering bait and tackle rental (with a deposit). If you have a good day, you might catch snook, mackerel, barracuda, grouper, shark, snapper, and blue runners. **Tips:** Ask about a 30-day pass. Snack bar open from 7 A.M. to 6 P.M.

◆ Pompano Fishing Pier

222 Pompano Beach Boulevard, Pompano Beach. (305) 943-1488. Open 24 hours. With gear: adults, $2.07; children 10 and under, $1; sightseeing, $.80. Additional charges for rentals.

Catch snook, snapper, grouper, mackerel, cobia, sand perch, blue runner, and bluefish varieties at this over-1,000-foot pier at Fisherman's Wharf Restaurant.

A restaurant, playground, and bait and tackle shop are all located right on the Atlantic Ocean.

◆ Sawgrass Recreation Park

5400 North U.S. 27, Fort Lauderdale. Mailing address is P.O. Box 291620, Fort Lauderdale 33329. (305) 389-0202 or (800) 457-0788. Daily, 6 A.M.–6 P.M. Boats and motors: $36/4 hours; $55/7 hours; rowboats: $25/5 hours. DIS, Honor, MC, and V accepted.

Licenses, bait, tackle, and fishing guides are available. Life jackets can be used free of charge for children under 6 years of age. There is a cookhouse that serves hot and cold sandwiches, drinks, and other snacks. For tour information, see the listing in "By Land, Sea, and Air."

HORSEBACK RIDING

Davie and an area near Kendall are considered the prime horse spots. Many ranches offer riding lessons and trail rides. Special programs for the handicapped are also available. Check with your local park district. Look in your yellow pages for a complete listing of stables and farms offering riding lessons.

◆ Horses and the Handicapped of South Florida

417 NE Third Street, Delray Beach 33483. (407) 278-2441. Call for details about weekly sessions.

Children ages 4 and up with cerebral palsy, Down's syndrome, and other special needs ride at two facilities: Trails West Riding Academy in Palm Beach Gardens and Tradewinds Stables in Coconut Creek. Riders are matched to horses compatible with their needs. The skills learned here carry over to other parts of the children's lives. A physician's referral is necessary for admission to the program. **Tip:** For more information about Tradewinds Stables, see listings in this chapter and in "Under the Sun."

◆ Jimaguas Ranch

12201 SW 80th Street, Miami 33183. (305) 271-4289. Weekends and some holidays, 8 A.M.–5 P.M. Trail rides, $10 per hour; buggy rides (mornings only), $5 per person.

Even the natives don't realize that a unique place called "Horse Country" is nestled between some of the busiest streets of the suburbs. The Jimaguas Ranch is just one of many ranches that has remained untouched by suburban development in this area that is bounded by Bird Road and Kendall Drive between SW 118th and SW 127th avenues. The entire family can enjoy a relaxing trail ride directed by a guide or a horse-drawn carriage ride through the Horse Country area. The horses here are all very gentle. **Tips:** The antique buggy may be rented for parties. Riding lessons are available, and party arrangements can be made.

◆ Tradewinds Stables

Located at northern entrance of Tradewinds Park, 3600 West Sample Road, Coconut Creek 33073. (305) 968-3875. Pony rides (under 52"): Monday through Thursday, 11 A.M.–3 P.M.; weekends, 11 A.M.–3:30 P.M. Trail rides: Saturday and Sunday, 10 and 11:30 A.M. and 1, 2:30, and 4 P.M. $13/per person.

Weekend riding is offered here, but it is a very popular program. You must go to the General Store at 9 A.M. on the morning you desire to ride. Your reservation must be made in person and paid for in advance. The cost is $13 per person for ages 9 and above (or 52" tall). Your time in the saddle will be a one-hour guided trail ride. For more information on Tradewinds Park, see listing in "Under the Sun."

◆ Valmaron Equestrian Center

16891 Jupiter Farms Road, Jupiter Farms 33478. Go west on Indiantown Road to Jupiter Farms Road. Valmaron is about one quarter mile on right. (407) 746-8229. Shows take place second Sunday of every month at 8:30 A.M.

A nice drive in the country will take you to Valmaron Country Store and Equestrian Center. There are small bleachers to sit on, and you can get a snack and watch the show on the deck of the Country Store. Inquire about classes for beginners and more experienced riders. Parking is available behind the Valmaron Country Store under the trees.

◆ Vinceremos Riding Center

8765 Lake Worth Road (one mile west of Florida Turnpike), Lake Worth 33467. (407) 433-5800.

Fully accredited by the North American Riding for Handicapped Association, Vinceremos provides riding therapy for people with disabilities and special needs. Horses are specially selected and trained for this purpose. The programs teach riding skills and help students meet therapeutic goals by working on balance, muscle tone, posture, coordination, confidence, and concentration. A professional therapist and certified riding instructor develop individual therapy plans for each student.

ICE SKATING

Skating provides good aerobic exercise for children. Remember to dress warmly in these rinks, even gloves would be smart for young children. Perhaps a skating party would go over well for your child's next birthday party!

◆ Gold Coast Ice Arena

4601 North Federal Highway, Pompano Beach 33064. Located two miles south of Boca Raton, almost a mile north of Sample Road on Federal Highway. (305) 943-1437. Open daily, hours vary. $4 to $5; skate rental, $1.50.

Dress warmly (it's about 50 degrees rinkside) and think winter when you visit this skating facility. Competitions and ice shows are held periodically throughout the year. For small children, try the "Tiny Tots" class on Saturday mornings. Ice hockey clinics for all levels of play are offered.

◆ Miami Ice Arena

14770 Biscayne Boulevard, North Miami Beach 33162. (305) 940-8222. Open daily, hours vary. $6 to $8; skate rental, $2.

This is one of the largest ice skating rinks in the area, and it may become a family favorite, especially when you think the long, hot summer days will never end.

◆ Scott Rakow Youth Center Ice Rink

2700 Sheridan Avenue, Miami Beach 33140. (305) 673-7767. Call for schedule information. Miami Beach resident, $1.50; nonresident, $3. Skate rental, $1.50.

Children in grades 4 through 12 can get a feel for the ice at this neighborhood youth center. Group and private lessons are available.

♦ Sunrise Ice Skating Center

3363 Pine Island Road, Sunrise. Take I-95 to Oakland Park Boulevard and go west 6.5 miles; west of University Drive. (305) 741-2366. Hours vary with sessions. $5.50 (includes skates).

One of South Florida's largest rinks, this skating center is 17,000 square feet and offers special family-discount nights, classes for all ages, and occasional spectator events, such as hockey games. A snackbar offers refreshments.

ROLLER SKATING

♦ Hot Wheels

12265 SW 112th Street, Miami 33186. Hotline, (305) 595-3200; information, 595-2958. Call for schedule information. Admission, $5.25; skates, $.75.

Special scheduled events include tot skates, family skates, all-day skates, Christian music night, rock night, and sleep-overs. The facility is available for party rentals. **Tip:** Smallest skate size is a child's size 8.

♦ In-line Heaven Skate Shop

1122 East Atlantic Boulevard, Delray Beach 33444. (407) 279-0222. $9 per hour.

Skate along Ocean Boulevard with rentals from this shop. Safety equipment can be rented as well. Adult and child sizes available.

♦ The Palace

6016 Old Congress Road (one mile west of I-95), Lantana 33462. (407) 967-0311. Hours and cost ($3–$5) vary depending on sessions.

This popular spot hosts lots of special events. Private party rooms are available when you have your birthday bash here. Twins' nights, two-for-one nights, and family nights are great fun.

♦ Roller Skating Center of Coral Springs

2100 University Drive, Coral Springs 33071. (305) 755-0011. Hours and cost vary depending on sessions. $1 skate rental.

A popular spot for the whole family, and a big hit for birthdays, this skating rink offers family-discount night, tiny tot classes, all-day skates, and more. Inquire about special group rates for schools, camps, and religious organizations.

SWIMMING

There is an endless list of swimming pools in South Florida. We have
listed a few for you to try, but if you desire more information, call your
local parks department, your local college or junior college, or a nearby
country club.

◆ **International Swimming Hall of Fame Pool**

*501 Seabreeze Boulevard (located one block west of the beach and one block
south of Las Olas Boulevard), Fort Lauderdale 33316. (305) 523-0994.*

The Hall of Fame Pool is open daily to the public except during special swimming events and competitions. Many types of classes are offered,
from infant water orientation to synchronized swimming. Summer camps
are also offered. Call for a complete schedule.

◆ **University of Miami**

*1 Hurricane Drive, Coral Gables 33146. (305) 284-3593. Half-hour
private lessons daily for a week begin at $100.*

For 40 years University of Miami swim coach Jack Nelson, a former
Olympic coach, has been providing swim lessons to Miami's youngsters.
Together with his staff of coaches from around the world, Nelson has
created a top-notch program. Classes are held in the university pool or in
your pool at home. Group and private lessons are available and are recommended for children ages 1 and up.

During the summer, UM hosts a swim camp for children ages 2 to 7.
It is available three times a week in the afternoon and is primarily a confidence builder (or "organized chaos!") for small children.

Don't forget that a swimming meet, with college students compet-
ing, is a fun event to attend!

◆ **Venetian Pool**

*2701 DeSoto Boulevard, Coral Gables 33134. (305) 460-5356. June
through August: Monday through Friday, 11 A.M.–7:30 P.M.; September,
October, April, and May: Tuesday through Friday, 11 A.M.–5:30 P.M.;
November through March: Tuesday through Friday, 11 A.M.–4:30 P.M.
Weekends throughout year: 10 A.M.–4:30 P.M. Coral Gables residents: adults,
$3; teens, $2; children, $1.60. Nonresidents: adults, $4; teens, $3.50;
children, $1.60. Call for updated class schedules and fees.*

Kids will feel they're in another world when they swim here. Nearly
$2.5 million was spent in 1989 to totally restore this historic gem listed
in the National Register of Historic Places. The pool was carved from a

rock quarry in the late 1920s. The original coral architecture that was popular then can still be seen. A "sandy beach," waterfalls, and swim-through caves will make a trip to this swimming hole, fed by natural, refreshing springs, a big hit! Swimming lessons for children 5 and above are offered by the Venetian Aquatic Club during the summer months. Call for information. **Tips:** Accessible to handicapped. Vending machines and a cafe are available.

COME AND GET IT!

South Florida's tropical environment, with its fresh seafood, colorful tropical fruits, and locally grown produce available year round, combines with the area's many cultural influences to produce great places to eat. From Jupiter to Key West, you can dine near the water on the catch of the day, choose down-home country cookin' at family-style restaurants, learn about different ethnic groups through their special dishes, savor the flavor of fresh-picked fruits and vegetables, or just cool off with an ice cream treat.

This chapter describes a variety of special eateries that will provide your children with culinary adventures. Most are reasonably priced and can provide more for your money than the standard burger-and-fries meal. Visits to "real" restaurants, as opposed to fast-food, play-while-you-nibble establishments, give children opportunities to practice social skills and table manners. Two other options for family dining are chain restaurants, which usually provide children's menus, balloons, and high chairs, and hotel restaurants. We've found that some of the restaurants we listed in the first edition, such as The Beverly Hills Cafe and the Latin American Cafeteria, became popular enough to open at several locations. Other popular chains in South Florida include Dalts, Denny's, Kenny Rogers Roasters, Perkins, Bennigan's, Cracker Barrel, Fuddruckers, Houlihan's, Raffles, Red Lobster, El Torito, Morrison's Cafeteria, the Olive Garden, Pollo Supremo, Pollo Tropical, Tony Roma's, Gepetto's Tale of the Whale, TGIFriday's, Piccadilly Cafeteria, and Shoney's.

Hotel restaurants are often overlooked, but remember that, since they have families staying as guests, hotels are usually equipped for and accustomed to children. The buffet meals are great for children, and are usually offered at discounted prices.

If you have young children, a few preparations will help make eating out more pleasurable for everyone.

- Bring a few finger foods that you know your child will like.
- Bring small activities (crayons, notepads, puzzles).
- Collect menus from your favorite restaurants. If you go out for pizza, for example, call ahead to order so that you don't have to wait when you arrive.

- Pack a wet cloth or wipes to clean sticky fingers during and after meals.
- Avoid restaurant rush hours if possible. Friday and Saturday nights after 6:30 P.M., lunch hour in business areas, and Sundays at noon usually mean long waits that result in understandably squirmy children.
- When you order, be specific about your needs for drinks (large or small, with or without ice and/or straws), additional small plates for sharing meals, or cups to share soup. You may want to bring your child's own cup with lid/sipper seal, too.

When you visit Cuban/Latin restaurants, you may find that at 5 or 6 P.M. they're not very crowded; don't assume they're not popular. By 8 or 9 P.M., they're usually full of couples, extended families (including toddlers who seem to have no problem staying awake), and others who enjoy Latin cuisine. The restaurant staff in these places is usually very happy to accommodate your children's special requests. You also may find that regular patrons tend to dress a little more formally than in other family restaurants. At the end of this chapter you'll find a glossary of Spanish terms often found on South Florida menus.

If you need a breath of fresh air and a taste of really fresh-off-the-vine food, your family might have fun taking a trip to the country to bring home some of that just-picked freshness. Tourists and natives alike enjoy picking their own strawberries, tomatoes, peppers, and squash in the winter months. For information about tours to agricultural areas, see listings in "By Land, Sea, and Air." See listings in "Exploring Science and Nature" for information about working citrus groves where you can sample interesting native fruits.

The fields are open mostly on weekends during the winter. Bring your own baskets or plastic containers, one for each member of the family. The field operators are helpful about picking techniques and ripeness of vegetables and fruits. Remember that the law prohibits children under 10 years of age from entering most fields.

DADE COUNTY

◆ American Classics

8701 Collins Avenue (in the Dezerland Surfside Beach Hotel), Miami Beach 33139. (305) 865-6661. Daily, 7 A.M.–11 P.M. Major credit cards accepted.

Take a seat in one of the dining room's five 1959 Chevys and order up a burger-fries-shake combo. An old Wurlitzer jukebox plays '50s music to keep you in the mood. Very novel, and good food, too. **Tips:** There is no children's menu, but you can request half-orders for half price. Burgers are only available on the lunch menu, so plan accordingly. High chairs and booster seats are available.

◆ Andalusia Bake Shop and Food Emporium

248 Andalusia Avenue, Coral Gables 33134; (305) 445-8696. 8603 South Dixie Highway (in the First Union Bank building), Miami; (305) 667-CAKE. 100 South Biscayne Boulevard (One Bayfront Plaza), Miami; (305) 358-9001. 2220 NW 82nd Avenue, Miami; (305) 470-CAKE. Check the phone directory for information about a new location in Aventura Mall. Open Monday through Saturday, 7 A.M.–6 P.M. Major credit cards and local personal checks accepted.

If you consistently provide delicious food and great service, people keep coming back and your fame spreads. Begun 30 years ago as a single bakery, Andalusia now offers take out hot and cold entrees, salads, and appetizers, as well as their delectable cakes and pastries. They've also opened several locations throughout Dade County.

◆ Angie's Place

404 SE First Avenue (at South Dixie Highway, one-quarter mile south of end of Florida Turnpike), Florida City 33034. (305) 245-8939. Daily, 6 A.M.–2 P.M. Cash payment only.

Angie's is run by sisters Angie, Tina, and Joyce, who were born and raised in Florida City. They serve up home-style breakfasts and lunches, using locally grown fresh vegetables. Ask about the daily specials.

◆ The Big Cheese

8080 SW 67th Avenue, South Miami 33143. (305) 662-6855. Monday through Thursday, 11 A.M.–11 P.M.; Friday, 11 A.M.–midnight; Saturday, noon–midnight; Sunday, 4–10 P.M. Cash payment only.

When you see a place that's always crowded with people of all ages, including families with young children, you know you've found a safe place to dine. The pizzas are incredible (by the pie or by the slice), and kids love to watch the chefs twirl the dough in the air. Sub sandwiches come with a variety of fixings and are plenty big to split between siblings. Dinners include tortellini, ziti, lasagna, stuffed eggplant, stuffed shells, and more. The meals are enough to stuff even a Miami Hurricane football player, and you may see the whole team in here.

◆ Big Fish Restaurant

55 SW Miami Avenue Road, Miami 33161. Take Second Avenue south from East Flagler Street, cross bridge over Miami River, turn right at foot of bridge, turn right again at first street, follow sign to restaurant. (305) 372-3725. Monday through Saturday, 11 A.M.–3 P.M. AE, MC, V accepted.

Children will enjoy the view of the Miami River, complete with tug boats, pelicans, and a draw bridge that opens and closes for the riverboat traffic. Try to get a table in the back next to the river. The seafood here is reasonably priced. Try the fish fingers and fries for the kids.

◆ Biscayne Miracle Mile Cafeteria

147 Miracle Mile, Coral Gables 33134. (305) 444-9005. Lunch: 11 A.M.– 2:15 P.M.; dinner: 4–8 P.M.; Sundays, 11 A.M.–8 P.M. Cash payment only.

This restaurant provides a delicious selection of salads, vegetables, meats, and fresh-baked breads and desserts. Children seem to love to put together their own meals. Waiters will carry high chairs and trays to the table and bring coffee refills or additional food if you need it. They'll also bring doggie bags if anyone's eyes are bigger than their stomachs.

◆ Cami's Seafood Place

6272 South Dixie Highway, South Miami 33143; (305) 665-1288. 869 SW 107th Avenue (across from Florida International University), Miami 33152; (305) 227-2722. Sunday through Thursday, 5–10 P.M.; Friday and Saturday, 5–11 P.M. MC, V accepted with $20 minimum.

The paper plates and plastic forks will make the kids think they're at a picnic. If they like shrimp, scallops, and other seafood, this is a great place to try. For dessert, try the mini sundaes or the fresh strawberries with whipped cream.

◆ Carolina Café

201 NW First Avenue (in front of Government Center Metrorail station), Miami 33136. (305) 579-0930. Monday through Friday, 7 A.M.–10 P.M.; Saturday, noon–10 P.M.; closed Sunday. IGT accepted.

If you're downtown and get the urge for barbecue, this is your best choice. The fried chicken, Brunswick stew, barbecue beans with chunks of meat, and shredded barbecue pork are outstanding. Leave room for dessert—they're homemade and delicious.

◆ Casa Larios

7929 NW Second Street (a few blocks west of Palmetto Expressway, just off Flagler Boulevard), Miami 33136. (305) 266-5494. Daily, 7 A.M.–11 P.M. Major credit cards accepted.

Delicious Cuban sandwiches, *arroz con pollo, caldo gallego,* and more await you here. The black bean soup can be served over white rice for a delicious meal for children; add a tropical fruit shake and they may never go back to the golden arches.

♦ Casita Tejas
10 South Krome Avenue, Homestead 33030. (305) 248-8224. Monday, Tuesday, and Thursday, 11 A.M.–9 P.M.; Friday, 11 A.M.–10 P.M.; Saturday, 9 A.M.–10 P.M.; Sunday, 9 A.M.–2 P.M. MC, V accepted.

The high ceilings and hardwood floors make you feel like you're in old Homestead, but the Mexican music, Tex-Mex food, and staff take you elsewhere. The portions are plentiful, and children always seem to enjoy the fresh tortilla chips that appear on your table as soon as you're seated. This is a popular place for family celebrations, and staff are happy to accommodate children. Take-out is available.

♦ Chuck Wagon Restaurant
7628 SW 117th Avenue, Miami 33173. (305) 274-2263. Saturday through Thursday, 6 A.M.–3 P.M.; Friday, 6 A.M.–9 P.M. Cash payment only.

The food is good here anytime, but it seems to be one of the most popular places in the Kendall area to take children for breakfast. During the week you can get two fresh-baked hot biscuits, two eggs, and home fries for around a dollar, and waiters are happy to bring extra plates if you want to share your meal with your toddler. Another breakfast favorite is the special plate of home fries covered with melted cheese, with two eggs on the side. High chairs and booster seats are available.

After your meal, wander through the feed store located at the front of the complex. This part of town used to be Dade County frontier—children might enjoy a drive through the area known as Horse Country (go north one block to Sunset Drive, turn left to drive under the Florida Turnpike). There are several ranches along this route that offer horse boarding and pony rides—look for them on your drive. For more information, see listings for horseback riding in "Under the Sun."

♦ Coopertown Restaurant
22700 SW Eighth Street (Tamiami Trail, in the Everglades), Miami 33929. (305) 226-6048. Daily, 8 A.M.–6 P.M. Cash payment only.

If your children simply must try alligator meat or frogs' legs, and you don't mind looking at the stuffed alligator heads, skulls, and other such trophies on the walls, then this is the place to dine. The above-mentioned specialties are available morning, noon, or night.

◆ The Crab House

1551 79th Street, Miami 33141. (305) 868-7085. Sunday through Thursday, 4:30–11 P.M.; Friday and Saturday, 4:30–midnight. Major credit cards accepted.

The view of Biscayne Bay is wonderful, but long after your visit here your kids will remember the mallets they used to bang open their crabs on the newspaper-covered table. It's different, it's fun, and it's definitely delicious. Fresh fish and pasta are also on the menu. The children's menu includes chicken, burgers, tuna salad, fish, and shrimp.

◆ David's Cafeteria

8288 Biscayne Boulevard, North Miami 33161. (305) 751-0631. Sunday through Friday: lunch, 11:30 A.M.–2 P.M.; dinner, 4–8 P.M. Cash payment only.

The home-style cooking at David's will appeal to young and old alike, and they usually have several children's selections. High chairs and booster seats are available.

◆ Deli Lane

7230 SW 59th Avenue, South Miami 33143; (305) 665-0606. 1401 Brickell, Miami; (305) 377-8811. Monday through Thursday, 8 A.M.– 11 P.M.; Friday and Saturday, 8 A.M.–midnight; Sunday, 8 A.M.–9 P.M. Major credit cards accepted.

Delicious and unusual menu choices will bring you here often, even if your kids just stick with the children's pizza ("I ate the whole thing, Mom!"). This is a very popular spot for lunch, so try going before or after the business lunch hour.

◆ East Coast Fisheries

360 West Flagler Street, Miami 33131. (305) 373-5516. Daily, 10 A.M.– 10 P.M. AE, MC, V accepted.

This dockside fresh-fish market and restaurant provides good food at fairly reasonable prices year after year after year. Try the crab cakes and crabmeat salad on crackers. The best part is watching the boats come in loaded with fresh fish.

◆ El Cid

117 NW 42nd Avenue (LeJeune Road), Miami 33126. (305) 642-3144. Daily, noon–midnight. Major credit cards accepted.

For all the young princesses and princes who dream of living in a castle, a meal here is a wonderful treat. The restaurant is inside a medieval castle, only a few miles south of Miami International Airport. As you enter, be sure to take time to admire the grilled and roasted food on display, as well as the whole dressed pigs, hams, and sausages hanging from the ceiling. The food is medieval Spanish-style (try the roast goose or lamb), and the servings are generous. Children's menu available. Ask if you can climb the winding stone staircase to see the upper rooms, which are generally used for groups. **Tip:** It's best to take children for late lunch or early dinner.

♦ 11th Street Diner

1065 Washington Avenue, Miami Beach 33139. (305) 534-6373. Monday through Thursday, 7 A.M.–3 A.M.; Friday and Saturday, 24 hours.

If trendy food is not your idea of a meal, and you find yourself in trend-mecca South Beach, this diner is probably a good choice. Hamburgers you'll love to bite into, thick chocolate shakes that taste perfect on hot Florida days, and all your other diner faves are on the menu.

♦ El Inka

11049 Bird Road, Miami 33175. (305) 553-4074. Tuesday through Sunday, noon–10 P.M. Major credit cards accepted.

This wonderful Peruvian eatery is set in a somewhat unappealing strip shopping center, awaiting the adventurous. Try the delicious *ceviche* (marinated fish), *papas a la huancaina* (potatoes prepared with vegetables and sauce), and finish off your meal with *picarones* (fried and sweetened puffy dough).

♦ El Pub

1548 SW Eighth Street, Miami 33130. (305) 643-2651. Daily, 8 A.M.– 1 A.M. AE, DIS, MC, V accepted.

Serving delicious and inexpensive Cuban food in the heart of Little Havana, this is a popular place for who's who in Miami's Latin circles. The staff is very helpful with children and is happy to provide extra plates, crackers, or whatever you need. There's no children's menu, but kids might like to try the black bean soup with white rice (you pour the thick soup over the rice) or the *caldo gallego*. High chairs and booster seats are available.

♦ Firehouse Four

1000 South Miami Avenue, Miami 33131. (305) 379-1923. Lunch: Monday through Saturday, 11:30 A.M.–2 P.M.; dinner: Monday through Thursday, 5:30–10 P.M.; Friday through Sunday, 5:30–11 P.M. Bar and grill open daily, 11:30 A.M.–midnight, for soups and sandwiches. Major credit cards accepted.

Listed on the National Register of Historic Places, Miami's oldest surviving fire station, built in 1923, houses this American cuisine restaurant. The original tile and pine floors remain intact, and the firehouse poles and other decorations appeal to children's imaginations. **Tips:** No children's menu, but sandwiches are available. No high chairs; just boosters. The happy hour after work here is popular with downtowners, so plan your visit accordingly.

◆ Granny Feelgood's

Metrofaire, 111 NW First Street (second floor of Government Center), Miami 33128; (305) 579-2104; Monday through Friday, 7 A.M.–5 P.M.; cash payment only. 190 SE First Avenue, Miami 33131; (305) 358-6233; Monday through Friday, 7:30 A.M.–6 P.M.; Saturday, 11 A.M.–3 P.M.; MC and V accepted. Cultural Center Plaza in downtown Miami; Monday through Saturday, 10:30 A.M.–3:30 P.M.; cash payment only. 647 Lincoln Road, Miami Beach 33139; (305) 673-0403; Monday through Thursday, 7:30 A.M.–10 P.M.; Friday and Saturday, 7:30 A.M.–11 P.M. AE, MC, V accepted.

This is the only place we've seen children really enjoy spinach (in lasagna)! The salads and fresh fruit juices and shakes are delicious. Granny's is a great place to stop for lunch if you're on a downtown outing on Saturday—not many places are open, and you'll feel so healthy when you finish your meal. The staff is very helpful with menu selections and special servings for children, so don't be afraid to ask. No high chairs, but booster seats are available.

◆ Gyro King

18315 West Dixie Highway, North Miami Beach 33180. Look for a hot-pink and green building on the east side of West Dixie Highway. (305) 935-9544. Daily, 9 A.M.–5 P.M. No credit cards accepted; checks accepted only when they get to know you.

This open-air eatery has a long counter with stools that older children will enjoy. Whether you eat in or take out, the Greek food and fruit drinks are delicious. Choose from *falafel* (a combination of chick peas, herbs, and spices deep-fried in sunflower oil and served in pocket bread), *gyros* (barbecued spiced lamb served in pocket bread), stuffed grape leaves, *baklava,* or other specialties. The smoothies (chunks of pineapple, banana, and strawberries blended with apple juice) are wonderful.

♦ Hard Rock Café

401 NE Biscayne Boulevard (adjacent to Bayside Marketplace), Miami 33132. (305) 377-3110. Daily, 11–2 A.M. AE, DC, MC, and V accepted.

You'll have no problem finding this restaurant—just look for the 60-foot Fender guitar on top. Finding a table will be much harder at this world-famous burger joint. Children will be amazed to see their parents sing along with the rock music, and parents will wax nostalgic as they tell stories about their rock 'n' roll music heroes. All this and great food, too.

♦ Island Delight

12618 North Kendall Drive, Miami 33186. (305) 598-0770. Monday through Saturday, 10 A.M.–9 P.M. Cash payment only.

Enjoy a meal of delicious Jamaican food at one of the small tables at the back of this grocery store, or take some home with you. Children will like trying the jerk chicken or pork (the meat is shredded and served in a spicy sauce)—just be sure to ask them to serve the hot Scotch Bonnet peppers on the side on your first trip! The food gets good reviews from the large Jamaican population in Miami, and if you choose to eat in, your children will hear English spoken with a different accent.

♦ Johnny Rockets

3036 Grand Avenue (near Cocowalk), Coconut Grove 33133; (305) 444-1000. 7497 North Kendall Drive (in Dadeland, on south side between The Limited and Saks), Miami 33156; (305) 663-8864. Monday through Thursday, 11 A.M.–10 P.M.; Friday and Saturday, 11 A.M.–11 P.M.; Sunday, 11 A.M.– 9 P.M. IGT accepted.

Grab a seat at the counter and watch the chef prepare your burger, fries, and shake. Grilled cheese, peanut butter and jelly, and egg salad sandwiches are the alternatives on the kid's menu. Individual jukeboxes are set up along the counter, so you can choose your music ("La Bamba" is always a favorite), or just listen to the crooning waiters. Call for information about birthday parties.

♦ King's Ice Cream

1831 SW Eighth Street (Calle Ocho and Tamiami Trail) in the Tamiami Plaza, Miami 33135. (305) 643-1842. Daily, 10 A.M.–11 P.M. Cash payment only.

Open since the 1960s, this is a wonderful place to get kids to try new tropical fruit flavors. The ice creams and sorbets are made with natural ingredients. Try their thick, homemade hot chocolate and crunchy *churros,* or the half coconuts filled with coconut sorbet. There are no tables, so plan to walk around or take your treats home. **Tip:** This is a great place to practice your Spanish, but English is also spoken.

◆ Knauss Berry Farm

15980 SW 248th Street (across from Redlands Junior High School), Homestead 33031. (305) 247-0668. Open from Thanksgiving to last week of April, Monday through Saturday, 8 A.M.–5:30 P.M. Cash payment only.

Don't miss a delightful trip to this countrified bakery. They've been selling delicious homemade pies and bread, all kinds of beautiful fresh vegetables, and huge fresh strawberries since 1956. Children may be interested in the staff's clothing (the women all wear long dresses and bonnets); explain that they are members of a Protestant denomination called German Baptists or "Dunkers." **Tips:** Stop here for cinnamon rolls and a fresh strawberry shake, then travel west to the Preston B. Bird and Mary Heinlein Fruit and Spice Park. For more information about the park, see listing in "Exploring Science and Nature."

◆ La Lupita's Mexican Bakery

8 East Mowry Street, Homestead 33030. (305) 248-7165. Daily, 7 A.M.– 5 P.M. Cash payment only.

Freshly baked *pan dulce* and giant Mexican-style cookies make this a tempting stop. The sweet rolls are not really that sweet, but they are delicious with a hot chocolate or a cup of *café con leche*.

◆ La Rosa Bakery

4259 West Flagler Street, Miami 33134. (305) 443-2113. Monday through Saturday, 7 A.M.–8 P.M.; Sunday, 7 A.M.–5 P.M. Cash payment only.

This is an excellent bakery where you'll find all kinds of Cuban and Latin goodies. They also have an amazing collection of plastic miniature cartoon figures to use on birthday cakes or cupcakes. Order a theme cake for a party, or buy the miniatures and come up with your own creation.

◆ Las Tapas

401 Biscayne Boulevard (near flag entrance to Bayside Marketplace), Miami 33132. (305) 372-2737. Sunday through Thursday, 11 A.M.–midnight; Friday and Saturday, 11 A.M.–1 A.M. Major credit cards accepted.

Little dishes (*tapas*) of Spanish-style foods can make a wonderful meal for both children and adults. Spicy sausages, fried calamari, Spanish omelettes, and seafood sauteed in garlic butter are favorites. You can choose several *tapas* from the menu to make a meal everyone shares. The black bean soup comes with a dish of white rice—children can make a meal of this by adding a few bites of what the adults order.

◆ Los Ranchos

135 SW 107th Avenue (original location), Sweetwater 33165; (305) 221-9367. In main building at Kendall Town & Country Mall (near Sears), Miami 33183; (305) 596-0098. 401 Biscayne Boulevard, in Bayside Marketplace (North Pavilion), Miami 33132; (305) 375-0666. Next to El Torito in The Falls shopping center at 8888 SW 136th Street, Miami 33176. Monday through Friday, 11:30 A.M.–11 P.M.; Saturday, noon–midnight; Sunday, 1–11 P.M. AE, DC, MC, V accepted.

Los Ranchos serves excellent Nicaraguan-style food, such as marinated beef, thinly sliced fried plantains, thickly sliced and fried sweet plantains, black beans and rice, special sauces (try the parsley-garlic *chimichurri* sauce on your meat!), all in huge portions. Mondays through Fridays, they feature two-for-one specials from 5 to 7 P.M., and live entertainment begins at 7 P.M. There's no children's menu, but waiters are very willing to provide extra plates and even extra rice and beans for toddlers. They have plenty of booster chairs and high chairs.

◆ Meatballs

8800 Miller Road (SW 56th Street), Miami 33165. (305) 598-3200. Lunch: Monday through Friday, 11:30 A.M.–2:30 P.M.; dinner: Monday through Thursday, 5–10 P.M.; Friday and Saturday, 5–11 P.M.; Sunday, 4–10 P.M.

Delicious Italian food is served family-style, so choose appetizer and entree platters (each one serves at least two adults) that will appeal to more than one person in your group. The sauces are seasoned with fresh herbs and make you realize how far canned pasta for kids is from real Italian food.

◆ Miccosukee Restaurant

North side of Tamiami Trail (near Shark Valley entrance to Everglades National Park, about 30 miles west of the Florida Turnpike SW Eighth Street exit). (305) 223-8380. Daily, 8 A.M.–4 P.M. AE, CB, DC, MC, V accepted.

Children will enjoy trying out the specialty foods served here, including Indian fry bread (dough deep-fried in peanut oil), Indian burgers (fry bread stuffed with ground beef and deep-fried), and breaded catfish and

frogs' legs deep-fried in peanut oil. The murals of Indian scenes are interesting, and you may learn a few things while you dine.

After you eat, don't miss spending some time looking for alligators,
turtles, freshwater otters, and several species of birds and waterfowl in the
canal north of the restaurant or in the large pond on the south side of the
highway. Remember to pack the binoculars! For information about the
Miccosukee Indian Village and Airboat Tours, see listing in "On Safari in
South Florida."

◆ Muffin Tin

*12655 South Dixie Highway (in South Park Centre), Miami 33156.
(305) 235-9020. Daily, 6:30 A.M.–2:30 P.M. Personal checks accepted.*

Here's a good stop for breakfast, lunch, or a midmorning snack of
muffins and hot chocolate. For the best service and shortest wait, avoid
arriving between noon and 1 P.M. during the week; weekend mornings are
always busy, but worth the wait.

◆ Mutineer

*U.S. 1 and SW 344rd Street (in Gateway Village, at end of Florida
Turnpike), Florida City 33034. (305) 245-3377. Daily, 11 A.M.–11 P.M.
Major credit cards accepted.*

This upscale restaurant offers delicious seafood from local and international waters, as well as beef. The dinner service includes a children's
menu. High chairs and booster seats are provided. In addition to the Mu-
tineer, Gateway Village includes the Galley, a snack bar that serves fruit
shakes, hot dogs, and more in an outdoor cafelike setting. There is a little
pond outside (complete with ducks and a turtle) between the dining room
and cafe.

◆ Natural Eats

*9477 South Dixie Highway (Dadeland Plaza, across from the last Metrorail
station), Miami 33156; (305) 665-7807. 8720 Mills Drive (Kendall
Town & Country Mall), Miami 33176; (305) 271-7424. Monday through
Saturday, 7:30 A.M.–9 P.M.; Sunday, 10 A.M.–9 P.M. Cash payment only.*

If you or your child are on a restricted diet, or if you just prefer
a more natural, wholesome meal, you'll enjoy this place. The menu of
delicious salads, sandwiches, soups, breads, desserts, and juices includes an
analysis of the calories, carbohydrates, protein, fiber, and grams of fat per
serving. It also provides meal suggestions based on specific diet restric-
tions ("stress control," "sugarless," "low calorie," or "for a healthy heart").

◆ Nature's Garden Bakery

600 Collins Avenue, Miami Beach 33139. (305) 534-1877. Sunday through Thursday, 8 A.M.–5 P.M.; Friday, 8 A.M.–2:30 P.M. Cash payment only.

Children will enjoy trying out different health food selections from this kosher bakery. Special diet meals are available.

◆ 94th Aero Squadron

1395 NW 57th Avenue, Miami 33126. (305) 261-4220. Monday to Friday, 11 A.M.–3 P.M., 5–11 P.M.; Saturday, 5–10 P.M.; Sunday, 11 A.M.–3 P.M., 4:30–10 P.M. AE, MC, V accepted.

Children can watch the airport activities while they eat. They will enjoy putting together their own meals at the lunch buffet and at Sunday brunch.

◆ Oak Feed Restaurant

2911 Grand Avenue (in the Mayfair), Coconut Grove 33133. (305) 446-9036. Lunch: Monday through Friday, 11:30 A.M.–3 P.M.; Saturday and Sunday, 11:30 A.M.–4:30 P.M. Dinner: Monday through Thursday, 5:30–10:30 P.M.; Friday and Saturday, 5:30–11 P.M. AE, MC, V accepted.

If your children cringe at the thought of "health foods," this is a great place to change their minds. The menu is mostly vegetarian but also includes fish and chicken (free range, of course), so there should be something for everyone.

After your meal, wander through the Mayfair, a gorgeous mall featuring exclusive shops, restaurants, movie theaters, and a hotel. Note the incredible tile work (be sure to look under the staircases) and green copper sculptures (even on the elevator doors). You'll also want to browse in the Oak Feed Market next door.

◆ Patacon

7902 NW 36th Street, Miami 33166; (305) 591-8866. 13720 SW Kendall Drive (88th Street), Miami 33186; (305) 382-3717. 6734 Collins Avenue, Miami Beach 33141; (305) 865-5695. Daily, noon–10:30 P.M. MC, V accepted.

Colombian food is what they do here, so start with *patacon pisao*, a plate-sized, flattened, fried green plantain *(plátano verde)* that you spread with a variety of fillings. Or try the *sancocho de cola* (oxtail stew), and add some salsa if it's not spicy enough. Even the beverages are out of the ordinary; try the blackberry juice and milk or the passion fruit nectar.

◆ Picnics at Allen's

4000 Red Road (corner of Red and Bird roads), South Miami 33143. (305) 665-6964. Monday through Friday, 6 A.M.–9 P.M.; Saturday, 6 A.M.– 7 P.M.; Sunday, 6 A.M.–3 P.M. Cash payment only.

If you're looking for a place to drink a thick milk shake or eat a banana split at the soda fountain, Picnics is the real thing. It's been in business over 40 years, and many customers bring their children here and tell them about the times they ate at the same table 30 years ago. Readers of *Harriet the Spy* can watch a dumb waiter in action as orders are sent upstairs. If you sit in the upstairs section the kids can watch their meal being prepared.

◆ Pineapples

530 Arthur Godfrey Road, Miami Beach 33140. (305) 532-9731. Monday through Friday, 11 A.M.–10 P.M.; Saturday and Sunday, 10 A.M.– 11 P.M. AE, IGT, MC, V accepted.

Even junk food junkies will enjoy the Chinese egg rolls and most desserts at this health food restaurant and store. Weekend brunches include Belgian waffles and overstuffed omelettes.

◆ The Pit Bar-B-Q

16400 SW Tamiami Trail (U.S. 41), Miami 33184. (305) 226-2272. Daily, 11 A.M.–10 P.M. Major credit cards accepted.

"Our barbecue comes from pigs that made perfect hogs of themselves." Plan to make a pit stop here on your next trip across Tamiami Trail. Everything's delicious, even the Everglades frogs' legs. This is a serve-yourself-and-take-your-food-out-to-the-picnic-tables kind of place, so come casual.

◆ Pizza Loft

6917 West Flagler Street, Miami 33144. (305) 266-5111. Monday through Thursday, 11 A.M.–11 P.M.; Friday and Saturday, 11 A.M.– midnight; Sunday, noon–11 P.M. AE, MC, and V accepted.

The sign at the top of the stairs welcomes you to the "World's Best Pizza," and it is definitely better than most. Order from the chatty menu to eat in or take out. Choose your favorite toppings for a pizza, or bring them from home if you don't see what you want—the chef will bake them on for no extra charge. Whole wheat crust is available at no extra charge. This is a good place to get the kids to try something a little different from the standard spaghetti and lasagna. The Fugazza Pizza, for example, stuffs lots of cheese, sauce, and onions between layers of thin crust. If you have room for dessert, the creamy, chocolaty, coffee-flavored *tiramisu* is great, but the kids might not like the liqueur, so they should probably stick to the homemade *cannoli*.

◆ Planet Hollywood

2911 Grand Avenue (in the former site of Burdines at Mayfair), Coconut Grove 33133. (305) 448-1700 (Mayfair office). Call for hours of operation. AE, MC, V accepted.

Scheduled to open in June 1994, this is where to come to find out how Mom Schwarzenegger prepares apple strudel for her little Arnold. Arnold and pals Sylvester Stallone and Bruce Willis are among the owners of this movie-themed restaurant chain. If you're in the mood for a movie after your meal, stop by the adjacent 10-screen theater.

◆ Potlikker's

591 Washington Avenue (one block east of Krome Avenue, behind the post office), Homestead 33030. (305) 248-0835. Daily, 7 A.M.–9 P.M. MC, V accepted.

The name comes from "pot liquor," which is the broth left over from boiled greens. Try the "Bahama Mama Sausage" and "Flap Jacks" for breakfast (although the sausage might be too spicy for some). For dinner, tempt your children with fried Okeechobee catfish, or chicken and dumplings, or fresh vegetables and sweet potato pie. Let the Key lime pie thaw a bit before you eat it.

◆ The Rascal House

17190 Collins Avenue, Miami Beach 33160. (305) 947-4581. Daily, 7– 1:45 A.M. Cash payment only.

This landmark Jewish deli is always the same, always busy, and always delicious. If a crowd is waiting outside when you get there, be sure to get in the right line for the number of people in your party. Once you get in take time to read the menu, but if you like corned beef in any form, potato *latkes* with sour cream, New York cheesecake, and crunchy dill pickles, you'll be happy you came. No children's menu, but there are lots of choices they'll enjoy.

◆ Roasters 'n Toasters

11293 South Dixie Highway, Miami 33156; (305) 251-4848; Monday through Saturday, 7 A.M.–7 P.M.; Sunday, 7 A.M.–3 P.M. 2910 NW 79th

Avenue, Miami 33122; (305) 470-9898; Monday through Friday, 7 A.M.–
3 P.M. Major credit cards and local personal checks accepted.

If you've never heard of a bagel ball, rush right over to Roasters 'n
Toasters and try their trademark delight. We even buy them unbaked and
store them in plastic bags in the refrigerator, ready for that moment when
we just have to have some (never just one). This establishment also serves
delicious sandwiches, muffins, and all kinds of flavored coffees. There are a
few seats inside, and takeout is available.

♦ Robert Is Here Fruit Stand

19900 SW 344th Street, Homestead 33034. (305) 246-1592. Monday
through Friday, 11 A.M.–7 P.M.; Saturday and Sunday, 8 A.M.–7 P.M. Local
checks accepted.

In existence for nearly 30 years, this fruit stand has it all: unusual and
delicious tropical fruits, a snack area, and plenty of good advice from
Robert himself. Try a Key lime milkshake or taste a Monstera Deliciosa.
Also, pick up a brochure and check out the handy chart on the back that
tells when fruits are in season.

♦ Romano's Macaroni Grill

12100 SW Kendall Drive (SW 88th Street), Miami 33183. (305) 270-
0621. Monday through Friday, 5–11 P.M.; Saturday and Sunday, noon–
midnight. Major credit cards accepted.

Enjoy but don't fill up too much on the *focaccia,* a flat bread seasoned
with rosemary that you dip in olive oil and freshly grated black pepper.
Everything on the menu is delicious, so plan on visiting often. The individual pizzas, or the one on the children's menu, easily feed two children.
If you like salad, be sure to ask for the Caesar salad—with optional ancho-
vies—with your entree. **Tips:** If you ask for house wine, your server will
bring a full jug and glasses; they use the honor system to charge you.
You'll want to make at least one trip to the restrooms here to learn a little
Italian (lessons play continuously on the restrooms' PA system).

♦ Shorty's

9200 South Dixie Highway, Miami 33156. (305) 665-5732. Daily,
11 A.M.–10 P.M. Cash payment only.

Huge servings of finger-licking good food, served on long wooden
tables, have made this a great place to take the family for barbecue for
many years. Children's menu and booster seats that attach to the tables are
available.

◆ The Soup Exchange

20301 Biscayne Boulevard, North Miami Beach 33162. (305) 936-1930. Daily, 11 A.M.–9:30 P.M. Cash payment only.

If your family loves to graze at one-of-a-kind, all-you-can-eat restaurants, this place is a must. Come hungry to appreciate the tremendous variety of fresh salads, soups, breads, entrees, side dishes (including baked potatoes and corn on the cob), fresh fruit, and desserts. **Tips:** You might want to mention to the kids that this is not a take-out (or a doggie bag) restaurant—what they eat now is what they get. Note also that this place is known in some circles as the "Dress Size Exchange."

◆ Sundays on the Bay

5420 Crandon Boulevard, Key Biscayne 33149. (305) 361-6777. Monday through Saturday, 11:30 A.M.–11:45 P.M.; Sunday, 10:30 A.M.– 11:45 P.M. Major credit cards accepted.

The setting is beautiful here on the key, and the food is delicious. There is no children's menu, but the appetizers make good children's meals. There are lots of boats, pelicans, fishermen, and people to watch during your meal.

Sunday brunch is usually crowded, but the food is good, and the live music is entertaining. Reservations are suggested on the weekends. There are several high chairs and booster seats.

◆ Tiffany's

22 NE 15th Street, Homestead 33030. (305) 246-0022. Monday through Saturday, 7:30 A.M.–3 P.M.; brunch buffet on Sunday, 11 A.M.–3 P.M. Major credit cards accepted.

Dress up for a delightful and delicious experience in cottage dining. The children's lunch menu features ham and cheese, turkey club, and grilled cheese sandwiches, with a side order of salad. The more adventurous might want to try hot crabmeat augratin, or fettucini Alfredo. The breakfast menu includes omelettes, Georgia pecan waffles, peaches and cream French toast, plantation shortcake, strawberry and cream crepes, and more. After your meal you may want to carefully browse in the adjacent antique and collectibles shop.

◆ Uncle Tom's Barbecue

3988 SW Eighth Street (near corner of Tamiami Trail and LeJeune Road), Coral Gables 33134. (305) 446-9528. Wednesday to Monday, 10 A.M.– 10 P.M. Cash payment only.

Uncle Tom (aka Tom Fantis) has been serving delectable barbecued ribs, chicken, and other delicious "down-home" meals since before 1948. Seat yourself in this small, informal, inexpensive eatery. There are booster seats and high chairs, but older children may enjoy sitting at the counter. There is no children's menu, but hot dogs and hamburgers, served in a basket with french fries, are available, and corn on the cob and baked beans can be ordered à la carte.

♦ Unicorn Village Restaurant

3565 NE 207th Street (in the Waterways), North Miami Beach 33180. (305) 933-8829. Lunch: Monday through Saturday, 11:30 A.M.–3:30 P.M.; dinner: Monday through Saturday, 4:30–10 P.M.; Sunday, 4–9:30 P.M. Major credit cards accepted.

The Unicorn Village establishment includes a health food store, delicatessen, and waterfront restaurant. The menu includes such healthy food as tofu lasagna, vegetables, poultry, fish, and several daily vegetarian specials. There is no children's menu, but many of their side dishes would be suitable. High chairs and booster seats are available. If the weather is great, ask for a table on the patio to take advantage of the passing entertainment on the Intracoastal Waterway.

♦ Versailles

3555 SW Eighth Street, Miami 33135. (305) 445-7614. Monday through Thursday, 8 A.M.–2 A.M.; Friday and Saturday, 8 A.M.–3 A.M.; Sunday, 9 A.M.–2 A.M. Major credit cards accepted.

When you visit Little Havana, you might want to plan a meal at what has been called the most famous Cuban restaurant in the country. Lots of mirrors, lights, noise, and delicious food characterize this unique place. *Mariquitas* in *mojo* sauce, pork chunks, black beans and rice, and *batidos* are specialties. High chairs and boosters are available.

♦ Whip 'n' Dip

1407 Sunset Drive (across from Audubon House), Coral Gables 33143. (305) 665-2565. Monday through Thursday, 11 A.M.–10:30 P.M.; Friday and Saturday, 11 A.M.–11:30 P.M.; Sunday, 1–10:30 P.M. Local personal checks accepted.

Ice cream and frozen yogurt creations are served here. One specialty includes whipped fresh frozen fruit with frozen yogurt for a refreshing treat. A few tables and chairs are available.

BROWARD COUNTY

◆ Cami's Seafood Place

7996 Pines Boulevard (corner of University and Hollywood boulevards), Pembroke Pines 33024. (305) 987-3474.

See listing under Dade County.

◆ Cap's Place Island Restaurant

2765 NE 28th Court, Lighthouse Point Yacht Basin 33064. Take North Copans Road exit off I-95; drive east to Federal Highway, turn left; turn right at NE 24th Street (first stoplight) and drive toward the ocean. Follow the restaurant signs. After you park, wait for a boat that will take you to Cap's Island. You can dock your own boat at the restaurant, turning at Marker 69, just north of Hillsboro Inlet. (305) 941-0418. Sunday through Thursday, 5:30–10 P.M.; Friday and Saturday, 5:30–11 P.M. Major credit cards accepted.

This is a fun place to take children for a special occasion (the prices are somewhat higher than most restaurants listed here). Tell them that Marilyn Monroe, Franklin D. Roosevelt, Winston Churchill, Jack Dempsey (and other famous folk that they may never have heard of) have eaten there. If that doesn't impress them, the adventure of getting there will. The food is good, too!

◆ Cheeseburger Cheeseburger

708 East Las Olas Boulevard, Fort Lauderdale 33301. (305) 524-8824. Sunday through Thursday, 11 A.M.–10 P.M.; Friday and Saturday, 7 A.M.– 11 P.M.

Don't you hate having to ask for cheese on your burger, and then having to pay for that slice? At this restaurant you have to request no cheese, and they don't even charge for taking it off. Standard American cheese, spicy jalapeño (which may be too hot for your child), Swiss and cheddar are your choices for whichever burger you order. While you wait, let the kids play Trivial Pursuit with the cards on the table, or use the paper and pencil to draw their dream burger. A simply brilliant touch is the roll of paper towels on each table to keep everyone's face and hands fairly clean.

◆ Grandma's

3404 North Ocean Boulevard (Galt Ocean Mile), Fort Lauderdale 33308. (305) 564-3671. Sunday through Thursday, noon–10 P.M.; Friday and Saturday, noon–11 P.M. Cash payment only.

Indoor seating is available at this old-fashioned ice cream parlor.

♦ Hooper's Choice

1100 Federal Highway (corner of Sunrise Boulevard and Federal Highway), Fort Lauderdale 33309. (305) 760-4393. Open daily, 24 hours a day. AE, MC, V accepted.

Everything is fresh (as opposed to frozen), including the burgers, fries, pizza, roast beef, and other choices.

♦ Joe's 17th Street Diner (aka Joe's Bel-Air Diner)

1717 Eisenhower Boulevard (across from Ocean World), Fort Lauderdale 33309. (305) 527-5637. Daily, 24 hours. MC and V.

The atmosphere is from the 1950s, with a game room, jukebox, and waitresses that look and act like characters from a '50s diner. It's a fun place for families. Burgers, Sloppy Joe Bel-Airs, double decker peanut butter and jelly sandwiches, fresh-baked fruit pies, and other old favorites for a new generation are on the menu.

♦ Jungle Queen

801 Seabreeze Boulevard (Route A1A), docked at Bahia Mar Yacht Basin, Fort Lauderdale 33316. (305) 462-5596. Departs at 7 P.M. for long cruise, 10 A.M. and 2 P.M. for shorter cruises. Adults, $7.50/day, $21.95/barbecue dinner cruise; children under 10, $4.95/day, $21.95/barbecue dinner cruise. Cash or personal checks (from Florida) accepted.

Cruise up the New River, where you'll see everything from plush homes to a bit of the Everglades. The four-hour dinner cruise includes a vaudeville show, a sing-along, and an "all you wish to eat" dinner of shrimp, chicken, and barbecue, served on Tropical Isle (owned by the Jungle Queen organization). On the island you'll tour the Jungle Queen Indian Village, where rare trees and birds may be seen, as well as watch professional alligator wrestlers in action. Birthday parties may be held during the daytime cruise. **Tips:** Reservations recommended. Sails rain-or-shine. Stroller and wheelchair access provided. The dinner cruise may not be appropriate for small children. Gifts, film, and restrooms available. For information, see listing in "By Land, Sea, and Air."

♦ Lou's Pizza and Subs

1547 East Commercial Boulevard, Fort Lauderdale 33316. (305) 491-5600. Monday through Thursday, 10 A.M.–11 P.M.; Friday and Saturday, 11 A.M.–midnight; Sunday, 1 P.M.–midnight. AE accepted.

This small, family-oriented restaurant provides good Italian-style food and live entertainment. On Sunday evenings, from 6 to 8 P.M., Chuckles (a clown/magician) performs one-on-one magic tricks and creates balloon animals at table side. Kids really enjoy it!

◆ Mai-Kai

3599 North Federal Highway, Fort Lauderdale 33308. (305) 563-3272. Sunday through Thursday, 5–10 P.M.; Friday and Saturday, 5–11 P.M. Dance performances: adults, $7.95 daily; children 12 and under, free Sunday through Thursday, regular price on Friday and Saturday. Major credit cards accepted.

Children enjoy the Polynesian decor and especially like watching the waterfalls at this five-star restaurant. The best part, however, is the Polynesian dance performance. Sunday through Thursday a children's menu is offered, and on Sunday nights children are treated to a performance just for them. Booster seats are available.

◆ Sadie's

3400 University Drive, Davie 33315. (305) 476-0205. Sunday, 11 A.M.– 8 P.M.; Monday through Thursday, 11 A.M.–3 P.M., 4–8:30 P.M.; Friday and Saturday, 11 A.M.–3 P.M., 4–9 P.M. Fixed rates for adults and children 3 to 10; children under 3 eat free. MC, V accepted.

Many factors combine to make this a great place to eat with children. The "all you care to eat" buffet with a good selection of not-too-spicy food (the salad section includes gelatin), the make-your-own-sundae in the dessert section, the unlimited refills of drinks, and the reasonable prices will encourage you to come here often.

Tips: This is a very popular, crowded place to eat at the peak lunch and dinner hours. Try to come for late lunch or early dinner to avoid a long wait. Also, bring your own baby spoons—they only supply soup spoons.

◆ Shorty's

5989 South University Drive, Davie 33328. (305) 680-9900.

See listing under Dade County.

◆ Spiced Apple

3281 Griffin Road, Fort Lauderdale 33312. (305) 962-0772. Monday through Thursday, 11:30 A.M.–10 P.M.; Friday and Saturday, 11:30 A.M.– 10:30 P.M.; Sunday, 11:30 A.M.–9:30 P.M. AE, MC, V accepted.

Fried chicken, country ham, corn fritters, and deep-dish peach cobbler are a few of the country-style dishes offered in this restored country house full of antiques. They have a license to sell alligator meat, so you'll also find "Cross Creek Gator Tail" on the menu, along with "Frog Legs from the Glades." A children's menu is available for lunch and dinner. Be sure to make reservations, and take time before or after your meal to browse in the country store at the back of the parking lot. Beware if you have small children—there are several "If you break it, you pay" signs.

◆ The Sugar Plum

10137 West Oakland Park Boulevard (Welleby Plaza), Sunrise 33304.
(305) 748-6447. Daily, noon–10 P.M. Cash payment only.

This small, old-fashioned ice cream parlor has a few benches to sit on while you enjoy your frozen treats. New York pretzels and cotton candy are also on the menu. You can order ice cream cakes to go.

◆ Who Song & Larry's

3100 North Federal Highway, Fort Lauderdale 33306. (305) 566-9771.
Monday through Thursday, 11 A.M.–11 P.M.; Friday and Saturday,
11 A.M.–midnight; Sunday, 10 A.M.–11 P.M. Major credit cards accepted.

Part of the El Torito chain of Mexican restaurants, Who Song & Larry's is set up to entertain kids. The tablecloths are large squares of brown butcher paper, and each table has a can of crayons—instant entertainment! It's even okay to draw on the walls! Mariachis play typical Mexican music nightly at 7 P.M.

The food at Who Song & Larry's is bountiful and good—try the lunch buffet that includes chicken and steak fajitas, enchiladas, make-your-own tacos, rice and beans, salad, and tortillas. You can even watch the tortillas being made. Lunch is probably the best time to take small children—there are less people and service is faster, but you won't see the mariachis. **Tip:** Reservations are suggested for dinner and on weekends (the wait can be up to an hour).

◆ Zuckerello's Restaurant and Pizzeria

3017 East Commercial Boulevard, Fort Lauderdale 33308. (305) 776-
4282. Daily, 4–11 P.M. Major credit cards accepted.

Try this family pizzeria for new approaches to pizza. You can choose your favorite ingredients to create a family gourmet pizza, or order ziti, a chicken cutlet, or other items from the children's menu.

≡ PALM BEACH COUNTY

◆ Aleyda's

545 Northlake Boulevard, North Palm Beach 33408; (407) 844-0770.
1890 South Military Trail, West Palm Beach 33415; (407) 642-2500.
1890 Okeechobee Boulevard, West Palm Beach 33417; (407) 688-9033.
Sunday through Thursday, 11 A.M.–10 P.M.; Friday and Saturday, 11 A.M.–
11 P.M.; Northlake location closed Sunday. AE, DIS, MC, V accepted.

The sign above the main entrance proclaims "There's no place like this place anywhere near this place, so this must be the place." If you like Tex-Mex food, Aleyda's definitely deserves a visit. Mexican tile on the floors and walls, arched doorways, Mexican pottery, and flowers create a south-of-the-border look. Aleyda and her staff opened the the Northlake restaurant in 1975, and continue to prepare everything from scratch daily. The menu includes Mexican, Tex-Mex, and South American specialties. The children's menu includes delicious chunky chicken soup and scrumptious *yuca frita,* cottage fries made from yuca. On your way out you can buy a quarter's worth of sunflower seeds to feed to the tropical birds in the foyer.

◆ Boca Diner

2801 North Federal Highway, Boca Raton 33432. (407) 750-6744. Open daily, 24 hours. AE, MC, and V accepted.

Among the standard diner fare on the menu, you'll also find Greek specialties, deli-style sandwiches, seafood, and filet mignon. The children's menu on the placemats comes with crayons to keep little ones busy while waiting for their meal. This is a good place to know about for those days and nights when you need a good place to eat at odd hours!

◆ Bones Family Barbecue

3500 North Federal Highway, Boca Raton 33487. (407) 368-5515. Monday through Thursday, 11 A.M.–9 P.M.; Friday to Saturday, 11 A.M.– 10 P.M.; Sunday, noon–9 P.M. MC, V accepted.

The original location in Illinois opened in 1930, and Bones has been open in Boca since 1983. That's over 60 years of good barbecue, so come hungry. There's no children's menu, but high chairs and booster seats are available.

◆ Boston's Restaurant

40 South Ocean Boulevard (just south of Atlantic Boulevard), Delray Beach 33483. (407) 278-3364. Daily, 11 A.M.–2 A.M. AE, DC, MC, V accepted.

Here's a great place to watch the boats and feel the ocean breeze (the Atlantic Ocean is just across the street!) as you eat fresh seafood or a grilled cheese sandwich. Children will prefer to eat on the outdoor patio and may want hot dogs instead of fish, but there's something here for everyone. The staff really seems to enjoy having children stop by. **Tip:** This is a very popular eating place, so plan meal time accordingly in order to get an outside table.

◆ Cheeseburger Cheeseburger

Mission Bay Plaza, at corner of Glades Road and S.R. 7 (next to Starmaker Family Theatre Co.), Boca Raton 33428. (407) 451-8989. Sunday

*through Thursday, 11:30 A.M.–9 P.M.; Friday and Saturday, 11:30 A.M.–
10 P.M. MC and V accepted.*

See listing in Broward County. For more information about
Starmaker Family Theatre Co., see listing in "Adventures in the Arts."

◆ Hamburger Heaven

*314 South County Road, Palm Beach 33480. (407) 655-5277. From
November through April: daily, 7:30 A.M.–8 P.M. From May through
October: daily, 7:30 A.M.–4 P.M. Closed in September. Cash payment only.*

Everyone in town comes by to enjoy the fresh ground beef burgers.
You can also find sandwiches and salads here.

◆ Island Queen

*900 East Blue Heron Boulevard, Riviera Beach 33404. (407) 842-0882.
Lunch cruises depart Wednesday through Sunday, 11 A.M. and 1 P.M. Dinner
cruises depart the same days at 7 P.M. Cost varies according to cruise; children
under 12 pay half price. MC, V accepted.*

Enjoy a narrated sightseeing cruise along the Intracoastal Waterway
as you dine in an authentic Mississippi paddlewheel steamboat. Cruises
depart from the Phil Foster Steamboat Landing on Singer Island. **Tips:**
Reservations recommended a week in advance. Sightseeing tours also
available Wednesdays at 3 P.M., and at other times on Mondays and
Tuesdays.

◆ Log Cabin Restaurant

*631 North Route A1A, Jupiter 33477. (407) 746-6877. Daily, 7 A.M.–
10 P.M. Breakfast served Monday through Saturday, 7–11 A.M.; Sunday,
7 A.M.–noon. Major credit cards accepted.*

The Log Cabin has been serving barbecue and other specialties (baskets of frog legs or catfish and hush puppies) for a long, long time. High
chairs, sassy seats, and boosters are available, and the menu has several
things that children will like, such as the "Chili Jack," a bowl of french
fries covered with homemade chili. Daily "all you can eat" evening specials are available from 4:30 P.M. The breakfast menu includes homemade
sausage, biscuits, and pan gravy.

◆ Mario's of Boca

*2200 Glaces Road, Boca Raton 33431. (407) 392-5595. Sunday through
Thursday, 11 A.M.–10:45 P.M.; Friday and Saturday, 11 A.M.–11:45 P.M.
Major credit cards accepted.*

Enjoy the delicious salads and hot garlic rolls, but leave room for the rest of your meal, which you order from a seemingly endless menu. Depending on your children's appetite, an individual pizza with their favorite ingredients may be the perfect choice. Lunch at Mario's is a buffet, and endless is the adjective here, as well. Come with a big appetite.

◆ Rizzo's

5990 North Federal Highway, Boca Raton 33487. (407) 997-8080. Open Monday through Friday, 11:30 A.M.–10 P.M.; Saturday and Sunday, 4:30–10 P.M. Early dinner specials, 4:30–6:30 P.M. Major credit cards accepted.

Rizzo's is Boca's oldest restaurant (opened in 1966). The atmosphere is casual but very nice, and a children's menu is available. Meat, fish, fowl, and pasta are their main specialties. Reservations are encouraged.

◆ Spiced Apple

2700 North Federal Highway, Boca Raton 33483. (407) 394-3100.
See listing under Broward County.

◆ Tom Sawyer's Restaurant and Pastry Shop

1759 NW Second Avenue, Boca Raton 33483. (407) 368-4634. Daily, 6 A.M.–3:30 P.M. Major credit cards accepted.

If breakfast is one of your favorite meals (and breakfast is served, along with lunch, until 3:30 P.M. on weekends for all you late risers), you'll want to try this fun place. In addition to the regular menu, breakfast and lunch specials are written on a board each day. Stop in the pastry shop to buy homemade goodies to take home. You might want to tell the children a few tales about Huck Finn, Tom Sawyer, and Becky Thatcher before you go.

◆ Waterway Café

2166 Barnard Drive, Palm Beach Gardens 33410. On the west side of the Intracoastal Waterway and the south side of PGA Boulevard. Turn east off I-95 at PGA Boulevard, turn right just before you cross the bridge on the Intracoastal. (407) 694-1700. Monday through Saturday, 7–11 A.M., 11:30 A.M.–10 P.M.; Sunday, 7 A.M.–11 A.M., noon–10 P.M. Major credit cards accepted.

A splendid view of the Intracoastal Waterway makes this a fun place for children and adults alike. The outside patio is a great choice to sit if your child likes to see bridges, boats, and pelicans while eating. Buffet breakfasts are served from 7-11 A.M. Kid's menu, high chairs, and boosters are available. A reggae band plays on Sunday from 4 to 9 P.M.—it's fun to listen to, but be sure to make reservations to avoid a long wait.

◆ Zuckerello's Restaurant and Pizzeria

2700 North Federal Highway, Boca Raton 33431. (407) 391-9332. Daily, 11:30 A.M.–11 P.M. Major credit cards accepted.

See listing under Broward County.

MONROE COUNTY

◆ Angler's Seafood House

3618 North Roosevelt Boulevard, Key West 33040. (305) 294-4717. Sunday through Thursday, 11 A.M.–10 P.M.; Friday and Saturday, 11 A.M.–11 P.M. AE, MC, V accepted.

Here you'll find fresh seafood and delicious Key lime pie. There are special prices for children's portions, and booster seats and high chairs are available.

◆ BJ's Bar-B-Q Family Restaurant

Mile Marker 102.5, Key Largo 33037. (305) 451-0900. Daily, 11 A.M.– 9 P.M. Personal checks accepted.

As the name says, the specialty here is barbecue. Chicken and fish are also served. A children's menu is available, but side orders (chili, barbecue beans, conch fritters) are good choices for children, too. High chairs and booster seats are available.

◆ Brian's in Paradise

11050 Overseas Highway, Marathon 33050. (305) 743-3183. Daily, 6 A.M.–10 P.M. Cash payment only.

This is a casual, reasonably priced family restaurant. Children's menu, booster seats, and high chairs are available.

◆ Don Pedro Restaurant

Mile Marker 53, Marathon 33050. (305) 743-5247. Open Wednesday through Monday, noon–3 P.M., 5–9 P.M. AE, MC, V accepted.

In this Cuban restaurant, children will enjoy the *picadillo*, chicken chunks, and black beans and rice. High chairs and booster seats are available.

◆ The Eatery

1405 Duval Street, Key West 33040. (305) 294-2727. Breakfast buffet: daily, 8–11:30 A.M.; lunch buffet: daily, noon–4 P.M.; dinner buffet: 5–10 P.M.; early bird prices from 5–6 P.M. MC, V accepted.

The waterfront location is entertaining in itself, but this restaurant also gives children a special price, and they love to put their meal together from the buffet. Prices are moderate for breakfast and lunch, higher at dinner ($13 for buffet).

◆ Perry's of the Keys

Mile Marker 102.5, Key Largo 33037; (305) 451-1834. Mile Marker 82, Islamorada 33036; (305) 664-5066. Mile Marker 52, Marathon 33050; (305) 743-3108. 3800 North Roosevelt Boulevard (Mile Marker 2), Key West 33040; (305) 294-8472. Sunday through Thursday, 11 A.M.– 10 P.M.; Friday and Saturday, 11 A.M.–11 P.M. Upper Keys locations also serve breakfast 7–11 A.M. Major credit cards accepted.

This local restaurant chain offers delicious, moderately priced food, including a menu of "Lite-Bites" (for children and light eaters), as well as a raw bar and lots of fresh seafood dishes. **Tip:** Lunch is served here until 5 P.M., which is rare throughout the Keys—most places close from 2 to 5 P.M.

◆ Seven Mile Grill

1240 Overseas Highway (Mile Marker 47), Marathon 33050. (305) 743-4481. Friday through Tuesday, 11:30 A.M.–8:30 P.M. Cash payment only.

Stop by this open-air, very casual eatery on the Marathon side of the Seven-Mile Bridge. Try the fish sandwiches and fresh shrimp bisque, and you'll probably be back for more. The Key lime pie and chocolate peanut butter pie are winners, too.

◆ The Sunset Café

Mile Marker 48.5 (in the Buccaneer Lodge), Marathon 33050. (305) 743-9071. Daily, 11 A.M.–9:30 P.M. Major credit cards accepted.

Meals are reasonably priced, and the restaurant has a gulf view. If you're there at the right time, you can join in the nightly sunset celebration. High chairs and booster seats available.

◆ Turtle Kraals

Land's End Village (where Margaret Street meets the Gulf), Key West 33040. (305) 294-2640. Monday through Saturday, 11 A.M.–11 P.M.; Sunday, noon–11 P.M. MC, V accepted ($15 minimum).

This is an informal eatery where kids can eat, learn, and have fun at a very reasonable price (unlike most area restaurants!), for it's a place where injured sea turtles are brought for recovery. Live loggerheads are kept in tanks and in a small, enclosed bay—your young ones may enjoy watching these creatures more than eating their sandwiches (the fresh seafood and imported beer will appeal to the adults in the group). Don't miss the touch tank as well.

By the way, *kraal* comes from a Dutch/South African word that originally meant "enclosure for livestock." The enclosure here was once used as a holding pen for turtles before they were shipped off and slaughtered for soup. Now it serves the opposite purpose. For more information, see listing in "On Safari in South Florida."

◆ Whale Harbor Inn

Mile Marker 83.5 (at the Whale Harbor Docks), Islamorada 33036. (305) 664-4803. Tuesday through Saturday, 4:30–9:30 P.M.; Sunday, noon–9 P.M. MC, V accepted.

The menu features delicious fresh seafood and Key lime pie. A buffet is served upstairs; the regular menu is available downstairs, where a children's menu and high chairs are available.

◆ The Wharf and Shucker's Raw Bar

Mile Marker 24, Summerland Key 33042. (305) 294-8882. Shows at 10:30 A.M. and 12:30, 2:30, and 4:30 P.M.; dolphin shows: adults, $4; children, $2.50. MC, V accepted.

Formerly the home of Flipper's Sea School, this is now a great place for a meal with children. There are two restaurants here: The Wharf, open for fine dining in the evening, and Shucker's Raw Bar, with an inexpensive lunch and dinner menu. There's no children's menu, but hot dogs and other snack foods are available for kids to eat as they watch the sea lions (dolphins can only be seen during the show). There are no high chairs, but booths are located inside and picnic tables and umbrella tables are outside.

GLOSSARY OF SPANISH TERMS

When you feel adventurous enough to try one of South Florida's many Latin American and Spanish restaurants, but you don't speak Spanish, you and your children may want to look over this list of foods before trying out one of the many Latin American eateries described earlier in this chapter. Some restaurants provide English menus, and occasionally there is an English description of the dish, but it's fun to try to order in Spanish.

Arroz con pollo A mixture of saffron-seasoned rice and chicken decorated with peas and pimentos.

Batido A milkshake, often made with fresh tropical fruit.

Bollos Similar to hushpuppies, but made with ground black-eyed peas instead of cornmeal.

Brazo gitano Jelly roll–type dessert filled with liqueur-laced whipped cream.

Café cubano Strong black coffee, sweetened with lots of sugar and served in tiny cups. Usually served with a glass of water. Drink that first to prepare your stomach, and be prepared to feel very awake (it's delicious, but don't order two—you'll be awake all night!). This is what you see people selling and drinking in little plastic cups at take-out windows outside many Cuban restaurants and newsstands.

Café con leche "Coffee with milk," usually comes with a cup of hot milk and a small pitcher of Cuban coffee. Most places serve it already sweetened, so try it before you add more.

Caldo gallego Thick Basque soup made with white beans, sausage, and ham.

Carambola Yellow star-shaped fruit, usually served in slices.

Chimichurri Sauce made with garlic, parsley, vinegar, basil, and other spices. Served on grilled meat in many Central and South American restaurants.

Churros Deep-fried lengths of dough made of yuca (a potato-like vegetable), sprinkled with sugar and served hot. *Delicioso!*

Coquitos Macaroon-type pastries found in Cuban bakeries (*pastelerias*).

Cortadito Half a cup of hot milk mixed with half a cup of Cuban coffee.

Empanada Turnover filled with meat, potatoes, or other ingredients; varies according to nationality.

Fabada asturiana Thick Basque soup made with white beans and sausage—can be a meal in itself.

Granizado Snowcone flavored with tropical fruit syrup. Often sold from carts.

Lechon Pork roast, usually seasoned with garlic and sour oranges.

Maduros Very ripe, sweet plantains, sliced and fried. Often served as a side dish with black beans and rice.

Mamey Large brown fruit with sweet, rose-colored, avocado-like flesh; delicious in a *batido.*

Mariquitas Thinly sliced plantains, deep-fried and lightly salted.

Medianoche Sandwich made with sliced ham and cheese on a Cuban roll and heated until cheese melts.

Mojo A sauce made with sour orange, garlic, and other spices.

Moros Black beans, sometimes served in a thick soup along with white rice. You can pour the beans over the rice or eat them separately.

Moros con cristianos Literally "Moors and Christians," a mixture of black beans with white rice.

Paella A mixture of saffron-seasoned rice, seafood, sausage, chicken, rabbit, and vegetables.

Palomilla Thinly sliced steak (sometimes called "minute steak") that fills your plate, usually served with french fries.

Pastelito A flaky pastry filled with cream cheese (*queso*), guava paste, coconut (*coco*), or a meat mixture.

Picadillo Mixture of ground beef, capers, raisins, and spices in a sauce; served with white rice.

Ropa vieja Meaning "old clothes," the shredded beef looks like rags (ask your kids why they think it's called "old clothes") and is mixed with vegetables in a stew.

Tostones Thick slices of plantain, flattened, fried, and lightly salted.

Tres Leches Rich dessert made with a sponge-cake base soaked in a sweetened condensed milk mixture and topped with merengue and maraschino cherries.

BY LAND, SEA, AND AIR

Discover the treasures of South Florida by land, sea, and air. The following list gives you an overview of the endless possibilities for touring; choose from trolleys, airboats, helicopters, paddleboats, balloons, and more. (We've even included some places that *host* unusual tours.) Not all tours may be appropriate for young children, but older children may find it exciting and a change of pace to hear a guide explain about a certain attraction. Set up your child with binoculars, a map, and a camera…and play tourist, whether you're visiting from out of town or you live in a nearby neighborhood.

DADE COUNTY

◆ Agricultural Guided Tour

Farmer's Market, 300 Krome Avenue, Florida City 33034. Mailing address is 101 Gateway Estates, Florida City 33034. (305) 248-6798. Tours leave at 9 A.M. and 1:30 P.M. Adults, $8; children 12–18, $5. Group rates available.

Visit the southernmost farming area of the continental United States during the winter production months, from December 1 to April 1. Since 1977, this three-hour lecture and bus tour (popular with tourists and local residents alike) looks at the reasons why Dade County is among the top five counties in the United States for winter vegetable production and is the leading county for producing tropical fruit crops. A film describing the geology of the area, irrigation techniques, and more is shown to visitors. Children over the age of 10 may get off the buses to get a closer look at wells, machinery, and banana groves, or to pick a sample of vegetables in season. **Tips:** The bus is not easily accessible for wheelchairs or strollers. Florida state law prohibits children under the age of 10 from entering produce fields. There is a Farmer's Market restaurant at the entrance.

◆ Art Deco Tour

(305) 672-2014. Call for meeting spot. Saturdays, 10:30 A.M. Cost is $6 per person.

Offered on Saturday mornings through the Miami Design Preservation League, this wonderful 90-minute walking tour of the Art Deco

District gives you insight into the architecture of the 1920s and 1930s. Since this is now an extremely popular spot for tourists, models, movie stars, and musicians, you may want to bring your camera and an autograph book along! **Tips:** Groups can request tours at other times. Call for information. Since this tour is not recommended for young children, perhaps you could stop by the Art Deco Welcome Center and pick up a map and information to conduct your own walking tour of the area. For more information, see listings in "Tracing the Past," and "Mark Your Calendar."

◆ Carnival Cruise Lines

Departs from Port of Miami. Mailing address is 3655 NW 87th Avenue, Miami 33178-2428. (305) 599-2600 in Dade County, (800) 325-1214 in Florida, (800) 377-7373 nationwide. Cruises start at $349, plus port charge for a three-day cruise.

Most of the Carnival Cruise Lines' ships offer "Camp Carnival Programs" for children on board. Cruises head to the Bahamas, the Caribbean, and Mexico. Activities start with a special breakfast for children and the ship's crew. Activities last throughout the day and include such fun things as scavenger hunts, pizza pig-outs, fun club movies, "coketail" parties, and arts and crafts projects. Counselors and staff have teaching experience and know how to plan fun and educational activities for children. Evening babysitting is available for an additional charge. **Tips:** Not all cruises are appropriate for children. Call for information and recommendations for your family's particular needs.

◆ Catamaran Rides

Docked near Dockside Terrace Restaurant at Bayside Marketplace. Rides leave Friday through Sunday at 5, 7, and 9 P.M. Adults, $10; children, $5.

The 55-foot, 49-passenger *Pau Hana* takes you for rides on Biscayne Bay.

◆ Celebration

Departs from Bayside Marketplace at Miamarina. Mailing address is Celebration Excursions, Inc., 3239 West Trade Avenue, Suite 9, Coconut Grove 33133. (305) 445-8456. Adults, $10; children under 6 admitted free with adult. MC, V accepted. Call for availability.

A cruise in this new 92-foot, air-conditioned luxury yacht will take you through Biscayne Bay, Government Cut, and Millionaire's Row. The daytime cruises are more appropriate for families. Hot dogs and chips are available.

◆ Dade Helicopter Services

950 MacArthur Causeway, Miami Beach 33139. (305) 374-3737. Daily, 9 A.M.–6 P.M. Adults, $49 to $119 per person; children accompanied by two adults pay half price. MC, V accepted.

Fly over Miami Beach, Port of Miami, Virginia Key, and Bal Harbour for a bird's-eye view of the city and an experience you'll never forget! There is no age restriction on these flights.

◆ Dade Heritage Trust

Historic Preservation Center, 190 SE 12th Terrace, Miami 33131. (305) 358-9572.

Call the office or stop by to pick up their excellent materials designed to help children and adults get to know Dade County as it once was. The friendly staff is willing to help you provide age-appropriate outings that introduce children to the history around them. If you are interested in exploring old Dade County sites (rather than just driving past them), the staff can arrange tours for children ages 1 and older. They request that groups have at least 10 people. A coloring book for younger children, a preservation activity book for older children, and other materials describing Dade County's historic sites are available at the office. For more information, see listing in "Tracing the Past."

◆ Discovery Cruises

Port Everglades, Fort Lauderdale. (800) 937-4477. Prices vary for day cruises; call for times, destinations, and prices.

Sail away for a day to destinations like Freeport in the Bahamas. Children are treated to fun activities like arts and crafts, face-painting, and a tour of the ship. Lockers are available to rent for $6, or you can request a cabin for $15. Special rates are offered throughout the year.

◆ Dolphin Cruise Line

P.O. Box 025420, Miami 33102-5420. (800) 683-7447. Daily, 9 A.M.– 10 P.M. Cost starts at $195 for a three-day cruise. Call for schedule and prices.

Interested in a cruise? Inquire about "Camp Jellystone" activities for children on every Dolphin Cruise. Cruise to such ports-of-call as Blue Lagoon Island, Montego Bay, and the Panama Canal.

◆ Everglades Alligator Farm

40351 SW 192nd Avenue, Homestead 33090. Located at the main entrance of the Everglades National Park. From Florida Turnpike, take Florida City exit and go west on Palm Drive for two miles. Turn left on 192nd Avenue and *head south for four miles to entrance. (305) 247-2628. Daily, 9 A.M.–6 P.M. Tours run continuously. Airboat rides and farm tour: adults, $11; children 4–12, $6; children under 4, free. AE, DIS, MC, and V accepted.*

Whiz through the "river of grass" for half an hour. Watch for alligators, fish, turtles, birds, and other wildlife. A walk through an alligator farm is also included. No reservations are necessary except for groups of more than 15 people. For more information, see listing in "On Safari in South Florida."

◆ Gator Park

24050 SW Eighth Street, Miami 33187. Located 6 miles west of Krome Avenue and 12 miles west of the Florida Turnpike. (305) 559-2255. Daily, 9 A.M. MC, V accepted.

Tour the Everglades by airboat and stop for a snack break—wild boar, gator, and frog legs (among traditional fare) are on the menu. RV camping is offered.

◆ Gold Coast Helicopters

15101 Biscayne Boulevard, Miami 33161. (305) 940-1009. Daily, 9:00 A.M.–5 P.M. $60–$170 for 10 to 60 minutes. AE, MC, V accepted.

Routes can take you above the Miami Beach coastline, over the Everglades, or above the homes of stars. Only two passengers (plus pilot) per flight.

◆ Gondola Rides

Depart from center of Bayside Marketplace. $5 per person ($20 minimum).
Glide along the bay in an Italian-style gondola.

◆ Heritage of Miami

Docked at Bayside Marketplace, Miamarina. (305) 442-9697. Departs three times daily from September to May. Call to check daily schedule. Adults, $10; children under 12, $5. Personal checks accepted.

If a trip on a tall ship sounds exciting, you might try this 85-foot, steel-topsail schooner. Up to 49 passengers at a time can enjoy the two-hour cruise on Biscayne Bay. Bring your own food if you wish; snacks, soft drinks, and ice are available on ship. **Tips:** Birthday parties can be held on board for a minimum of $120; you bring the party supplies, they supply the boat and the bay!

◆ Historical Tours of Dade County

(305) 375-1625.

Paul George, a well-known historian and assistant professor at Miami-Dade Community College, conducts Saturday morning walking and boating tours that describe Dade County history. He includes such places as Calle Ocho, Coral Gables, and Coconut Grove. For more information about South Florida's history, see listing for Historical Museum of Southern Florida in "Tracing the Past."

◆ Horse-Drawn Carriage Rides

Depart daily from south end of Bayside Marketplace. $5 per person for short rides; $10 for long rides. Children, $3.

Children always enjoy horses, and this is a novel way to see them in action, and to see Miami as well.

◆ Metro-Dade Aviation Department

Mailing address is Miami International Airport, P.O. Box 592075, Miami 33159. Marketing and Communications, (305) 876-7017. Monday through Friday, 9:30 and 10:00 A.M. Free public service of Aviation Department.

Miami International Airport is one of the world's largest and busiest airports, with air services provided by over 100 airlines. Over 1,300 daily flights come and go from Miami. With all this activity, a trip around the airport is sure to be exciting for children. This 90-minute to two-hour tour takes kids onto the air field to watch takeoffs and landings, fueling of the planes, and cargo and baggage loading. They also tour the fire rescue area and the terminal building, where they stay in the international area in hopes of entering a major airline's plane. Children touring this facility are expected to behave responsibly and respectfully, as they will enter restricted areas of operation.

Tours are geared toward the children's particular age group. For preschoolers or groups wishing to avoid the hustle and bustle of the airport, the Aviation Department will bring slide presentations to groups. Coloring books are given as a token of the trip, and groups can request a lunch stop at the Burger King located within the airport; call for cost. **Tips:** Tours are only for groups of 10 to 40 people. Make reservations well in advance. Recommended for children ages 5 and up.

◆ Metromover

Twelve downtown stations along a 1.9-mile loop track. Connects with Metrorail at Government Center station. Monday through Friday, 6:30 A.M.–9 P.M.; Saturday, 8:30 A.M.–11 P.M.; Sunday, 8:30 A.M.–6:30 P.M. Extended service for some special events. Fare, $.25. Transfers available.

Ride 25 feet above the ground for a quick tour of downtown Miami, or to get to such places as Bayside Marketplace, Gusman Center for the Performing Arts, and other downtown destinations. Your ride is free if you transfer from Metrorail. It takes approximately 15 minutes to complete the loop! (New stops were added in 1993.)

◆ Metrorail

There are 20 stations along the 21-mile track that extends from Dadeland in Kendall to Okeechobee. Schedule and transfer information, (305) 638-6700; Maps-by-Mail, (305) 654-6033. Daily, 5:30 A.M.–midnight. Extended service for some special events. Full fare, $1; reduced fare, $.60. (Reduced fare available for seniors, students, children, and handicapped persons, but a pre-paid permit is required.) Change machines are available at the stations.

Local residents and tourists alike can get an overview of the Miami area, or they can get to places such as the Center for Fine Arts, Vizcaya, the Museum of Science and Space Transit Planetarium, and the Hialeah Racetrack by taking Metrorail. Children enjoy seeing the cars, buses, boats, houses, and more from above, and everyone will appreciate the air-conditioned and comfortable ride.

Strollers can be used on Metrorail, but they should be folded up during peak periods. Elevators are available to get to the platforms.

Transit Agency personnel suggest always holding the hands of small children when entering and leaving the vehicles. Step on and off together. Please remember that the platform is a dangerous area; keep your children behind the lines painted on the floor and away from the tracks at all times.

◆ The Miami Herald Publishing Company

One Herald Plaza, Miami 33132. (305) 350-2111.

Tour this Pulitzer Prize–winning newspaper facility. Call for information and ask about their program called "Newspapers in Education," which provides teachers with classroom materials.

◆ Miccosukee Indian Village and Airboat Tours

Miccosukee Reservation, U.S. 41 (Tamiami Trail). (305) 223-8380. Continuous tours daily, 9 A.M.–5 P.M. $5 for 15 minutes; $6 for 30 minutes. Children under 3, free. Cash payment only.

Both the short (15-minute) and long (30-minute) tours include a fast trip through the canals and over the "river of grass," where alligators, wading birds, and other wildlife can be seen. The long tour makes a 10-minute stop at an Indian camp on an island in the Everglades. **Tips:**

Rides are very noisy and may bother small children; cotton ear plugs are provided. Be sure to call in advance to confirm that the rides are being offered, as they are suspended when the water level in the Everglades gets too low. For more information, see listing in "On Safari in South Florida."

◆ Nikko Gold Coast Cruises

Haulover Park Marina, 10800 Collins Avenue (one mile south of 163rd Street), Miami Beach 33154. (305) 945-5461. Daily, 8:30 A.M.–5 P.M. Cost varies according to tour. Rainchecks available. Major credit cards accepted.

Two 150-passenger boats travel down the Intracoastal Waterway to Biscayne Bay to give you a peek at such sights as Millionaire's Row, Bayside Marketplace, Seaquarium, Vizcaya, Fort Lauderdale, and the Everglades. Tours are fully narrated. The seven-hour tour package may include stops at Seaquarium, Bayside, or Vizcaya. The trip from Fort Lauderdale includes a stop at an Indian village. **Tips:** Arrive 30 minutes prior to departure time. Snack bars and restrooms are available on board. Stroller and wheelchair access provided. Not recommended for restless children.

◆ Old Town Trolley Tours of Miami

Bayside Marketplace, 650 NW Eighth Street, Miami 33136. (305) 374-TOUR. Depart daily every 30 minutes, from 10 A.M.–4 P.M., from 14 convenient locations. Adults, $16; discounts available for children. Cash or traveler's checks only.

You'll have seen it all—or almost—after taking one of the tours offered by these popular red trolley cars. Choose from the City Magic Tour or the Miami Beach Tour. Some of the points of interest include Vizcaya, Parrot Jungle, and Calle Ocho. Your driver will point out the history of Dade County in buildings, streets, and even trees. And by the time you're back to your point of origin, you and your child will be ready for a game of "Dade Trivia."

The trolley leaves every half hour from Bayside Marketplace and takes about 90 minutes to complete its loop. You will stop at 12 different locations, where you can hop off, look around, and catch the next trolley that comes by to continue your tour.

◆ Port of Miami

1015 North America Way, Miami 33132. (305) 371-7678.

Known as the "cruise capital of the world," the Port of Miami hosts over one-third of the free world's fleet of cruise ships. All the well-known cruise lines can be seen here. Call for tour information.

♦ Reef Rover IV Glass-bottom Boat

Located at Biscayne National Park, 9700 SW 328th Street, Homestead 33030. Located nine miles east of Homestead at Convoy Point. From the Florida Turnpike Homestead/Key West Extension take Tallahassee Road (SW 137th Avenue) south to North Canal Drive (SW 328th Street) and head east. Mailing address is P.O. Box 1369, Homestead 33090-1369. Tour: daily, 10 A.M.; adults, $16.50; children under 12, $8. Snorkeling tours: daily, 1:30 P.M.; adults, $27.50; children under 12, $13.75. DIS, MC, and V accepted.

A very popular three-hour trip on this glass-bottom boat will give you a first-hand look at scenic underwater reefs. Call ahead for departure times and reservations. Reservations must be made one day in advance for off-shore snorkeling trips that depart daily from the park's headquarters. This trip lasts approximately four hours; rental equipment is included in the ticket price. For more information about the park, see listing in "Under the Sun."

♦ Shark Valley Tram Tours

Located 30 miles west of Miami on U.S. 41 (Tamiami Trail), adjacent to the Miccosukee Indian Village. Mailing address is P.O. Box 1729, Tamiami Station, Miami 33144-1729. (305) 221-8455. Daily. Call for reservations. Cash or traveler's checks only.

Open trams allow tourists to get great photographs of the Everglades and its wildlife. Passengers will cover 15 miles in the two-hour narrated tour, with a stop at a 50-foot observation tower. Bicycles are available to rent. **Tips:** Tours are accessible to strollers and wheelchairs. Reservations recommended December through March.

♦ Tropical Balloons

4408 SW 73rd Avenue, Miami 33155. (305) 666-6645. Weekends only by appointment. $140 per person.

Up, up, and away…this one-hour balloon ride at dawn lets you see the upper keys, Everglades National Park, Biscayne Bay, and downtown Miami.

♦ Water Taxi

Between NE 163rd Street and Shops of Bal Harbour. (305) 545-5051.

Known in Broward County for years, the Water Taxi made its debut in Miami in 1993. The brightly colored 26-foot taxi carries 25 passengers through the north Miami waterways. The taxi can pick up and deliver travelers at any safe dock (restaurants, homes, and marinas).

BROWARD COUNTY

♦ Billie Swamp Safari and Camping Village

Located off Alligator Alley (I-75) at exit 14 at the Seminole Indian Reservation. Drive north on Snake Road for 18 miles to the Big Cypress Seminole Indian Reservation and look for signs. (813) 983-6101; (800) 949-6101. Admission only: adults, $4; seniors, $2.50; children 12 and under, $1; Day trip or night tour: adults, $30; children 12 and under, $20.

Conquer the Everglades! Here's an opportunity for visitors to get to know the Everglades and Native American lifestyles and culture. Take a day trip or night tour that includes an orientation to the Everglades, meals, a 90-minute safari, and use of recreational facilities. The safari guide (on a four-wheel-drive all-terrain vehicle) takes passengers along rugged trails, marshes, and prairies looking for wildlife. Be sure to bring binoculars, camera, and water! While on the reservation, visitors can bird-watch, practice archery, hike, and canoe. Meals are served in a meeting-house-type restaurant, where displays of arts and crafts and Indian artifacts are displayed. Food choices include barbecued meats, hamburgers, frog legs, alligator, stew, and vegetables. Overnight stays are available and reservations must be made. Campers sleep on bunks in screened-in chickee-style bungalows and have use of a bath house. Campfire programs and alligator wrestling are on the ticket. For information about the Ah-Tha-Thi-Ki Museum, see listing in "Tracing the Past."

♦ Carrie B

SE Fifth Avenue and North New River Drive, Fort Lauderdale. Departs from Riverwalk on the New River. (305) 768-9920. Daily, 11 A.M., 1, and 3 P.M. Adults, $7.95 plus tax; children under 12, $3.95 plus tax.

Take a 90-minute narrated tour on a 19th century riverboat replica. Highlights include Millionaire's Row, Port Everglades, naval ships, and more. Food and drinks are available.

♦ Everglades Holiday Park and Campground

21940 Griffin Road, Fort Lauderdale 33332. Located at the eastern entrance of the Everglades, west of U.S. 27 and Fort Lauderdale. (305) 434-8111 in Broward. Park: free; open 24 hours a day. Airboats and alligator wrestling: adults, $12.50 plus tax; children 4 to 11, $6.25 plus tax; children 3 and under, free. Airboats run daily, 9 A.M.–5 P.M. MC and V accepted.

Take a fully narrated, 45-minute airboat tour of the Everglades at this park. Other offerings include bird-watching, fishing, picnicking, and camping. Group rates and private airboat tours are available. For more information about the park, see listing in "Under the Sun."

♦ Fort Lauderdale Sun-Sentinel

333 SW 12th Avenue, Deerfield Beach 33441. Located west of I-95 at the Hillsboro Boulevard exit. (305) 425-1076; (407) 243-6575.

Learn about the newspaper business in this interesting tour of the production facilities of this hometown paper. Children ages 6 and older and adults will enjoy walking through the facilities for a first-hand look at today's news.

♦ Hibiscus Tours

1848 SW 24th Avenue, Fort Lauderdale 33312. (305) 792-5518. Daily, 8:30 A.M.–1 P.M. Adults, $22; children under 12, $20. Cash payment only.

The tour bus picks up passengers from several hotels along Fort Lauderdale Beach. The tour includes a 45-minute airboat ride, an animal and alligator show, a trip to a working orange grove, and a stop at Everglades Holiday Park. Make reservations at your hotel, or call for information. Snacks and restrooms are available at most tour stops.

♦ Jungle Queen

801 Seabreeze Boulevard (Route A1A), Bahia Mar Yacht Basin, Fort Lauderdale 33316. (305) 462-5596 in Fort Lauderdale; (305) 947-6597 in Miami. Daily, 10 A.M., 2, and 7 P.M. Prices vary. Call for information.

Roving the waterways for over 45 years, this riverboat takes you on a three-hour tour to various locations, including Bayside Marketplace. The popular daytime cruise stops at an Indian village for an alligator wrestling show. For more information, see listing in "Come and Get It!"

♦ Las Olas Horse and Carriage

Catch them at corner of East Las Olas Boulevard and SE Eighth Avenue, or wherever you see them along their route in downtown Fort Lauderdale. (305) 763-7393. Tuesday through Sunday, 7–11:30 P.M. Twenty-minute New River ride: adults, $8; children, half price. Thirty-minute ride through Colee-Hammock Park (old residential area): adults, $12; children 4 to 10, half price. Cash payment only.

Children and adults will enjoy this novel way to see Fort Lauderdale. If you come without the kids, bring your own champagne—they'll provide the glasses. Doors on the carriage provide extra safety for children on board.

♦ Lolly the Trolley

A1A south of Las Olas Boulevard, Fort Lauderdale. (305) 768-0700.
Daily, 9:45, 11:45 A.M., and 2 P.M. Adults, $10; children 6 to 12, $5.

Tour Fort Lauderdale in an open-air trolley car.

♦ *Miss Ocean World*

1701 SE 17th Street Causeway, Fort Lauderdale 33316. Located at Ocean
World. (305) 525-6612. Daily at 12:30, 2:50, and 5:05 P.M. Adults, $6
plus tax; children 4 to 12, $5 plus tax; under 4, free. DC, MC, and V
accepted.

This one-hour trip up the Intracoastal Waterway to Port Everglades
is offered three times daily. A ride on *Miss Ocean World* is offered to visitors of Ocean World for an additional charge. A snack bar is on board the
double decker, 99-passenger tour boat. For more information about Ocean
World, see listing in "On Safari in South Florida."

♦ *Paddlewheel Queen*

2950 NE 32nd Avenue, Fort Lauderdale 33316. (305) 564-7659. Lunch
cruise, daily, 1 P.M. $14.95.

Take the lunch cruise on this popular riverboat to see the sights while
you savor your meal. A trip up the Intracoastal Waterway is planned
daily.

♦ Port Everglades

Take I-95 to I-595 to Port Everglades exit and follow signs east. (305)
523-3404.

This is the second busiest cruise port in the world, next to the Port of
Miami. Nearly 2 million passengers a year sail from this 2,100-acre sea-
port on over 23 major cruise lines. If a naval vessel or freighter happens to
be docked when you drive over for a look, you might get to hop aboard
and sneak a peek. This is just by chance, but it's worth investigating.

♦ Pro Diver II

Bahia Mar Yacht Basin on A1A (just south of Las Olas Boulevard),
Fort Lauderdale. (305) 467-6030. Departs Thursday through Saturday,
9:30 A.M.; Sunday, 2 P.M. Adults, $15; children under 12, $10; under 5,
free. Adult snorkelers (equipment included), $20; children under 12, $15.
Cash only.

A daily glass-bottom boat trip to Fort Lauderdale's Twin Ledges coral
reef (off the beach near the Sheraton Yankee Trader) gives adults and

children a chance to view the underwater world, either through the boat's glass bottom or "up-close and personal" with snorkeling equipment. The two-hour trip gives passengers a look at the Intracoastal Waterway, Port Everglades, and the reefs and fish of the Atlantic Ocean a half-mile offshore. **Tips:** Parking available in the Bahia Mar parking lot. Pro Dive shop will stamp parking ticket for discount. Food and drinks are available.

♦ Rickshaw Express

Downtown Fort Lauderdale. (305) 522-4640. Weekends only: Friday, 6 P.M.–midnight; Saturday, noon–midnight; Sunday, noon–9 P.M. Twelve-minute ride: adults, $3; children, $1.50. Twenty-five-minute ride: adults, $6; children, $3. Cash payment only.

This is a fun way to see the sights of downtown Fort Lauderdale. And part of the fun is in walking downtown and waiting for the rickshaws to come by.

♦ Sawgrass Recreation Park

5400 North U.S. 27, Fort Lauderdale. Mailing address is P.O. Box 291620, Fort Lauderdale 33329. (305) 389-0202 or (800) 457-0788. Tours: daily, 9 A.M.–5 P.M. Adults, $12; children 6 to 12, $6.50; children under 6, free. Fishing: daily, 6 A.M.–6 P.M. DIS, Honor, MC, and V accepted.

Allow at least 90 minutes for this three-in-one tour presentation, featuring an airboat ride, reptile exhibit, and Florida Indian Village. Each phase of the tour is 30 minutes. Alligators, crocodiles, and snakes are highlighted in the reptile exhibit. The 18th century Indian Village explores the history and culture of native Floridians. A cookhouse offers hot and cold sandwiches and "Gator Tidbits." Camping facilities can be reserved. For fishing information, see listing in "On Your Mark, Get Set, Go!"

♦ Water Taxi

1900 SE 15th Street, Fort Lauderdale 33316. (305) 565-5507. One-way taxi service: adults, $5; children 12 and under, $3. Roundtrip: $10 per person. All-day pass: adults, $13; children, $9. Cash only.

Call from any waterside location along the Intracoastal Waterway between Commercial Boulevard and Port Everglades, or from the New River to downtown, and this bright yellow taxi with a surrey on top will take you to your destination. Any place with a dock will do. A 30-minute, narrated eco-float tour of the New River is offered on weekends every 30 minutes between 11 A.M. and 5 P.M. Adults, $3; seniors, $2.50; children, $2. To participate on this trip, meet at the Performing Arts dock. **Tips:** Allow about 30 minutes for the taxi to pick you up, and remember that water conditions may affect travel time.

◆ Water Tours of the New River

(305) 463-4431. Saturdays. $16 per person. Call for times, reservations, and meeting place. MC, V, and personal checks accepted.

Hosted by the Fort Lauderdale Historical Society, this narrated tour of the New River is offered on Saturdays for people interested in finding out more about the river and its surroundings. At least 10 people must be signed up for the tour for it to be offered. Schools and other groups may request tours at other times. Call for further information.

☰ PALM BEACH COUNTY

◆ Canoe Outfitters of Florida

4100 Indiantown Road, Jupiter 33478. Located at River Bend Park. (407) 746-7053. Monday through Friday, 8:30 A.M.–3:30 P.M.; weekends, 8 A.M.–5 P.M. Prices vary, call for information. Checks and cash only.

See the wildlife of the Loxahatchee River and Jonathan Dickinson State Park—raccoon, otter, opossum, and deer—while you get a workout! Paddles and life jackets are provided, and you can even request a bus pick-up if you run out of energy down river.

◆ Glider Rides of America

Lantana Airport. (407) 965-9101. Call for prices.

Take a ride in a vintage plane or a helicopter for a view of the coast and city!

◆ Hallpatee Seminole Village at Knollwood Groves Airboat Rides

8053 Lawrence Road, Boynton Beach 33032. Located off Lawrence Road, between Hypoluxo Road and Boynton Beach Boulevard. (407) 582-5947; (800) 624-2730. Adults, $5; seniors, $4.50; children 12 and above, $3. Group rates available. MC, V accepted.

Seminole Indian culture is highlighted at this Indian village. Take a tram ride through the citrus groves, walk the paths of the natural jungle hammock, and inquire about airboat rides. Don't miss the alligator wrestling show offered throughout the day! **Tip:** Gift shop, snack area, and restrooms are available.

◆ Loxahatchee Everglades Tours

15490 West End Lox Road, Boca Raton 33434. Located west of the Florida Turnpike off S.R. 7 (S.R. 441), six miles west on Lox Road. (407) 482-6107 or (800) 683-5873. Daily, 9 A.M.–5 P.M.

Get out your calendar and "pencil in" an airboat ride on the "river of grass" for next week. The rides may be noisy, but they are definitely worth a try. Look for alligators, wood storks, anhingas, and other creatures roaming around.

◆ *Ramblin' Rose* Riverboat

Veteran's Park, 801 East Atlantic Avenue, Delray Beach 33483. (407) 243-0686. Adults, $8.95; children, $3.75.

Take a two- to four-hour narrated cruise along the Intracoastal Waterway. Snacks or a pleasurable lunch in the dining room are offered. Reservations are required.

◆ *Star of Palm Beach*

Phil Foster Park, 900 East Blue Heron Boulevard, Singer Island 33404. From I-95 take exit 55 (Blue Heron Boulevard) and drive east four miles. At the east end of the Blue Heron Bridge, turn left into Phil Foster Park. From the Florida Turnpike, take the PGA exit, travel east seven miles and turn right into Phil Foster Park. Look for the large white statue of a sailor. (404) 848-STAR. Costs start at adults, $8.95; children, $4.25. AE, MC, and V accepted.

This 300-passenger Mississippi River paddlewheeler offers such a variety of cruises that it's difficult to list them all. Here are some suggestions particularly geared to families. The Lil' Skipper Sightseeing Specials are offered every Tuesday at 3:00 P.M. The children on board receive a captain's hat, and a child is selected as "Captain of the Day," with special duties and prizes awarded to the lucky winner. Family Dinners are offered Thursday evenings, when a Dixieland band complements the cruise. Special theme cruises are offered on just about every holiday, but those with special interest to children are offered on Presidents' Day (February), Easter, Mother's and Father's days, Fourth of July, Thanksgiving, and Christmas.

◆ Water Taxi

Operates in north Palm Beach County from December to May. (407) 775-BOAT.

Taxi! This is a fun and unusual way to be delivered to your favorite restaurant on the water. Also, there are 30- and 90-minute cruises. Call for information.

 **MONROE COUNTY**

◆ Captain Buddy's Family Fun Trips

Mile Marker 28, P.O. Box 1488, Big Pine Key 33043. (305) USA-3572. Open daily at various times. Cost for adults starts at $29; first child age 5 or under free with adult; additional children pay half price. MC, V accepted.

This customized four-hour tour explores the coral reef and outer islands. Snorkeling equipment is available to rent.

◆ Chalk's Seaplanes

Departs from the end of Duvall Street at Pier House. (305) 292-3637 in Key West; (305) 371-8628 in Dade County; (305) 359-7980 in Broward County. Costs vary from $39.50 to $139.

The famous "flying boats" have been flying over South Florida waters for over 70 years. Water take-offs and landings are exciting for first-time seaplane flyers, and by flying at low altitudes (500 feet), passengers get a bird's-eye view of the water and marine life. Take a tour of Key West or Fort Jefferson National Monument in the Dry Tortugas National Park. Snorkeling can be enjoyed on the Fort Jefferson tour, but you'll need to bring your own equipment.

If you'd like to bring a boxed lunch, sodas will be provided for you on the Fort Jefferson tour. If you'd like to order lunch to go from the Pier House, call (305) 296-4600 to make your request.

◆ Conch Classic Air Tours

(305) 296-0727. $40-$120; children under 2, free. AE, DC, MC, V accepted.

Put on your helmet, goggles, and complimentary scarf to take a flight in a 1987 WACO open-cockpit plane. Fly over Key West to the coral reefs and outer islands. You'll get a great view of the sea life below. Flights last 20 to 40 minutes. Call for reservations and directions.

◆ Conch Tour Train

Departs from Mallory Square and Roosevelt Depot at 301 Front Street, Key West. For information and reservations, 1 Key Lime Square, Key West 33040. (305) 294-5161. Daily, 9:30 A.M.–4:30 P.M. Adults, $11; children, $5. Group rates for 20 or more available with reservations.

This 90-minute narrated ride highlights over 60 historical and unusual sights. Along the 14-mile route you will see such points of interest as the Hemingway House, the Audubon House, Mel Fisher's Treasure Exhibit, Truman's Little White House, and the southernmost point.

Some of the most interesting stories capture the days of pirates, conquistadors, and Old Key West.

♦ Fireball Glass-bottom Boat

Departs from north end of Duval Street. Mailing address is 2 Duval Street, Key West 33040. (305) 296-6293. Open year round, 8 A.M.–sunset. Boats leave daily, 10 and 11:30 A.M., 1 and 2 P.M., and sunset. Additional trips during the winter. Prices vary. Group rates and rainchecks available. MC, V accepted.

Don't forget your camera on this one! During this two-hour trip you'll get a narrated history lesson as you pass by Fort Zachary Taylor, live coral reefs, and shrimp boats. Children can feed the fish off the deck of this 65-foot boat. **Tips:** A water cooler is brought on board and film is available to purchase. There are also two restrooms on board. Strollers may be brought on board. Sunscreen is advisable.

♦ John Pennekamp Coral Reef State Park

Mile Marker 102.5, U.S. 1, Key Largo 33037. (305) 451-1621. Daily, 9:15 A.M., 12:15, and 3 P.M. Adults, $14; children under 12, $9; under 3, free. MC, V accepted.

Cruising by glass-bottom boat lets visitors peek into the underwater world. You'll be sure to see plenty of colorful coral and fish, maybe even a shark! The boat ventures out about eight miles to the coral reefs. Soft drinks are available on board the boat.

♦ Key Largo Princess Glass-bottom Boat

Mile Marker 100, Holiday Inn Docks, Key Largo 33037. (305) 451-4655. Departs at 10 A.M., and 1 and 4 P.M. Adults, $14; children 2–11, $7; under 2, free. MC, V accepted.

This company has been touring the coral reefs since 1953. The trip out to the reefs on this 70-foot motor yacht is about two hours in length. Lobsters, turtles, tropical fish, and sharks are plentiful. The boat can take out as many as 125 passengers, and drinks, snacks, and restrooms are on board.

♦ Key West Seaplane Service

5603 Jr. College Road, Key West 33040. Between Mile Markers 5 and 6. Turn west to bayside and drive past landfill (highest point in the Keys). (305) 294-6978. Departs daily, 8 A.M. and noon. Extra flights on Sunday if necessary. Adults, $99; children 6 and under, $50. AE, MC, V accepted.

This 40-minute, low-flying flight gives you a view of shipwrecks and marine life as it takes you to Fort Jefferson and the Dry Tortugas, located

70 miles west of Key West. You can spend two hours swimming around and exploring the island. A cooler with soft drinks is provided, but take a picnic along. For more information about Fort Jefferson National Monument at the Dry Tortugas National Park, see listings in "Tracing the Past" and "Under the Sun."

◆ Mosquito Coast Kayak Guides

1107 Duvall Street, Key West 33040. (305) 294-7178. $45/day per person.
Older children will enjoy the thrill of using all their senses in this "back to nature" experience. Not only will they hear about their surroundings from a guide, but they'll get to participate in the tour itself! Experience is not necessary. You'll explore mangroves, islands, and the strikingly clear waters off the Keys. Your ticket price includes snorkeling equipment and bottled water.

◆ Old Town Trolley Tours

Old Town Trolley Car Barn, 1910 North Roosevelt Boulevard, Key West 33040. (305) 296-6688. Departs from Mallory Square in Old Town every half hour beginning at 8:45 A.M., with the last tour at 4:30 P.M. Adults, $10; children 4 to 15, $4; children under 4, free. MC, V accepted.
Narrated tours last 90 minutes, but you can get off at any point and rejoin a tour at 30-minute intervals. Over 100 points of interest are covered, and all-weather transportation is provided. Foreign language tours are available. Free parking is also available at the Key West Welcome Center, 3840 North Roosevelt.

◆ Pelican Path

Located in historic Key West 33040. Stop by the Key West Chamber of Commerce at Mallory Square, 402 Wall Street. (305) 294-2587.
This footpath leads hikers throughout historic Key West. Pelican signs point the way. A map is available at the Key West Chamber of Commerce.

◆ Sundiver Station

Two locations: Mile Marker 103 (bayside) and Mile Marker 100 (oceanside), Key Largo. Mailing address is P.O. Box 963, Key Largo 33037. (305) 451-2220 or (800) 654-7369. Daily trips, 9 A.M., noon, and 3 P.M. Cost starts at $19.95 per person. Family rates available.
Snorkeling trips to shallow-water reefs are offered by the crew of the *Sundiver* luxury yacht. Only small groups will be taken out to the reefs. Masks, snorkels, fins, and underwater cameras are available. Safety vests are provided free of charge.

MARK YOUR CALENDAR

Festivals, arts and crafts fairs, annual cultural and sporting events, and musical, historical, and holiday happenings can be opportunities for families to get out and get to know South Florida and each other. This listing is by no means exhaustive; investigate on your own and you'll find that something is happening near you this week. Note that not all listings include addresses, phone numbers, or admission prices. Check your local newspapers for details.

 **DADE COUNTY**

JANUARY

◆ Art Deco Weekend

(305) 672-2014. Free admission.

Relive the 1920s and 1930s in the historic Art Deco District in Miami Beach. Here you'll find period artwork, memorabilia, and collectibles, along with music from the Big Band era and other entertainment. The festival is very crowded, and maneuvering with strollers is difficult. For more information about the Art Deco District, see listing in "Tracing the Past."

◆ Homestead Frontier Days and Rodeo

(305) 247-2332 or 372-9966. Admission charged.

This is the biggest event of its kind in South Florida, with rodeo events, parade, arts and crafts, and food.

◆ Our Lady of Lebanon Lebanese Festival

(305) 856-7449. Admission charged.

As the name implies, you'll find Lebanese foods, live music, dancing, gifts, and an indoor gameroom. Parking is free.

◆ Pig Bowl

Admission charged.

This is the annual police football competition between Metro-Dade/ Miami Police and a visiting out-of-state team, held at the Orange Bowl. Watch local newspapers for details. No strollers allowed.

♦ Redlands Natural Arts Festival
(305) 247-5727. Admission charged.

Held at the Preston B. Bird and Mary Heinlein Fruit and Spice Park in Homestead, this festival's theme reflects the pioneer spirit of the region, with craft demonstrations, foods, clowns, pony rides, and Indian and pioneer exhibits. For more information, see listing in "Exploring Science and Nature."

♦ Ringling Brothers/Barnum and Bailey Circus
(305) 673-7300. Admission charged.

The famed circus comes to town at the Miami Beach Convention Center. Try to get downtown for their annual Elephant Walk.

♦ Three Kings Parade
(305) 856-6653. Free admission.

This parade takes its path down the famous SW Eighth Street as part of the Latin Festival. Enjoy Latin rhythms and colorful floats and costumes. Don't forget to taste the food in Little Havana.

FEBRUARY

♦ Around the World Fair
(305) 854-4247. Admission charged.

Tropical Park hosts this juried art exhibition, along with entertainment, international foods, rides, and a flea market. The Small World children's area includes pony rides, puppets, and face-painting. The fair is sponsored by the Patrons of the Miami Museum of Science.

♦ Black Heritage Celebration
(305) 347-3003 or 347-3007.

Events showcase the history and contributions of African-Americans and take place all month at schools, libraries, festivals, and other locations. Check your local newspapers for event information.

♦ Coconut Grove Art Festival
(305) 447-0401. Free admission.

Each year this event gets bigger and better, but harder to get around with children, especially with strollers. This juried art fair displays excellent work, and the accompanying entertainment in the park by the bay makes this a great way to spend a day.

◆ Doral/Ryder Open PGA Golf Tournament

(305) 477-GOLF or (305) 592-0570. Admission charged.

Here's one of the best known PGA golf tournaments, held annually at the "Blue Monster" course at the Doral Hotel and Country Club. Older children will probably enjoy seeing the pros and celebrities. Usually the first few rounds are free to the public; after that tickets are needed.

◆ Hialeah Spring Festival

(305) 888-8686.

Enjoy 10 days of entertainment at Hialeah Race Track, with ethnic foods, games, rides, and fireworks.

◆ Ryder Pitch, Putt, and Drive

(305) 665-8292. Free admission.

This junior golf competition is for boys and girls ages 17 and under and is located throughout Dade County. Golf clubs are available if needed.

◆ Scottish Festival and Games

(305) 757-6730. Admission charged.

At Crandon Gardens, Key Biscayne, the events include Highland dance, bagpipe competition, and traditional foods and crafts.

◆ Superstars

(305) 579-2676. Free admission.

Watch sports celebrities compete in various events.

MARCH

◆ Arti Gras

(305) 893-6511. Free admission.

Theater, opera, ballet, dance, jazz, puppets, and other children's shows make this a very popular arts event.

◆ Beaux Arts Festival

(305) 284-3536. Free admission.

Beaux Arts is the longest running outdoor arts festival in Greater Miami. Look for art classes in the children's area. For more information, see Lowe Art Museum listing in "Adventures in the Arts."

♦ Carnaval Miami

(305) 324-7349. Admission charged to some events.

Carnaval Miami offers an excellent way to taste the city's Latin flavor. Almost two weeks of events, with 60 stages for music and over 500 food vendors, culminate with "Calle Ocho," the world's largest and most famous block party. Look for entertainment and activities for kids. Events become quite crowded, so use discretion with children.

♦ Dade County Youth Fair

(305) 223-7060. Admission charged.

Begun as a 4-H Fair in 1950, Dade County now hosts the largest youth fair in the country; you'll find a showcase of student projects, plus entertainment, rides, and science and agriculture exhibits at Tamiami Park. A new "agriplex" exhibition hall to house the agricultural division and an arena for horse shows is scheduled to open for the 1995 fair. **Tip:** Discuss and decide how much you want to spend on rides and food before you go.

♦ Italian Renaissance Festival

(305) 759-6651. Admission charged.

A 16th-century marketplace is re-created at Vizcaya, with crafts, merchants, and food. Entertainment includes jugglers, jesters, madrigal groups, troubadours, and a living chess tournament (the players are people!), all in period costumes.

♦ Lipton International Players Championships

Admission charged.

The best tennis players in the world compete on the courts during this two-week tournament at picturesque Key Biscayne.

♦ Miami Grand Prix

(305) 662-5660. Admission charged.

Downtown Miami becomes a race course for the many drivers and spectators from around the world who come for this event. Crowd size makes it difficult to bring young children.

♦ St. Patrick's Day Parade and Festival

(305) 949-8400. Free admission.

This parade down Flagler Street will give you an even bigger excuse to wear green! Enjoy foods, live entertainment, and more.

◆ American Traditions Festival

(305) 347-2582. Free admission.

At Miami-Dade Community College's South Campus, you'll find two days of music, hot-air balloons, ethnic foods, children's games and theater, helicopter rides, and fireworks.

◆ Dade Heritage Days

(305) 358-9572. Admission to some events.

Get to know all there is to know about the place we call home by participating in this month-long celebration of Miami's history. Historic neighborhoods hold festivals, tours, and parades. Events for kids include storytelling, workshops, and some hands-on activities. Organized by the Dade Heritage Trust; for more information, see listings in "Tracing the Past" and "By Land, Sea, and Air."

◆ Oceans Miami/Bounty of the Sea

(305) 361-5786. Free admission.

The Bounty of the Sea Festival offers a month-long celebration with exhibits and demonstrations that help us better understand our ocean, as well as a full lineup of music, children's activities, and arts and crafts.

◆ River Cities Festival

(305) 887-1515. Free admission.

This three-day, five-community event includes bike shows, a dog show, a "chili cookoff," a torchlight parade, a beauty contest, and arts and crafts activities.

◆ Tropifest

(305) 887-8838. Free admission.

Tropical Park comes alive for everyone during this annual sports and arts festival, featuring area celebrities and sponsored by SCLAD (Spinal Cord Living-Assistance Development, Inc.).

MAY

◆ Cornucopia of the Arts

(305) 579-2680. Admission charged.

Young artists and performers are featured in this art show on the grounds of Vizcaya. Enjoy artworks and performances by dancers, actors, youth symphonies, sculptors, and more.

◆ Great Sunrise Balloon Race and Festival
(305) 245-6204. Admission charged for some events.

This event takes place at Harris Field in Homestead, with hot-air balloon races, country and western music performances, and arts and crafts demonstrations.

JUNE

◆ Diabetic Children's Camp
Diabetic Children's Camp, Coral Gables Youth Center, Coral Gables. (305) 285-2930.

Sports, exercises, movies, and arts and crafts are supervised by trained nurses and counselors.

◆ Goombay Festival
(305) 445-8292. Free admission.

The Goombay Festival is one of the largest black heritage festivals in the U.S. This weekend event features Bahamian arts, foods, a colorful parade, and musical entertainment in Coconut Grove. Several blocks of the neighborhood are closed to traffic during the festival.

◆ Hispanic Theatre Festival
(305) 446-7144. Some events are free; call for ticket information; tickets also available from Ticketmaster.

Held annually since 1985, most plays in the festival are for adults, and most are in Spanish. At least one day of plays and other activities for children is scheduled.

◆ Royal Poinciana Fiesta
(305) 371-2723. Admission charged to some events.

For over 50 years, this fiesta has celebrated the blooming of the breathtaking Poinciana trees. A week of events includes a folkloric variety show featuring music and dance from 12 nations, an art exhibition, and a bus tour of areas rich with the red, yellow, and orange blooms of the Poinciana.

JULY

♦ **Bayside Marketplace's Fourth of July Celebration**

(305) 577-3344. Free admission.

Biscayne Bay is the backdrop for this celebration and fireworks display. It's held at the popular Bayside Marketplace, where food and fun go hand in hand.

♦ **International Music and Crafts Festival**

(305) 223-8388 (weekends), 223-8380 (weekdays). Admission charged.

Musicians and craftspeople from many countries around the world share their art, crafts, music, dance, and foods. Held at the covered amphitheater at the Miccosukee Indian Village. For more information, see village listing in "On Safari in South Florida."

♦ **PACE/Hammocks July Fourth Festival**

(305) 382-3377. Free admission.

The area adjacent to Hammocks Junior High School becomes the site of a petting zoo, a children's corner with face-painting and games, dance performances, and plenty of music. This is a great way for the entire family to celebrate our nation's birthday. The event is sponsored by PACE, a nonprofit organization that supports the work of South Florida's performing artists. Traditional fireworks and a special concert are the highlights.

♦ **Pops by the Bay**

(305) 361-6730. Admission charged.

Enjoy this summer concert series at Miami Marine Stadium. It's fun to see the people on the boats who are watching the concert on the barge.

AUGUST

♦ **Lee Evans Bowling Tournament of the Americas**

(305) 652-4197. Free admission.

Amateurs compete from 24 countries. This spectator event may interest older children.

SEPTEMBER

♦ **Catch-a-Cure**

(305) 477-3437.

Adults and children alike can compete in this fishing tournament to benefit diabetes research.

♦ Festival Miami

(305) 284-3941. Admission charged.

Jazz, opera, chamber music, and piano pieces are showcased in this two-week celebration of performing and visual arts, with concerts by University of Miami and international performers. No stroller access.

OCTOBER

♦ Baynanza

(305) 662-4124.

Over a week of celebration and salute to Biscayne Bay. Enjoy music, arts and crafts, seafood dishes, and boating events.

♦ Campus Life Haunted House

(305) 271-2442. Admission charged.

This carnival features shows, magic, and rides, along with a Haunted House at Metrozoo/Gold Coast Railroad Museum. Not recommended for young children.

♦ Electric Island Run

(305) 477-3437.

This 15K race held on Miami Beach is a benefit for diabetes research. Moms and dads can walk in the race with strollers.

♦ Friends of Germany Oktoberfest

(305) 374-7610. Free admission.

Enjoy this German street festival that features music, food, and drink.

♦ Hispanic Heritage Festival

(305) 541-5023. Admission charged for some events.

Celebrate Miami's Hispanic roots with this month-long series of cultural events, which includes a re-enactment at Bayfront Park of Columbus's arrival in America.

♦ Miami Air Show

(305) 685-7025. Admission charged.

Runways become exhibit and display areas, with special entertainment by the U.S. Navy Blue Angels.

♦ Miami Museum of Science Fine Arts Show

(305) 667-0500. Free admission.

There's a new theme each year at this popular and educational museum. Not recommended for young children.

◆ Oktoberfest

(305) 255-4579.

In Homestead you'll find a celebration with folk dancing and German oom-pah-pah bands!

◆ Paella Festival

(305) 347-3205. Admission charged.

This is part of the Hispanic Heritage Festival, held at the Wolfson Campus of Miami-Dade Community College. Enjoy Latin food at its best, prepared in the largest *paella* pans you've ever seen. For a list of Spanish food terms, see glossary at the end of "Come and Get It!"

◆ South Florida Auto Show

(305) 758-2643. Admission charged.

See the latest trends in cars at the Miami Beach Convention Center. The show floor is often too crowded for strollers.

◆ Sunday in the Park with Art

(305) 238-4575.

This family-oriented fine arts show is held at the Charles Deering Estate. Look for the kids' tent, which holds all-day activities and art competitions. For more information on the Charles Deering Estate, see listing in "Tracing the Past."

NOVEMBER

◆ Asiafest

(305) 577-3378. Free admission.

You'll be delighted by the Far East treasures at Bayfront Park, from countries such as Japan, India, China, Korea, Thailand, and Singapore. Highlights include performing arts, cultural and craft pavilions, and distinctive cuisine from each of the countries represented.

◆ Fall Festival at Cauley Square

(305) 258-0011. Free admission.

Fall Festival features over 125 arts and crafts booths and a variety of foods and music. Can get a bit crowded at times. For more information on Cauley Square, see listing in "Tracing the Past."

◆ The Harvest
(305) 375-1492. Admission charged.

Take a walk back in history as you experience this weekend celebration of South Florida's folk culture on the Dade County Youth Fairgrounds. Events include re-enactments and folklife performances and demonstrations. Children will learn firsthand about various crafts such as woodcarving, cooking over a fire, soapmaking, and more. There's lots of music and other forms of entertainment at Tamiami Park. It's put on in conjunction with the Historical Museum of Southern Florida; for more information about the museum, see listing in "Tracing the Past."

◆ Junior Orange Bowl Festival
(305) 662-1210. Admission charged for some events.

Young athletes from around the world participate and compete in this largest sports and cultural festival for children and teens. The eight-week-long event includes golf, tennis, racquetball, gymnastics, cheerleading, football, running, writing, photography, fine arts competitions, as well as sports ability games for the physically challenged. The Junior Orange Bowl Parade concludes the event through the streets of Coral Gables on the Thursday before New Year's Day.

◆ Miami Book Fair International
(305) 347-3258 or call Books and Books, (305) 442-4408. Free admission.

For eight days in the fall, the Wolfson campus of Miami-Dade Community College becomes a mecca for writers and readers of all ages. The Miami Book Fair International, a nonprofit organization, has hosted this week-long event since 1984. On the last three days (Friday through Sunday) you can take young readers to the Children's Alley section of the Book Fair—a wonderful place for kids to explore. Past fairs have included booths with children's books authors, illustrators, and publishers, as well as a petting zoo, a moon walk, train rides, face-painting, puppet shows, arts and crafts, storytellers, mimes, and more.

The "Young People's Crossing" events, such as dance and karate demonstrations, take place in the atrium, and are appropriate for junior or senior high school students.

◆ St. Sophia Greek Festival
(305) 854-2922. Admission charged.

Join this celebration of Greek heritage at St. Sophia's Greek Orthodox Cathedral, complete with food, entertainment, and dancing.

DECEMBER

♦ Christmas at the Biltmore
(305) 445-1926. Free admission.
Celebrate the holidays with a festive flair at Miami's famous Biltmore Hotel. For more information on the Biltmore, see listing in "Tracing the Past."

♦ Christmas Lights at Vizcaya
(305) 579-4626. Admission charged.
Holiday lights trim the trees and gardens around Vizcaya—a magical and simply gorgeous celebration of Christmas.

♦ Fairchild Tropical Gardens Ramble
(305) 667-1651. Admission charged.
Highlights include exhibits by plant societies, sales of rare plants, and foods and crafts relating to plants. Some exhibits and hands-on activities for children are offered. For more information on the gardens, see listing in "Exploring Science and Nature."

♦ Garden Christmas at Vizcaya
(305) 854-6559. Admission charged.
Punch and cookies add a special touch to this great holiday event for kids. Costumed characters and choral groups perform. Stroller access is difficult. For more information about Vizcaya Museum and Gardens, see listing in "Tracing the Past."

♦ Hometown Tree Lighting
(305) 667-5511. Free admission.
A 30-foot-high Christmas tree lights up South Miami. Caroling, candy canes, and a reading of the Nativity story delight children.

♦ Miccosukee Annual Indian Arts Festival
(305) 223-8380 (weekdays), 223-8388 (weekends). Admission charged.
Representatives from nearly 20 tribes gather at the Indian village for song, dance, and performances. For more information, see Miccosukee Indian Village listing in "On Safari in South Florida."

♦ Orange Bowl Festival
(305) 642-1515 or 642-5211, or (800) 634-6740. Admission charged for some events.

Greater Miami's largest festival, which includes over 25 different events, begins midmonth with the Orange Bowl/Rolex International Tennis Championships and the Junior Orange Bowl Festival and Parade. The festival continues with the Orange Bowl Regatta Series and the world's largest nighttime parade (the King Orange Jamboree Parade). Then follows the Fiesta by the Bay, with music, fireworks, and food. The Orange Bowl stadium is the site for (you guessed it!) the Orange Bowl Football Classic, where two of the nation's top-rated college teams fight it out on the turf!

◆ Santa's Enchanted Forest

(305) 226-8315. Admission charged.

Over one million lights cover Tropical Park and convert it into a magical forest. See a laser show, visit a petting zoo, and take your child's picture beside a 50-foot snowman.

◆ Winter Reflections on the Bay

(305) 947-3525. Free; parking fee charged.

Boats decked in holiday lights make their way down the Intracoastal Waterway, taking off from Bayfront Park. Fireworks and live music top off the evening.

BROWARD COUNTY

JANUARY

◆ Gulfstream Park Annual Family Day

(305) 454-7000, in Broward; (305) 944-1242, in Dade. Admission charged.

Youngsters get a chance to saddle up for the day and even try on jockey silks. Watch the horses work out and meet famous jockeys.

◆ Trading Post Days

(305) 524-4736. Free for children.

Come dress up in Civil War–period clothes, make small metal ball bullets over a fire, and learn about pioneer life in South Florida back when Stranahan House, on the New River, in what is now downtown Fort Lauderdale, was a trading post. For more information about Stranahan House, see listing in "Tracing the Past."

♦ Orange Blossom Festival and Pro Rodeo

(305) 581-0790. Free admission.

One of the oldest cultural events in South Florida offers fun for the entire family with a pro rodeo, country fair, parade, street dance, and hot-air balloon race in Davie.

♦ Seminole Tribal Fair and Rodeo

(305) 584-0400. Admission charged.

Alligator wrestling, snake shows, Indian dancers, and craftspeople make up this cultural event. A rodeo features barrel racing, bull riding, calf roping, and steer wrestling. Find wonderful handmade items like patchwork jackets, palmetto fiber dolls, and sweetgrass baskets.

♦ Sistrunk Historical Festival

(305) 765-4663.

Join in the celebration with the ethnic black community in commemoration of Dr. James Sistrunk, Broward County's first black physician. Festival includes art exhibits and cultural contributions from the African-American and Caribbean communities.

MARCH

♦ Art in the Sun Festival

(305) 941-2940. Free admission.

Features work from over 250 artists, plus live entertainment and children's attractions, all in Pompano Beach.

♦ Flamingo Gardens Easter Egg Hunt and Spring Arts Festival

(305) 473-2955. Admission charged.

Children, divided by age groups, hunt for traditional Easter eggs. Arts and crafts are also on display. For more information, see listing in "On Safari in South Florida."

♦ Florida Derby

(305) 454-7000, in Broward; (305) 944-1242, in Dade. Admission charged.

This horse race is held at Gulfstream Park. Activities for children include a petting zoo, a wild animal race, jousting, and music. For more information, see listing in "On Your Mark, Get Set, Go!"

◆ Riverwalk Art Festival
(305) 764-2005. Free admission.
   Bubier Park on the New River is the setting for this arts festival. With a visit to the special "Kids' Art Korner," even the tiniest of visitors can participate in art activities.

◆ St. Patrick's Parade and Festival
(305) 764-4393.
   Wear your green and attend this festive parade in downtown Fort Lauderdale.

◆ South Florida Irish Festival
(305) 429-1542. Admission charged.
   Highlights of the festival include traditional Irish foods, a shoppers' bazaar, a carnival, and arts and crafts activities. Continuous children's entertainment consists of puppet shows, clowns, magic, and sports. Contests are held to determine who has the most freckles or the reddest hair.

APRIL

◆ Fort Lauderdale Downtown Festival of the Arts
(305) 761-5360.
   There are lots of things here for children to enjoy, such as hands-on booths and communal arts projects. Mimes and clowns provide entertainment.

◆ Week of the Ocean
(305) 462-5573.
   In conjunction with National Week of the Ocean, this event is held in various educational settings, with contests, exhibits, and ecology-focused events that children will enjoy.

MAY

◆ Festival of Nations
(305) 527-8489. Free admission.
   Memorial Day weekend is when this family-oriented festival takes place. On the campus of Broward Community College, you will find international foods and performances of all kinds. Over 40 ethnic groups are represented. Children can listen to storytellers, make flags from around the world, and enjoy kiddie rides.

◆ Kite Flight

(305) 477-3437. Admission charged.

On Dania Beach you'll find lots of kites, as children gather for demonstrations and give-aways.

◆ Pompano Beach Seafood Fest

(305) 941-2940. Free admission.

Great way to introduce new food to the children. Sample shrimp, chowders, conch, and other kinds of seafood!

JUNE

◆ Automania

(305) 921-3404. Free admission.

Here's a chance to see classic cars from yesteryear, displayed at Young Circle Park in Hollywood. Entertainment and food booths can be found here as well.

◆ Seminole Arts Festival

(305) 583-2435, 548-0400. Admission charged.

Head to the Seminole Festival Grounds, U.S. 441 and Stirling Road, Hollywood. You'll enjoy intertribal Native American dancing, food, art, and alligator wrestling. The Florida High School Rodeo Association State Championships are also held during this festival.

◆ International Submarine Races

(305) 351-4175. Free admission.

Get over to the Fort Lauderdale beach at the Bahia Mar to watch over 50 teams compete in homemade underwater vessels. They're created by serious engineering students worldwide. Major sponsors include the H. A. Perry Foundation and Florida Atlantic University. Underwater videographers film the races, and you can watch the live action from a large-screen TV on the beach. The competition takes place every other year.

JULY

◆ City of Fort Lauderdale July Fourth Sandblast

(305) 761-5388. Admission charged.

For nearly 40 years, young and old have enjoyed the sand sculptures of "Sandblast." Contests have categories—and winners!—for all ages.

◆ Hollywood Hoe Down

(305) 921-3404. Free admission.

Here you'll find down-home country western fun with hayrides, a petting farm, amusements, and a children's stage area.

◆ Turtle Races

(305) 467-6637. Free admission to race; admission charged for museum.

Watch as 100 turtles race in the Museum of Discovery and Science's Grand Atrium. Bring your own, or borrow one of the free loaner turtles, available on a first come, first serve basis. The goal of the event is to teach the public about turtles and the dangers to them caused by man. For more information about the Museum of Discovery and Science, see "On Safari in South Florida" and "Exploring Science and Nature."

OCTOBER

◆ Fort Lauderdale Oktoberfest

(305) 761-5388. Free admission.

Traditional Bavarian and German food, authentic dancers, and music are all on tap, along with a petting zoo and performances by a children's theatrical group.

◆ Oktoberfest at the American German Club

(305) 967-6464. 511 Lantana Road, Lantana.

NOVEMBER

◆ Broward County Fair

(305) 923-3248. Admission charged.

This traditional county fair at Gulfstream Park has a midway, student exhibits, and lots of music and food.

◆ Florida Championship Rodeo

(305) 797-1145. Admission charged.

In addition to the professional cowboys, watch for pony rides, clogging demonstrations, and even Santa!

◆ Candy Cane Parade

(305) 921-3404. Free admission.

Here's a beachside parade that children can participate in—so does Saint Nick!

◆ Christmas in Old Fort Lauderdale

(305) 761-5360. Free admission.

As the holidays approach, this downtown historical district lights up with Christmas trees and menorahs. Horsedrawn carriages wend their way around the area while carols are sung. Activities to interest children include hands-on art projects, crafts, displays of Christmas scenes from years gone by, and a special puppet show.

◆ Festival of Trees

(305) 525-5500. Admission charged.

Join the Museum of Art for a holiday display of designer Christmas trees. Serenades, tours, and refreshments (including the very popular, reservation-required "Teddy Bear Tea") are offered. For more information, see Museum of Art listing in "Adventures in the Arts."

◆ Fort Lauderdale Winterfest

(305) 522-3983. Admission charged for some events.

This month-long festival is a mix of holiday activities and beach parties. The seven-mile boat parade down the Intracoastal Waterway tops off the festival—a night of fun and fireworks!

◆ Holiday Enchantment at Flamingo Gardens

(305) 473-2955. Admission charged.

At this time of year, the gardens are transformed into an enchanted forest! Take a tram ride for a closer look. For more information, see listing in "On Safari in South Florida."

◆ Pompano Beach Holiday Boat Parade

(305) 941-2940. Free admission.

See the oldest holiday boat parade in the nation. Over 250,000 spectators watch each year as decorated boats follow a five-mile parade route along the Intracoastal Waterway.

PALM BEACH COUNTY

♦ Downtown Festival of the Arts

(305) 472-3755. Free admission.

Atlantic Plaza in downtown Delray Beach hosts 200 artists and craftspeople from across the country. Live entertainment is also featured.

♦ South Florida Fair and Exposition Showcase

(407) 793-0333 or (800) 527-FAIR. Admission charged.

This showcase of agricultural, industrial, and educational progress features rides, shows, contests, livestock, 4-H exhibits, and handmade crafts. Events such as horse shows, auto races, concerts, and antique shows are held throughout the year.

♦ ArtiGras

(407) 694-2300. Admission charged.

This celebration of arts, held at NorthCorp Parkway in Palm Beach Gardens, includes 350 juried fine artists and craftspeople. Children's activities and live entertainment are also on the schedule.

♦ Black Awareness Parade and Events

(407) 738-7444.

In celebration of Black History Month, the city of Boynton Beach Recreation and Parks Department sponsors events throughout the month.

♦ Flagler Museum Anniversary Open House

(407) 655-2833. Free admission.

This popular open house has taken place yearly since the late 1950s. The program varies from year to year, and may include shows, historical re-enactments, exhibits, mimes, clowns, refreshments, and other activities. Arrive early to find convenient parking. For more information, see listing for Whitehall/Henry Morrison Flagler Museum in "Tracing the Past."

♦ *Hatsume* Fair at the Morikami

(407) 495-0233. Admission charged.

This festival celebrates the "first bud of spring" with ethnic foods and entertainment. There are demonstrations to interest children and adults of all ages. The fair gets quite crowded, and stroller access can be difficult. For more information about the Morikami Museum and Japanese Gardens, see listing in "Tracing the Past."

◆ Winter Equestrian Festival

(407) 793-5867. Admission charged.

Over 300 riders from around the world compete in three grand prix events at the Palm Beach Polo and Country Club. For more information, see listing in "On Your Mark, Get Set, Go!"

MARCH

◆ Finlandia Days

(407) 586-3713. Free admission.

Come to Bryant Park in Lake Worth to enjoy this ethnic celebration featuring arts, entertainment, and food.

◆ G.A.L.A. (Great American Love Affair)

(407) 738-7444.

Sponsored by the Boynton Beach Recreation and Parks Department, this arts and crafts festival takes place in downtown Boynton Beach and includes KidsKorner, a special area for children's activities, a youth art exhibit, entertainment, food, and displays about local businesses.

◆ Meet Me Downtown

(407) 395-4433. Free admission except for children's rides.

Browse Palm Beach County's largest juried art show, and enjoy entertainment, food, and children's activities.

APRIL

◆ BOOKFEST! of the Palm Beaches

(407) 731-0398. Free admission.

Authors, booksellers, and thousands of books for children and adults take over the South Florida Fairgrounds. Special events for children are included.

◆ The Delray Affair

(407) 278-0424. Held on East Atlantic Avenue, between the Intracoastal Waterway and Swinton Avenue, Delray Beach.

Street performers, concerts, and other entertainment join more than 400 exhibitors of arts and crafts.

♦ Mizner Festival KidsFest
(407) 832-2989.

The Children's Museum of Boca Raton hosts this celebration of the arts for children. Cartoon characters, live entertainment by children's theater companies, clowns, and more provide lots of family fun.

MAY

♦ KidFest: A Celebration of Children and the Arts
(407) 575-7336.

Carlin Park, at the corner of A1A and Indiantown in Jupiter, is the setting for this celebration that features something for everyone in the family.

♦ Ocean Encounter
(407) 832-1988. Free admission.

Shell collections, touch tanks, tours, saltwater aquarium displays, and more are featured in this joint effort by the South Florida Science Museum and the Marine Aquarium Society of the Palm Beaches.

♦ Seafare
(407) 747-6639. Jupiter Lighthouse.

Celebrating the history of Jupiter at this great event, organized by the Loxahatchee Historical Museum. This may be your only chance to climb inside the lighthouse, and children will be fascinated by the historical re-enactments from the Spanish Conquistadors, the Seminole Indian Wars, and the Civil War. The children's area lets visitors try their luck at digging for archaeological finds and at arts and crafts activities. **Tip:** No parking is available at the festival site, so you'll need to park at one of the area shopping centers and take the bus.

♦ Sunfest
(407) 659-5980. Admission charged.

West Palm Beach hosts this four-day event, with jazz performances by big-name entertainers, power boat races, a "For Kid's Sake Park" art show, and fireworks! This street fair is Florida's largest outdoor jazz festival.

JUNE

♦ Kite Flying Festival

(407) 627-2000.
One of the PGA Sheraton Resort's golf courses provides the backdrop for this annual kite-flying extravaganza. Entertainment, food, and games are also on tap.

♦ Turtle Walks

(407) 627-8280 for Marinelife Center of Juno Beach at Loggerhead Beach; (407) 338-1473 for Gumbo Limbo Nature Center; (407) 686-6600 for Pine Jog Environmental Education Center; (407) 624-6950 for John D. MacArthur Beach State Park.
Make reservations early for these popular events that only take place in June and July. You'll meet at dusk for an orientation and slide show. Scouts are sent down to the beach to locate a female turtle, then the whole group heads down to watch her lay 75 to 100 eggs before she returns to the ocean. Turtles return from points all over the world to lay their eggs here. **Tips:** It's about a three-hour program, so you won't be home until midnight. You'll need to bring sweaters and flashlights. For more information about the locations listed above, see listings in "Exploring Science and Nature" and "Under the Sun."

JULY

♦ Fourth on Flagler

(407) 659-8004. Free admission.
Head over to Flagler Drive between Banyan Boulevard and Lakeview Avenue in West Palm Beach for South Florida's largest Independence Day festival. The Grand Old Flagler Parade, four entertainment stages, a Kids Kamp area, and much more. Be sure the kids take a nap so that they'll be awake for the grand finale fireworks show.

AUGUST

♦ Boca's Festival Days

(407) 395-4433. Free admission for most events.
This month-long celebration has activities geared for everyone. The schedule changes yearly, so be sure to watch the newspaper for detailed information. Past events have included sand sculpting, concerts, art shows, and fun parades.

♦ *Bon* Festival at the Morikami

(407) 495-0233. $5 admission.

Don't miss this unique street festival that features Japanese dancing, drum music, fireworks, and a lantern-floating ceremony! For more information about the Morikami Museum and Japanese Gardens, see listing in "Tracing the Past."

OCTOBER

♦ Fiesta on Flagler

(407) 582-6515. Admission charged to some events.

Celebrate Hispanic Heritage Month at this international festival. Don't miss the Plaza de Niños, mini–World's Expo, folk music and dance, crafts, food, and more.

NOVEMBER

♦ Florida Heritage Festival

(407) 832-6397. South Florida Fairgrounds, West Palm Beach.

Five-day celebration of Florida's rich cultural heritage takes place at the South Florida Fairgrounds.

♦ Harvest Fest

(407) 278-0424. Intracoastal Waterway and East Atlantic Avenue, Delray Beach. Free admission.

This two-day craft and agricultural festival includes an open-air farmers' market, petting zoo, and old-fashioned entertainment.

DECEMBER

♦ Boca Raton Holiday Boat Parade

(407) 395-4433. Free admission.

You can park in Red Reef Park or Silver Palm Park and watch over 50 decorated boats float down the Intracoastal Waterway. Parade travels between C-15 Canal and the Hillsboro Bridge in Boca Raton.

♦ Enchanted Kingdom

(407) 793-0333. Admission charged.

The grounds of the South Florida Fairgrounds are filled with holiday arts and crafts.

◆ Holiday Boat Parade and Fireworks in West Palm Beach

(407) 659-8004. Free admission.

Watch the decorated boats as they go down the Intracoastal Waterway between Banyan Boulevard and Lakeview Avenue.

◆ Holiday Boat Parade of Lights in Boynton Beach

(407) 734-6103. Free admission.

Get out the binoculars and find a place on the water between the Delray Beach Intracoastal Waterway and the Boynton Beach Intracoastal Waterway. Better yet, find someone with a balcony or backyard on the parade route and offer to bring dinner in exchange for the front row seats.

◆ Lake Worth Christmas Parade

(407) 582-4401. Free admission.

This charming parade, along with fun holiday arts, crafts, and food festival, makes for an enjoyable outing.

◆ *Osho Gatsu* (Japanese New Year) at the Morikami

(407) 495-0233. Free admission.

The Morikami Museum and Japanese Gardens is the stage for a series of Japanese cultural demonstrations and workshops in celebration of the New Year. Activities may include kite making and kite flying, and designing and making holiday ornaments, decorations, and New Year's greeting cards. For more information about the Morikami Museum and Japanese Gardens, see listing in "Tracing the Past."

≡ **MONROE COUNTY**

JANUARY

◆ Florida Keys Renaissance Faire

Marathon hosts this festival of arts and crafts, jousters, jesters, and "kingly feasts."

FEBRUARY

◆ Civil War Days

(305) 292-6713.

Re-enactments of Civil War battles, complete with cannon fire, take place at Fort Zachary Taylor State Historic Site. For more information about Fort Zachary Taylor, see listing in "Tracing the Past."

◆ Old Island Days
(305) 294-2587.

Celebrate Key West's unique history and architecture through festivals, tours, and contests. There's something here for everyone.

APRIL

◆ Conch Republic Days
(305) 294-4440.

A salute to island living! Enjoy the annual Kite Festival, fishing tournaments, and other traditional festival activities.

◆ Indian Key Festival
(305) 664-4815. Free admission.

This event focuses on the 1830s, when this key was the Dade County seat, and offers free boat rides, island tours, archeological displays, and native foods.

MAY

◆ Pirates in Paradise Festival
(800) 842-9580. Admission charged.

"It's a pirate invasion!" Events include a thieves market and pirate encampment at the Museum of Natural History of the Florida Keys. Food, crafts, and entertainment are part of the two-day event. For more information about the museum, see listings in "On Safari in South Florida" and "Exploring Science and Nature."

◆ Sand Castle Building Contest
(305) 664-2321.

Islamorada is the host for this fun family event, usually held on a weekend just before school is out. Come celebrate the beginning of summer!

AUGUST

♦ World Cup Jet-Ski Races

(305) 664-2321.

Top jet-skiers from around the world compete and entertain the entire family!

NOVEMBER

♦ Festival of the Continents

(305) 296-5882. Admission charged.

In Key West, this performing arts celebration focuses on dance, musicals, symphonies, folklore, drama, and opera. Events run continuously through April.

♦ Island Art Fair

(305) 872-2411.

Held on grounds of Lower Keys Chamber of Commerce, Mile Marker 31.

DECEMBER

♦ Arts Expo

(305) 292-7832.

Activity sites for this festival run 105 miles from Key Largo to Key West! Painting, dance, music, and literature are the main highlights.

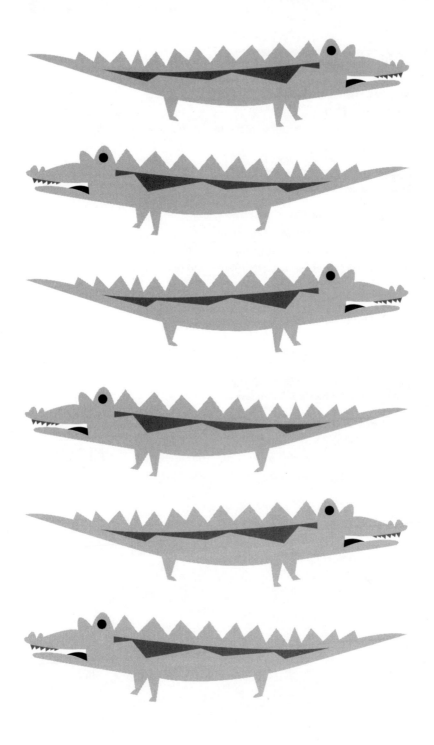

ACROSS ALLIGATOR ALLEY

Just beyond the western boundaries of the Everglades—148 miles west of Miami—lies Florida's unspoiled gulf shores and the areas of Naples, Fort Myers, and Marco and Sanibel islands. Voted by many as a "golfer's paradise," the "shelling capital of the world," the "best beaches anywhere," and the "top tourist destination in the world," this section of Florida definitely has its advantages. You be the judge!

We guarantee that visitors will be quite pleased with the sandy white beaches, the incredible shelling opportunities, the exotic wildlife and foliage, and the plentiful menu of things for families to do. A trip to this subtropical paradise is a must for anyone visiting or living in the state. Here is a list of places to explore, but once you make your way to *this* coast, we're sure you'll find your own special destinations to entice you back year after year.

As you travel across either Alligator Alley (U.S. 75) or Tamiami Trail (U.S. 41) you'll see a number of airboat concessions and bait shops. Boaters and fishermen will notice several rest areas that include boat ramps and parking areas and picnic tables. If you need to stop to stretch your legs, remember that both of these highways are busy and you should not stop your car along the side of the road.

♦ Babcock Wilderness Adventures
8000 S.R. 31, Punta Gorda 33982. Take exit 26 off I-75. (813) 338-6367. Reservations: (813) 489-3911. Hours and tours are seasonal; call for times and reservations. Adults, $16; seniors, $15; children under 12, $8. MC and V accepted.

In 1914 E. V. Babcock, a logging tycoon, bought this 90,000-acre ranch and during the 1930s logged the abundant cypress trees that covered the property. Today, visitors can tour Telegraph Cypress Swamp by swamp buggy (they're actually 32-seat, refurbished truck bodies!) with experienced naturalists, who often have the opportunity to point out bison, alligators, an occasional Florida panther, and other wildlife on this working cattle ranch. It is best to call for a schedule of the 90-minute tour and to make a reservation. Picnic facilities are available; no vending machines or snack shop on the premises. **Tips:** Allow at least two hours to tour. Group rates are available.

◆ Cayo Costa State Park

Mailing address is P.O. Box 1150, Boca Grande 33921. The island is located directly south of Boca Grande. (813) 964-0375. Daily, 8 A.M.– sunset. Entrance to island: $2 per group.

Located on a primitive barrier island, this state park is accessible only by private boat or passenger ferry. Boats at Boca Grande, Pine Island, and Punta Gorda offer round trips to the island for a fee. For information, call or write the park office.

Once on the island, visitors will find 12 primitive camping cabins, boat docks, wonderful beaches, and picnic areas. A tram makes round trips from the bayside to the gulfside beaches periodically throughout the day (round trip is $.50 per person). Hiking is particularly nice, with several nature trails to choose from. If you venture down the Quarantine Trail (begins near the Bayside Dock), you'll eventually get to a picnic area on Pelican Bay. Try the Cemetery Trail and you'll get a close-up view of a pioneer grave site. Several Indian mounds can be seen along the way. Bird-watching is encouraged—brown and white pelicans, ospreys, and bald eagles are often sighted.

◆ Cecil M. Webb Wildlife Management Area

Take exit 27 off I-75 and drive east to entrance. You must have the appropriate permits or licenses for fishing, camping, or hunting. Call the Game and Fresh Water Fish Commission, (813) 648-3203, for information. Open daily, 8 A.M.–sunset.

If your family enjoys camping, boating, fishing, archery, target practice, and hunting, plan a visit to this area. Stop at the entrance for a map of the area's 65,770 acres and a brochure that describes the various permits and licenses required for fishing and hunting.

◆ Children's Science Center

2915 N.E. Pine Island Road, Cape Coral 33909. (813) 997-0012. Tuesday through Friday, 9:30 A.M.–4:30 P.M.; Saturday, 9 A.M.–5 P.M.; Sunday, noon–5 P.M. Adults, $3; children 3 to 11, $1.50; children under 3, free.

Built by the Math, Science, and Technology Foundation of Florida, this five-acre center offers an outdoor science park with xeriscape garden, nature walkways, bubble bins, hopscotch, and hands-on exhibits. A picnic area is available, and special events are always on the calendar.

♦ Collier Automotive Museum

2500 South Horseshoe Drive, Naples 33942. (813) 643-5252. Hours are seasonal; call ahead. Adults, $6; children 5 to 12, $3; children under 5, free. MC and V accepted.

The *New York Times* called this sports car collection the "finest in America," so this is a must-see for the sports car enthusiasts in your family. You'll see the country's first Ferrari, a 1934 Alfa Romeo, and much more. For a big thrill, sit behind the wheel of a race car and pretend to be at the Indy 500! **Tip:** Allow about 40 minutes to tour.

♦ Collier County Museum

3301 Tamiami Trail East, Naples 33962. (813) 774-8476. Monday through Friday, 9 A.M.–5 P.M. Free.

This five-acre historical park explores tracts of history beginning with the Calusa Indians. Annual events include the Florida Heritage Days Festival in March, and an American Indian Powwow in November.

♦ Collier-Seminole State Park

Mailing address is Route 4, Box 848, Naples 33961. Located 17 miles southeast of Naples at junction C.R. 92 and U.S. 41. (813) 394-3397. Boat tours: (813) 642-8898. Daily, 8 A.M.–sunset. Admission, $3.25 per vehicle, up to eight passengers.

The vegetation and wildlife in this park are representative of the Everglades. Cypress swamps, tropical hammock (hardwood forest), salt marshes, and pine flatwoods are the botanical features that make up the area. Thirteen miles of canoe trails meander through the park. A limited number of people are permitted in the preserve each day, so call ahead to reserve your space.

From the park, visitors have boating access to the Ten Thousand Islands in the Gulf of Mexico. Camping, picnicking, hiking (over six miles of trails), and canoeing are activities offered here. Tours on pontoon boats are conducted daily, while paddleboats and canoes can be rented. Bring your binoculars for an up-close glimpse of bald eagles, Florida black bears, pelicans, crocodiles, and manatees. A small museum is housed in an 1830s army blockhouse replica. **Tip:** Remember your bug spray in the summer months!

♦ The Conservancy
Naples Nature Center

1450 Merrihue Drive, Naples 33961. (813) 262-4202. Monday through Saturday, 9:30 A.M.–4:30 P.M. Free.

This is a 14-acre nature center, which includes nature trails, a natural history museum, and an animal rehabilitation program for injured and sick native animals and birds. Boat rides, summer camp, and field trips are offered here.

The Briggs Nature Center

Located in the Rookery Bay National Estuarine Research Reserve between Naples and Marco Island. (813) 775-8569. January through March: Monday through Saturday, 8:30 A.M.–5 P.M.; Sunday 1–5 P.M. April through September: Monday through Friday, 8:30 A.M.–5 P.M. October through December: Monday through Saturday, 8:30 A.M.–5 P.M. Adults, $2; children 6 to 15, $1.

This is also part of "The Conservancy" and offers educational programs. Call for more information.

◆ Corkscrew Swamp Sanctuary/National Audubon Society

Route 6, Box 1875A, Naples 33964. Take exit 17 off I-75, head east 15 miles to Sanctuary Road, and follow the signs. (813) 657-3771. Daily, 7 A.M.–5 P.M. (November through April); 8 A.M.–5 P.M. (May through October). Adults, $5; children, $2.50.

This rich environment offers exotic flora and fauna in abundance. Two miles of nature trails take hikers through parts of the 11,000-acre sanctuary. You'll see 500-year-old trees draped with airplants, orchids, lichens, large quantities of snails (as well as the shells of those already eaten by the Everglades kite), and the country's largest stand of bald cypress trees.

In the early 1900s, the Audubon Society recognized the area's importance when poachers came here to prey on wood storks and osprey for feathers. Today the area is a breeding ground for wood storks in the winter, and the largest colony of its kind in the United States. A nature center is open daily from 9 A.M. to 5 P.M. Be sure to ask about special events and naturalist-led interpretive programs. **Tip:** You'll also run into more than a few mosquitos, so be prepared.

◆ Del-Nor Wiggins Pass State Recreation Area

11100 Gulf Shore Boulevard North, Naples 33940. Off S.R. 846, 11 miles northwest of Naples. (813) 597-6196. Daily, 8 A.M. to sunset.

Boardwalks, nature trails, and shell-covered beaches await young explorers here. Fishing, swimming, shelling, and boating are popular at this 166-acre park. Picnic facilities are featured here as well.

◆ J. N. "Ding" Darling National Wildlife Refuge

Located on Sanibel Island, off S.R. 867 west of Fort Myers. Mailing address: P.O. Drawer B, Sanibel 33957. (813) 472-1100. Refuge: daily, sunrise to sunset. Visitors' Center: Monday through Saturday, 9 A.M.–4 P.M. Admission: $4 per vehicle; $1 for bikers or walkers.

Drive, walk, or canoe through this 5,000-acre refuge abounding in wildlife and native plants. Raccoon, otters, and alligators can be seen routinely, as well as an amazing number of bird species. Visit in the morning hours if sighting wildlife is your goal.

The preserve was named for 1920s Pulitzer Prize–winning editorial cartoonist and environmentalist Jay Norwood Darling. A pamphlet, available at the interpretive center, provides a nice map and information about the area.

At Tarpon Bay Road, inside the refuge, you can catch an open-air tram that will take passengers on a journey through the refuge. The tour costs $7 for adults and $3.50 for children. Bikes, canoes, and fishing boats are available to rent. **Tip:** There is a $3 access fee to Sanibel Island.

◆ ECHO (Educational Concerns for Hunger Organization)

17430 Durrance Road, North Fort Myers 33917. Located off S.R. 78, one mile east of I-75 at exit 26. (813) 543-3246. Tours: Tuesday, Friday, and Saturday at 10 A.M. (Call for winter hours.) Free.

This attraction is actually a working interdenominational Christian ministry working to develop new agricultural techniques and seeds to help fight world hunger. Gardeners will be interested to know that this organization has one of the largest collections of tropical food plants in the state. Take a walk through a simulated rain forest and see rice, sesame, black pepper, and other interesting crops being grown with and without soil. The organization sends seeds, materials, and other goods, including educational resources, to over 100 countries in Africa, Asia, and Latin America.

◆ Edison Ford Complex

2350 McGregor Boulevard, Fort Myers 33901. (813) 334-3614. Monday through Saturday, 9 A.M.–5:30 P.M.; Sunday, noon–5:30 P.M.; last tour leaves at 3:30 P.M. Closed Thanksgiving and Christmas. Combined tickets: adults, $10; children 6 to 12, $5; children under 6, free.

Two of the world's most famous 20th century industrialists, inventor Thomas A. Edison and automobile magnate Henry Ford, lived as wintertime neighbors in the homes that now make up the Edison-Ford complex. Tour the estates with a guide and see the many displays of inventions and collections the men treasured.

Edison's 14-acre riverfront estate, which he visited for 46 winters, will take about 80 minutes to tour. Visitors tour his home, tropical gardens, and laboratory, where he turned goldenrod into rubber! His inventions include the light bulb, phonograph (over 200 are on display), and cement. He had over 1,000 patents to his name. Make sure you look for the banyan tree that ranks as the third largest specimen in the world— it's 400 feet around.

Ford's home, called "Mangoes," has been restored, and it offers an insight into his life. A few of his autos are on display at this three-acre estate.

Each February Edison's birthday is celebrated with a "Pageant of Light Festival." **Tip:** Allow about one hour and 45 minutes to tour.

◆ Everglades Wonder Gardens

27010 Old U.S. 41, Bonita Springs 33923. (813) 992-2591. Daily, 9 A.M.–5 P.M.; last tour at 4 P.M. Adults, $8; children 3 to 12, $4.

Florida panthers, black bear, crocodiles, alligators, deer, otters, snakes, and birds can be observed at this wildlife attraction. It has been in operation since 1936.

◆ Fakahatchee Strand State Preserve

Mailing address is P.O. Box 548, Copeland 33926. Located off U.S. 41 in the Everglades. (813) 695-4593. Daily, 8 A.M.–sundown. Free admission.

On your first visit here you may want to take the 12-mile one-way trip along W. J. Janes Memorial Scenic Drive. The trip along this gravel road may take up to an hour, and you'll only see a fraction of the preserve's 75,000 acres, but be on the lookout for Florida black bears, alligators, raccoons, bobcats, deer, southern bald eagles, peregrine falcons, and other wildlife.

For another view of the preserve, take U.S. 41 to S.R. 29 and go north about seven miles to Big Cypress Bend. A stroll down the 2,000-foot boardwalk here takes you into a strand of virgin cypress trees that reach up to 100 feet high. The observation area at the end of the walk overlooks a pond that's home to several alligators.

◆ Fort Myers Historical Museum

2300 Peck Street, Fort Myers 33901. (813) 332-5955. Monday through Saturday, 9 A.M.–4:30 P.M.; Sunday, 1–5 P.M. Closed Saturdays from May *through September. Adults, $2.50; children under 12, $1. MC, V accepted.*

This museum set up shop in the restored Peck Street Depot, which was used until 1971 as a rail passenger service. The collections inside include Calusa and Seminole Indian artifacts found in the area and a scale model of turn-of-the-century Fort Myers. Some of the historical displays document the area as far back as 1200 B.C. The last-built private Pullman car of the 1920s, the longest of its kind, "The Esperanza," has been restored and is on display. A furnished replica of a Cracker house is also on the grounds and can be toured with a guide. **Tip:** Allow about one hour to tour.

♦ Frannie's Teddy Bear Museum

2511 Pine Ridge Road, Naples 33942. Located one mile west of I-75, exit 16. (813) 598-2711. Wednesday through Saturday, 10 A.M.–5 P.M.; Sunday 1–5 P.M. Adults, $4.50; children 13-19 and seniors, $2.50; children 3-12, $1.50. AE, MC, V accepted.

Opened in 1990 by Frances Pew Hayes, a Naples philanthropist, this $2 million collection has nearly 2,000 teddy bears on display. (You might even find yourself talking to a few of the cute and cuddly ones!) Many of the bears are from Hayes's own collection. A bear theater and dioramas are open to view. **Tip:** It takes about 30 minutes to tour.

♦ Jungle Larry's Zoological Park at Caribbean Gardens

1590 Goodlette Road, Naples 33940. (813) 262-5409. Daily, 9:30 A.M.–5:30 P.M.; tickets sold until 4:30 P.M. Closed Thanksgiving and Christmas. Adults, $10.95; children 4 to 15, $6.95; children under 4, free.

This 53-acre zoological park was the brainstorm of Jungle Larry, a one-time Ohio television personality. Walk along the paths of the park, which take you to a petting zoo, animal shows (they run continuously throughout the day), a picnic area, and playground. When you are tired of walking, or need a breeze to cool you off, take a Safari Island Cruise or tram ride. About 150 animals live at the park, including lions, tigers, cougars, and leopards. Brave visitors can pet an alligator or snake at the "Wildlife Encounter." For show times and helpful information, call the number listed above.

♦ Museum of Charlotte County

260 West Retta Esplanade, Punta Gorda 33950. Located at corner of U.S. 41 south and Retta Esplanade, next to the Memorial Auditorium. (813) 639-3777. Tuesday through Friday, 10 A.M.–5 P.M. Saturday, noon–5 P.M. Free.

This small museum has five galleries that highlight African and American animals, local history, and special exhibits. Classes for children are offered periodically.

♦ Naples Depot Civic and Cultural Center

1051 Fifth Avenue South, Naples 33940. Located at junction U.S. 41 and Fifth Avenue in downtown. (813) 262-1776. Monday through Friday, 10 A.M.–4 P.M. Free.

This is a renovated 1927 train station that functions as an art gallery for traveling exhibits. Outside the depot is a caboose that houses railroad memorabilia.

♦ Nature Center of Lee County Junior Museum and Planetarium

3450 Ortiz Avenue, Fort Myers 33906. Located just north of Colonial Boulevard. (813) 275-3435. Planetarium: (813) 275-3616. Monday through Saturday, 9 A.M.–5 P.M.; Sunday, 11 A.M.–5 P.M. Nature Center: adults, $2; children under 12, $1. Planetarium: adults, $3; children under 12, $2. Laser light and music shows: $5 per person. Memberships available.

This active nature center offers indoor and outdoor study opportunities. Boardwalk trails take visitors through a subtropical wetlands environment. An Audubon aviary is a sight not to be missed—special aviary programs are offered on Thursday mornings. Guided walks covering many different topics are offered throughout the week, and daily wildlife presentations are on the schedule.

Permanent and changing exhibits on Southwest Florida are on display. In 1993, the center was awarded grant monies from the state to complete an exhibit called the *Year of the Indian,* which will focus on the Calusa Indians.

♦ Octagon Wildlife Center

41660 Horseshoe Road, Punta Gorda 33948. (813) 543-1130. Daily, 9 A.M.–5 P.M. Adults, $4; children under 12, $2.

Visit the endangered and injured panthers, mountain lions, tigers, and other animals under the care of the center's staff. If you plan to visit with a group of 10 or more, call ahead to schedule a guided tour.

♦ Sanibel Sealife Center

Fantasy Island Center, 2353 Periwinkle Way, Sanibel Island 33957. (813) 472-8680.

A 100-gallon touch tank, 15 aquariums, and sea life displays focusing on the Gulf of Mexico can be enjoyed at this small nature center. Beach walks and classes are offered periodically. For more information and a schedule of upcoming events, give the center a call.

◆ Six Mile Cypress Slough Preserve

Penzance Crossing at Six Mile Cypress Parkway, Fort Myers. (813) 338-3300. Daily, 8 A.M.–5 P.M. Parking fee: $2 per car. Admission charged to special events.

Over 2,000 acres of wetlands provide a safe home for local birds and animals. Call for a calendar of special events, including night tours, that are held here throughout the year.

◆ Sun Harvest Citrus

14810 Metropolitan Parkway South, Fort Myers 33912-4305. Located at the southwest corner of Six Mile Cypress and Metro Parkway. (813) 768-2686; (800) 743-1480. Open November through May: Monday through Saturday, 9 A.M.–6 P.M.; Sunday, 11 A.M.–5 P.M. Free.

Tours of this 16,000-square-foot packinghouse will give little ones a clearer picture of how orange juice gets to their breakfast table. The state-of-the-art packing line sorts the oranges (almost a half ton a minute!) and prepares them for shipping across the country. Visitors can also see the citrus as it is made into juice. Free samples of juice and citrus are offered, and a gift shop offers bags of the delicious products to take home. There is a playground next to the gift shop, which will allow the kids a chance to run and stretch while mom and dad relax for a moment. A "Packinghouse Pals FunPack" is a free bonus for the kids!

◆ Sun Splash Family Waterpark

400 Santa Barbara Boulevard, Cape Coral 33915-0027. (813) 574-0558. Hours are seasonal. Admission, $7.95 for guests 54" and taller; $5.95 for guests under 54"; children under 2, free. MC and V accepted.

Two giant water slides, a lazy river ride, Luna-Sea activity pool, Tot Spot Kiddie area, and sand volleyball are some of the fun activities offered at this family-oriented park. Call for special events and prices. Showers and lockers are available.

INDEX